Body Politics

MW01240905

The politics of the body is often highly contested, culturally specific, and controlled, and this book calls our attention to how bodies are included or excluded in the polity.

With governments regulating bodies in ways that mark the political boundaries of who is a citizen, worthy of protection and rights, as well as those who transgress socially proscribed norms, the contributors to this volume offer a systematic investigation of both theoretical and empirical accounts of bodily differences broadly defined. These chapters, diverse in both the populations and the political behaviours examined, as well as the methodological approaches employed, showcase the significance of body politics in a way few edited works in political science currently do.

Arguing that the body is an important site to understand power relations, this book will be of interest to those studying the unequal application of rights to women, racial and ethnic minorities, the LGBTQ community, and people with disabilities.

This book was originally published as a special issue of *Politics, Groups, and Identities.*

Nadia E. Brown is a University Scholar and an Associate Professor of Political Science and African American Studies at Purdue University, West Lafayette, USA. She specializes in Black women's politics and holds a graduate certificate in Women's and Gender Studies. Her research interests lie broadly in identity politics, legislative studies, and Black women's studies. While trained as a political scientist, her scholarship on intersectionality seeks to push beyond disciplinary constraints to think more holistically about the politics of identity.

Sarah Allen Gershon is an Associate Professor of Political Science at Georgia State University, Atlanta, USA. Her research focuses primarily on the incorporation of traditionally underrepresented groups (including women, and racial and ethnic minorities) into the American political system. In seeking to explain the challenges faced by these groups, her work emphasizes the role of communication, campaigns, and political attitudes.

Body Politics

Edited by
Nadia E. Brown and Sarah Allen Gershon

LONDON AND NEW YORK

First published 2020
by Routledge
2 Park Square, Milton Park, Abingdon, Oxon, OX14 4RN

and by Routledge
52 Vanderbilt Avenue, New York, NY 10017

Routledge is an imprint of the Taylor & Francis Group, an informa business

First issued in paperback 2021

© 2020 Western Political Science Association

All rights reserved. No part of this book may be reprinted or reproduced or utilised in any form or by any electronic, mechanical, or other means, now known or hereafter invented, including photocopying and recording, or in any information storage or retrieval system, without permission in writing from the publishers.

Trademark notice: Product or corporate names may be trademarks or registered trademarks, and are used only for identification and explanation without intent to infringe.

British Library Cataloguing-in-Publication Data
A catalogue record for this book is available from the British Library

ISBN13: 978-0-367-35813-6 (hbk)
ISBN13: 978-1-03-208933-1 (pbk)

Typeset in Minion Pro
by codeMantra

Publisher's Note
The publisher accepts responsibility for any inconsistencies that may have arisen during the conversion of this book from journal articles to book chapters, namely the inclusion of journal terminology.

Disclaimer
Every effort has been made to contact copyright holders for their permission to reprint material in this book. The publishers would be grateful to hear from any copyright holder who is not here acknowledged and will undertake to rectify any errors or omissions in future editions of this book.

Contents

Citation Information

The chapters in this book were originally published in *Politics, Groups, and Identities*, volume 5, issue 1 (March 2017). When citing this material, please use the original page numbering for each article, as follows:

For any permission-related enquiries please visit:
http://www.tandfonline.com/page/help/permissions

Contributors

Frank R. Baumgartner is a Professor of Political Science at the University of North Carolina at Chapel Hill, USA.

Ray Block Jr. is an Associate Professor of Political Science and African American and Africana Studies at the University of Kentucky, Lexington, USA.

Nadia E. Brown is a University Scholar and an Associate Professor of Political Science and African American Studies at Purdue University, West Lafayette, USA.

Florence Ebila is a Research Associate at the Makerere Institute of Social Research and School of Women and Gender Studies at Makerere University, Kampala, Uganda.

Derek A. Epp is an Assistant Professor in the Department of Government at the University of Texas at Austin, USA.

Andrew R. Flores is an Assistant Professor of Political Science and Legal Studies at Mills College, Oakland, USA.

Sarah Allen Gershon is an Associate Professor of Political Science at Georgia State University, Atlanta, USA.

Donald P. Haider-Markel is a Professor and the Chair of Political Science at the University of Kansas, Lawrence, USA.

Brian F. Harrison is an Adjunct Faculty Member in the Humphrey School of Public Affairs at the University of Minnesota, Minneapolis, USA.

Valerie M. Hennings is an Associate Professor in the Department of Political Science at Morningside College, Sioux City, USA.

Amber Knight is an Assistant Professor of Political Science and Public Administration at Saint Louis University, USA.

Daniel C. Lewis is an Associate Professor of Political Science at Siena College, USA.

Bayard Love is the Director of Development at the International Civil Rights Center and Museum, USA.

Brooke Mascagni is an Assistant Professor of Political Science and Gender Studies at Texas A&M University, College Station, USA.

Claire McKinney is an Assistant Professor in the Departments of Government and Gender, Sexuality and Women's Studies at The College of William & Mary, Williamsburg, USA.

Melissa R. Michelson is a Professor Political Science at Menlo College, USA.

Patrick R. Miller is an Assistant Professor of Political Science at the University of Kansas, Lawrence, USA.

Deborah J. Schildkraut is a Professor of Political Science at Tufts University, Medford, USA.

Elizabeth A. Sharrow is an Assistant Professor of Political Science and History at the University of Massachusetts, USA.

Kelsey Shoub is a Postdoctoral Research Associate at the University of Virginia, Charlottesville, USA.

Amy Erica Smith is a Professor of Political Science at Iowa State University, Ames, USA.

Barry L. Tadlock is an Associate Professor of Political Science at Ohio University, Athens, USA.

Jami K. Taylor is a Professor of Political Science and Public Administration at the University of Toledo, USA.

Jerry Thomas is an Assistant Professor of Political Science at the University of Wisconsin Oshkosh, USA.

Aili Mari Tripp is the Wangari Maathai Professor of Political Science and Gender and Women's Studies at the University of Wisconsin-Madison, USA.

Katherine Warming is a Graduate Assistant Teacher in the Department of History at Iowa State University, Ames, USA.

Body politics

Nadia E. Brown and Sarah Allen Gershon

Bodies are sites in which social constructions of differences are mapped onto human beings. Subjecting the body to systemic regimes – such as government regulation – is a method of ensuring that bodies will behave in socially and politically accepted manners. The body is placed in hierarchized (false) dichotomies, for example, masculine/feminine; mind/body; able-bodied/disabled; fat/skinny; heterosexual/homosexual; and young/old. Furthermore, these dichotomies illustrate that public/private borders are unstable. For example, governments either choose to recognize the rights for minorities or justify discrimination and marginalization for minorities. The denial of constitutional rights of women seeking abortions, racial/ethnic minorities, gay men, lesbians, and transgendered people, or people with disabilities have demonstrated the unequal application of free speech, due process, privacy rights, and the Equal Protection clause. Citizenship entitlements are not available for bodies that transgress cultural, social, sexual, and/or political boundaries.

Feminist scholars have argued that the body is both socially shaped and colonized.[1] The politics of the body, different from the body politic, argues that the body itself is politically inscribed and is shaped by practices of containment and control. Locating the body within a Western intellectual history perhaps starts with Marx but was popularized by Foucault.[2] Marx contended that the body was marked with a person's economic class which in turn affected his experiences. Foucault (1977) later argued that the body is a central point for analyzing the shape of power. Indeed, issues ranging from population size to gender formation and those that society has deemed deviant are inherently political. These issues, among others, define and shape the body. The "cultivation of the body is essential" to determine how one will behave in society (Johnson 1989, 6). Linda Zerilli has noted that Foucault's scholarship has guided feminist theorists to understand how the "body has been historically disciplined" as well as the basis for many essentialist claims (1991, 2).

In this way, examining the body provides scholars with a mode of subjectivity that was previously misrepresented. Social conditioning and normalization incorrectly assume a stable nature of identity and power relations. However, this reduces individual agency and subjectivity. As active subjects, marginalized bodies can confound the dominant discourse by opposing prevailing ideologies that have marked the body with meaning. To be sure, power relations are dynamic, nuanced, and highly contextual. Power is not manifested in a static form. As such, resistance and change are incessant. Analyzing the body as a site where power is contested and negotiated provides scholars with the ability to examine the fluidity of privilege and marginalization.

This special edition of *Politics, Groups, and Identities* includes innovative scholarship on body politics that examines epistemological and/or empirical accounts of bodily difference broadly defined. The theme of body politics directs our attention to how bodies are included or excluded in the polity. How do governments respond to the political demands of bodies that transgress normative boundaries? What ways do physical representations of difference impact power relations? How does the regulation of bodies, or the lack of regulation, impact society? In what ways do transgressive bodies that cross state boundaries challenge or reify national/international power relations? How do moral perspectives and virtues indicate how bodies need to be regulated and protected? This special issue also showcases the myriad of ways bodies can be studied theoretically, qualitatively, and quantitatively. The dialogues section expands on this theme, with authors exploring different approaches to the study of bodies. These pieces serve to remind us of the salient role bodies play in shaping political attitudes, actions, and rights and clearly highlight the need for great research in this field.

The work included in this special edition explores how and why different bodies are excluded, marginalized, or threatened. First, Miller, Flores, Haider-Markel, Lewis, Tadlock, and Tayolr's study illustrates that social and morality norms shape political attitudes. Diverging from other research into policy support, this study highlights the impact of body-centered considerations. As these authors illustrate – feelings of disgust toward transgendered bodies, as well as authoritarianism shapes attitudes toward civil rights and gender expression.

Sharrow and Knight explore the regulation of female bodies in distinct ways. Sharrow confronts the politicization of female athlete's bodies through Title IX. As her archival study reveals, the implementation of Title IX has complicated outcomes. On the one hand, this policy has increased opportunities for some women's bodies, yet it favors sex as a characteristic of bodies in such a way that marginalizes other bodies – such as those of transgender athletes. Knight expands our understanding of how disabled bodies are politicized and regulated, arguing that reproductive liberty – in particular, the right to motherhood – is constrained for disabled women. The practical implications for theoretically shifting how we articulate reproductive self-determination for women of color, poor women, and women with disabilities would protect these vulnerable populations from unwarranted government interference.

Considering the role of bodies in political engagement, Ebila and Tripp explore the display of the naked female body during land protests in Uganda. In their case study, the authors highlight the symbolic nature of women's and mothers' bodies, showing how the association between shame and nakedness was leveraged in political resistance to land grabs. This study further underscores the unique cultural beliefs and traditions which gave the naked female body particular symbolic power during these protests.

Moving to a focus on the inclusion of different bodies in government, Smith, Warming, and Hemmings explore the origins of support for women in office in the Americas, focusing on the role of pro-female stereotypes. As these authors illustrate, positive beliefs about female leadership styles increase voters' support for policies that will diversify government, such as gender quotas. Finally, two pieces explore the role of racial identity in shaping political attitudes and experiences. Taking a different approach to the concept of linked fate, Schildkraut explores the importance of whiteness in shaping political attitudes. As has often been found in studies of women, racial, and ethnic minorities, Schildkraut's work indicates that linked fate is common among whites and has electoral consequences. Baumgartner, Epp, Shoub, and Love explore the treatment of blacks and whites in police stops in North Carolina. Their data reveal that young men of color have been increasingly singled out for more frequent searches and arrests, compared with other drivers. The final essays in this issue explore how power, discrimination, and privilege are mapped onto racialized bodies.

In the dialogues section, Thomas, Harrison, and Michelson and Block discuss different approaches to the study of body politics. Harrison and Michelson explore the use of experimental methodology to study the role of framing and priming in shaping attitudes toward transgender bathroom access. Block's essay discusses his work (with Haynes) examining Michele Obama's media image. Block and Haynes employ novel data drawn from different polls and filmographies to identify media images and then use those images in controlled experiments to identify which media frames increase voter support for Obama. Thomas outlines queer sensibilities and methods, which he uses to analyze queer bodies, more specifically a sculpture Charles Ray. The invited review essay, written by Mascagni, explores movements that confront campus sexual violence. Centered on the case of Brock Turner, a Sanford University student, Mascagni argues that blatant white supremacist misogyny and respectability politics allow for certain perpetrators of sexual violence to receive leniency. Taken together, these manuscripts explore how certain bodies are subject to heightened and sustained scrutiny.

Notes

1. See Brownmiller (1975), Davis (1983), Dworkin (1974), Griffin (1978, 1979); and Rich (1980).
2. See Fraser (1989) and Hartsock (1990) for critiques of Foucault's conception of power.

Disclosure statement

No potential conflict of interest was reported by the authors.

References

Brownmiller, S. 1975. *Against Our Will*. New York: Bantam.
Davis, A. 1983. *Women, Race and Class*. New York: Vintage.
Dworkin, A. 1974. *Woman-Hating*. New York: Dutton.
Foucault, M. 1977. "The Eye of Power." In *Power/Knowledge*, edited by C. Gordon, 55–62. New York, NY: Pantheon.
Fraser, N. 1989. "Foucault on Modern Power: Empirical Insights and Normative Confusion." In *Unruly Practices: Power, Discourse and Gender in Contemporary Social Theory*, edited by N. Fraser, 73–94. Minneapolis: University of Minnesota Press.
Griffin, S. 1978. *Woman and Nature: The Roaring Inside Her*. New York: Harper Colophon.
Griffin, S. 1979. *Rape: The Power of Consciousness*. New York: Harper & Row.
Hartsock, N. 1990. "Foucault on Power: A Theory for Women?" In *Feminism/Postmodernism*, edited by L. Nicholson. New York: Routledge.
Johnson, D. 1989. "The Body: Which One? Whose?" *The Whole Earth Review*, Summer, 6.
Rich, A. 1980. "Compulsory Heterosexuality and Lesbian Existence." *Signs* 5 (4): 631–660.
Zerilli, L. 1991. "Rememoration or War? French Feminist Narrative and the Politics of Self-Representation." *Differences* 3 (1): 1–19.

Transgender politics as body politics: effects of disgust sensitivity and authoritarianism on transgender rights attitudes

Patrick R. Miller, Andrew R. Flores, Donald P. Haider-Markel, Daniel C. Lewis, Barry L. Tadlock and Jami K. Taylor

ABSTRACT
Transgender identity inherently involves body politics, specifically how transgender people may physically represent gender in ways that do not match their assigned sex at birth and how some may alter their bodies. Yet, political behavior research on transgender rights attitudes leaves unaddressed the role of transgender bodies in shaping those attitudes. Using an original, representative national survey of American adults, we analyze how authoritarianism and disgust sensitivity affect transgender rights attitudes. These two predispositions often reflect social norms and morality about bodies, especially those of stigmatized minority groups. First, we show that attitudes about transgender rights are multidimensional, forming civil rights and body-centric dimensions. Second, we demonstrate that disgust sensitivity and authoritarianism both positively predict opposition to transgender rights, and that they moderate each other's effects such that the greatest opposition is among those jointly scoring higher on both predictors. Finally, we show that disgust sensitivity and authoritarianism predict greater than average opposition to body-centric transgender rights policies.

In November 2015, Houston voters rejected Proposition 1, the Houston Equal Rights Ordinance (HERO). It proposed outlawing various forms of discrimination in the city based on sexual orientation and gender identity (Moyer 2015). Opponents dubbed it the "bathroom ordinance" and adopted the slogan "no men in women's bathrooms," an antagonistic reference to transgender individuals. The Campaign for Houston, a leading proposition opponent, aired radio ads repeating this bathroom attack and calling HERO "filthy," "disgusting," and "unsafe" (Wright 2015). Opponents also attacked HERO for supposedly upending gender lines and promoting immorality (Morris and Driessen 2015), pitting HERO against traditional norms.

HERO opponents likely perceived it advantageous to deploy messages involving disgust and social traditionalism, and to tie those messages to transgender bodies, perhaps believing that these sentiments resonated with how voters thought about the issue. However, given data limitations, current empirical research on transgender rights attitudes (e.g., Flores 2015; Norton and Herek 2013) gives little insight into what psychological dynamics – disgust, traditionalism, or otherwise – shape American attitudes on those issues. Indeed, the limited body of empirical studies specifically on transgender rights opinions scarcely goes beyond studying basic demographic and partisanship correlates of those attitudes.

Our research fills this gap by examining American attitudes on transgender rights, paying particular attention to psychological dynamics that may involve perceptions of transgender bodies. Given how the term "transgender" is commonly used in social discourse, average citizens likely associate that concept with the body, both how gender is presented via the body and how some transgender persons alter their bodies. First, we show that transgender rights attitudes are multidimensional, including a dimension that covers traditional civil rights debates and another dimension that deals with policies that we term "body-centric." By body-centric, we mean policies that involve how transgender people represent gender or gender roles with their bodies or how some transgender people employ medical interventions such as hormone therapy or surgery to change their bodies. Second, we demonstrate that disgust sensitivity and authoritarianism – both associated with traditional morality and body perceptions – influence those attitudes, and moderate each other's effects. Finally, we show that Americans are less supportive of transgender rights issues that are body-centric rather than traditional civil rights questions, and that disgust and authoritarianism partly explain that support differential.

Transgender politics as body politics

"Transgender" is often used as an umbrella term encompassing numerous subgroups: gender dysphoric individuals with psychological identities as male or female that are opposite of their sex assigned at birth, transsexual persons who seek medical intervention to alter their bodies, the genderqueer, two-spirited, drag queens, drag kings, and transvestites, among others (Tadlock 2015). Our goal is neither to adjudicate the "correct" usage of transgender nor to explore the complexities of transgender identity. Rather, we simply recognize that it is a broad, multi-faceted term encompassing substantial diversity.

It is unclear from research exactly how Americans understand the term "transgender." Many Americans may see transgender as primarily referring to transsexuals given their prominence in popular culture (Tadlock 2015). For many, transgender may lack precise definition given the breadth that it encompasses. Indeed, many individuals may not distinguish between distinct subgroups commonly labeled as transgender – for example, someone assigned male at birth who identifies as female or dresses in a feminine manner without altering their body versus someone assigned male at birth who undergoes hormone therapy or sex reassignment surgery. Most Americans may perceive both individuals as transgender without considering closely how gender expression via the body or the body itself differentiate subgroups.

A Public Religion Research Institute (PRRI) survey reinforces that Americans may indeed perceive "transgender" broadly (PRRI 2011), connecting the concept to both body self-presentation and physical alteration. Respondents recognizing the term – 91%

– were asked in an open-ended question to explain it. PRRI categorized the largest share of responses – 46% – as defining transgender as "someone who switches from one gender to another." It is unclear, however, whether this means switching gender presentation via dress or name, or switching physically via hormone therapy or surgery. Most Americans do not fully grasp the sex-gender difference and use the two terms interchangeably (Fausto-Sterling 2012), so the meaning of "switching" here is open to interpretation. Ten percent of respondents defined transgender as "born in the wrong sex" or "wrong body," and 20% as relating to gender identification or "living like" the opposite gender.

The breadth of how transgender is understood is likely important for assessing how individuals think about transgender rights. This may especially be true to the extent that those issues relate to "body politics," meaning how the body becomes a politicized object in power struggles over policies and practices that regulate it (Waylen et al. 2013), sometimes as an object for biological regulation, a target of political violence, or an object whose presentation through dress or the visible match of gender roles and sex is contested. Political behavior research has established in numerous contexts that understandings and perceptions of groups fundamentally shape how individuals evaluate policies related to those groups (for review: Ellemers, Spears, and Doosje 1999). We must consider, then, that given the common understandings of what transgender means to Americans, that an ingredient in transgender rights attitudes is perceptions of the body, both how some transgender people *present* their bodies and how other transgender people *alter* their bodies. Consequently, attitudes toward transgender rights may partly reflect body politics.

The concept of body presentation captures how individuals perceive and label transgender people who may present their gender in varying and sometimes gender non-binary ways that do not necessarily conform to their assigned sex at birth. For many, perceptions of transgender people likely often boil down to labeling their gender as either male or female and navigating how that perception matches the body. Assuredly, for some individuals, navigating that match invites no negativity. But for some, discomfort with transgender people may stem from expectancy violations related to gender ambiguity, eliciting disapproval of those who appear male but do not conform to "masculine" self-presentation expectations, or who appear female but do not conform to "feminine" standards (Miller and Grollman 2015).

Given the common understanding of transgender, these body-relevant perceptions may also include feelings about how others may alter their bodies physically. Americans likely vary in their comfort with the notion of transforming one's body via hormone therapy or sex reassignment surgery, often in lay-language called "sex change" surgery. Some persons assuredly hold more laissez-faire attitudes about these alterations and defer to transgender persons' autonomy to govern their bodies as they choose. Others likely view such body changes as unnecessary or problematic mutilations that violate norms of what is moral or natural (Raymond 1979), perhaps even reacting with emotions like fear or disgust.

However, given current research into transgender rights attitudes, there is little empirical evidence about how reactions to transgender bodies shape those attitudes. Quantitative research on this topic is scant (e.g., Flores 2015; Norton and Herek 2013). The few studies outline basic demographic and partisan cleavages in transgender rights attitudes, but due to limited data provide less insight into psychological factors that might channel reactions to transgender bodies. Here, we explore two such factors – disgust sensitivity and authoritarianism – that can broaden our understanding of transgender rights opinions, especially as they relate to body politics.

Disgust and transgender rights attitudes

Fundamentally, it is useful to know the demographic and political predictors of transgender rights attitudes. Flores (2015) shows that Republicans, biblical literalists, African-Americans, men, older people, and those not knowing transgender people are all less supportive of those rights. Existing theory, however, provides few clear narratives linking these correlates to perceptions of transgender bodies. For example, Republicans or older Americans may be less favorable toward transgender rights, but there is no clear psychological rationale for why those effects might reflect considerations of body politics. Integrating more psychological variables into this nascent research, though, can make those theoretical connections.

Emotions such as disgust may link reactions to transgender bodies – both how they are presented or altered – to transgender rights opinions. Disgust is "experienced in response to repulsive objects" (Schirmer 2013, 599), often stimuli that threaten contamination or body boundary violations (Rozin, Lowery, and Ebert 1994). Disgust allows subjective interpretation and social construction to influence emotional reactions. Piercings or body tattoos, for example, may be offensive because of an individual's personal tastes or dominant societal norms, but not induce disgust reactions for others.

Social psychology research has expanded on this notion of disgust as socially engineered, positing that for some it is a "behavioral immune system" (Schaller and Duncan 2007). This protection mechanism reacts both to stimuli viewed as physically infectious and those deemed morally contaminating (Haidt et al. 1997; Hodson and Costello 2007; Horberg et al. 2009; Miller 1997). Applied to attitudes toward social groups, the behavioral immune system generally elicits ingroup favoritism and outgroup derogation, a bias powerfully applied when the targeted outgroup is a stigmatized or relatively powerless minority (Faulkner et al. 2004; Navarette and Fessler 2006; Park, Faulkner, and Schaller 2003; Park, Schaller, and Crandall 2007; Schaller and Duncan 2007).

Importantly, disgust exists in both emotional state and trait forms (Spielberger 1972; Woody and Tolin 2002). State disgust means reactions to particular stimuli. This conceptualization matches cognitive-based appraisal models of emotion common in political behavior analyses (for review: Miller 2011) in which survey respondents are asked if certain attitude objects elicit particular emotions. However, a drawback of state assessments is that reported discrete emotions may actually reflect simple affect toward attitude objects rather than unique emotional states. Conversely, disgust trait analyses treat the emotion as a generic aversion to disgust-relevant objects. This trait is a relatively stable disposition over time, and predicts both disgust reactivity to myriad aversive stimuli and willingness to engage in disgust-inducing activities (Haidt, McCauley, and Rozin 1994; Olatunji 2008; Olatunji and Sawchuk 2005). We adopt the trait conceptualization of disgust, though this approach to emotion is less standard in political science than in psychology (exception: Miller and Conover 2015). This choice avoids problematic conceptual overlap between reported emotions and policy attitudes possible with a state approach. It also allows greater comparability to social psychology studies on disgust and gay rights that almost universally adopt the trait approach.

Among the groups under the LGBT umbrella, research has mostly linked disgust to gays and lesbians. Disgust sensitivity negatively predicts openness on sociosexual norms applicable to gays and lesbians (Druschel and Sherman 1999). Haidt (2001) argues that disgust is especially powerful in attitudes toward gays and lesbians because it activates "moral intuitions," moral judgments stemming from strong gut feelings of right versus wrong that are often deeply ingrained through socialization and that humans may find difficult verbally rationalizing. Thus, if social norms dictate that homosexuality is morally wrong, individuals who have long accepted that norm may feel disgust toward gays and lesbians both because of what they may do sexually and because their sexual orientations are seen as contaminating deeply held moral beliefs.

In affecting attitudes toward groups, disgust shifts moral judgments toward politically conservative positions, especially when social traditionalism is jeopardized (Haidt and Hersh 2001; Hodson and Costello 2007; Inbar et al. 2009; Olatunji 2008). Again, research on attitudes toward gays and lesbians may help link disgust to transgender persons. Disgust sensitivity positively predicts many forms of prejudice toward gays and lesbians (Dasgupta et al. 2009; Inbar et al. 2009; Olatunji 2008; Terrizzi, Shook, and Ventis 2010). Its effects also extend into policy attitudes. Those having stronger disgust orientations are less likely to support same-sex marriage (Adams, Stewart, and Blanchar 2014; Haidt and Hersh 2001; Inbar et al. 2009; Smith et al. 2011), controlling for other political orientations.

The theory underlying disgust suggests that it could channel reactions to transgender bodies into policy preferences, though little empirical work explores any connection between disgust and transgender rights opinions (exception: Casey 2016). Much like gays and lesbians whose bodies often defy old-fashioned gender roles and sexual standards, transgender people challenge traditional body norms derived from conservative moral principles, perhaps threatening moral intuitions about gender roles and body appropriateness akin to Haidt (2001). Individuals with stronger disgust dispositions may have more adverse reactions to transgender people who challenge body norms by displaying gender on their bodies – dress, makeup, or hair, for example – in ways that do not match their sex assigned at birth. Likewise, those strongly oriented toward disgust may react negatively to perceived body norm challenges from those who alter their bodies via hormone therapy or surgery. And given the literature on disgust and outgroup attitudes, disgust may be especially potent in this context given that transgender people are a relatively stigmatized minority group. *Thus, we expect that those with greater disgust sensitivity will be more strongly opposed to transgender rights policies* (H1).

Authoritarianism and transgender rights attitudes

Authoritarianism is a second psychological factor that may influence transgender rights opinions by channeling reactions to transgender bodies into policy preferences. Scholarship on authoritarianism is diverse and disjointed. There is no academic consensus on a single definition for the concept since it is often treated in behavioral analyses as an umbrella term encompassing numerous "authoritarian" traits. Many scholars have treated authoritarianism as a personality type, focusing on its negative, borderline pathological effects on behavior (e.g., Adorno et al. 1950; Altemeyer 1981; Stenner 2005). Recently, American politics scholars have deviated from pejorative treatments of authoritarianism, refashioning it as a disposition that most individuals possess to a degree, and that when activated powerfully affects political attitudes and behavior (for review: Hetherington and Weiler 2009).

Higher authoritarians possess several core characteristics relevant to applying the concept to transgender rights. First, they have greater need for order, seeing "the world in more concrete, black and white terms" (Hetherington and Weiler 2009, 3; also Altemeyer 1996; Stenner 2005). Conversely, lower authoritarians are more comfortable with ambiguity and complex evaluations. Second, higher authoritarians perceive stronger boundaries between ingroups and outgroups (Hetherington and Weiler 2009), suggesting a stronger tendency to emphasize group membership and attributions in attitude formation. Third, higher authoritarians place greater value on conforming to traditional social norms, and tend to perceive those norms as threatened by stigmatized and relatively less powerful minority groups (Altemeyer 1996; Stenner 2005). Lower authoritarians, however, tend to emphasize personal autonomy over social convention.

Authoritarianism positively predicts antagonism toward rights for minority groups, including gays and lesbians (Barker and Tinnick 2006; Hetherington and Weiler 2009; Laythe, Finkel, and Kirkpatrick 2001; Peterson, Doty, and Winter 1993). Scholars have argued that higher authoritarians value traditional gender roles and sexual norms, and that these attachments manifest in more conservative attitudes toward regulating bodies of minority groups (Adorno et al. 1950; Kelley 1985; Larsen and Long 1988; Rios 2013; Sales 1973; Whitley and Aegisdóttir 2000) – abortion, dress codes for women, or sodomy laws, for example. Lower authoritarians, conversely, emphasize greater fairness in dealing with outgroups while valuing social traditionalism less, pushing them toward politically liberal attitudes in evaluating minority rights.

Authoritarianism has a plausible connection to attitudes about transgender rights given these outgroup prejudice findings; indeed, Norton and Herek (2013) relatedly find that it predicts simple affect toward transgender people. Higher authoritarians may perceive transgender people as threatening traditional gender and body norms, in both how some present their gender and how others may alter their bodies. In defense of those norms, authoritarian predispositions may activate, inclining higher authoritarians toward more conservative transgender rights preferences. Lower authoritarians may conversely take more liberal policy positions, possibly viewing transgender people as less threatening to traditional norms, valuing those norms less in the first place, and being more apt to apply fairness norms to their political evaluations. *Thus, we expect that greater authoritarianism corresponds to greater opposition to transgender rights* (H2).

Further, authoritarianism and disgust sensitivity may interact, conditioning each other's effects on transgender rights attitudes. Hetherington and Weiler (2009) posit that the greater threat that higher authoritarians perceive from the social world discourages them from engaging in more complex cognition, making them rely more on emotion than lower authoritarians in attitude formation. This may be especially true for authoritarians and disgust. Adorno et al. (1950) describe moral disgust at "deviant" outgroups as central to the authoritarian personality, driving both the dehumanization of "others" and social antagonism toward minority populations (also: Hancock 2004). Social psychology research also suggests a moderating link between disgust sensitivity and authoritarianism in political contexts (Brenner and Inbar 2015; Hodson et al. 2013). *Thus, we expect that disgust sensitivity and authoritarianism demonstrate a moderated effect on transgender rights attitudes* (H3). We expect a statistical interaction such that those jointly expressing the highest levels of disgust sensitivity *and* authoritarianism should possess the most negative attitudes toward those rights. Conversely, those scoring lowest in *both* disgust sensitivity and authoritarianism should have the most positive attitudes on transgender rights.

Data

Data for this study are from an original nationally representative survey of 1020 American adults conducted by GfK. Data collection occurred October 9–11, 2015. The survey uses an online probability sample derived from address-based sampling to overcome coverage bias issues common in telephone-based polling. Selected respondents in non-Internet households are provided a laptop computer and online access to encourage participation. This sample also differs from those of many online survey providers since respondents do not opt-in to the panel, reducing demographic and political biases common in samples from other firms. All analyses herein employ weights compensating for demographic non-response. Missing data values were estimated via multiple imputation rather than allowing for listwise deletion which systematically biases data analyses.

Measures

Transgender policy attitudes

The survey included 14 statements covering various transgender rights policy sentiments. For each question, respondents rated how much they agreed or disagreed with the statement on a five-point scale ranging from "strongly agree" to "strongly disagree" with a neutral "neither agree nor disagree" midpoint. These statements were modeled on similar survey items on gay or transgender rights when possible, drawing on the General Social Survey, American National Election Studies (ANES), and the 2011 PRRI survey cited earlier.

We demonstrate below using principal components analysis that these 14 statements show dimensionality on a two-factor solution. The first dimension is termed "civil rights," and the second "body-centric," recalling our earlier definition of this term. Each statement is recoded on a ±2 scale, such that +2 indicates the greatest support of transgender rights and –2 the most opposition, with zero indicating neutrality. Policy statements are then combined into two additive scales based on their greatest factor loading along the two dimensions. On the scales, positive scores denote net support for transgender rights, and negative scores net opposition (civil rights scale: $\alpha = .90$, scored ± 14; body-centric scale: $\alpha = .92$, scored ± 14). On the civil rights scale, 24.71% of respondents have negative scores, 8.14% neutral, and 67.15% positive. For the body-centric dimension, 55.69% have negative scale values, 6.76% neutral, and 37.55% positive.

Authoritarianism

We employ the standard authoritarianism battery used in the ANES since 1992. Each question in this four-item scale poses two traits to respondents, who then choose which is "more important for a child to have." Listing authoritarian traits first, the four choices include: "respect for elders" versus "independence," "good manners" versus "curiosity," "obedience" versus "self-reliance," and "well behaved" versus "being considerate." The four questions are then combined into an additive index indicating how many authoritarian traits respondents preferred, with higher values indicating greater authoritarian dispositions (scored 0–4; $\alpha = .62$). Table 1 provides descriptive statistics and correlations of variables used in analyses. Though numerous authoritarianism measurement schemes exist, the child-rearing scale reflects core authoritarian sentiments, correlates highly with alternative measures, and significantly affects many political attitudes in the American context (Hetherington and Weiler 2009).

Disgust sensitivity

The survey included three questions from the 25-item disgust sensitivity scale (Haidt, McCauley, and Rozin 1994; Olatunji 2008). The longer battery measures variation in the tendency to feel disgusted across three dimensions: core disgust, contamination disgust, and animal-reminder disgust. All three dimensions correlate similarly with political behavior variables, including gay rights attitudes, so they are commonly combined into one scale in such analyses (Inbar et al. 2009; Terrizzi, Shook, and Ventis 2010).

The three-item subset comes from the contamination disgust dimension. Respondents evaluated how much they felt the three disgust statements accurately described them. Responses were on four-point scales ranging from "not like me" to "extremely like me." The three statements included: (1) "I never let any part of my body touch the toilet seat in a public washroom," (2) "I probably would not go to my favorite restaurant if I found out that the cook had a cold," and (3) "I use hand sanitizer on a daily basis." Responses were then combined into an additive scale, with higher values indicating greater disgust sensitivity (scored 0–9; $\alpha = .66$).

Controls

All models included standard demographic controls, including: age in years, church attendance (1/"never" to 6/"more than once a week"), education level (1/"less than high school graduate" to 7/"professional or doctorate degree"), LGBT (0/non-LGBT, 1/LGBT), household income (1/"less than $5000 annually" to 19/"$175,000 or more annually"), race (0/non-white, 1/white), and sex (0/male, 1/female). Also included were ideology (1/"very liberal" to 7/"very conservative") and partisanship (1/"strong Democrat" to 7/"strong Republican") measured via the standard ANES scales.

Results

Structure of transgender policy attitudes

Before testing our hypotheses, we first explore respondent attitudes on the policy statements that form our dependent variables. Table 2 provides the transgender rights question wordings. Responses are recoded into three categories: *supportive* positions favoring transgender rights, *opposed* positions against those rights, and *neutral* responses. Rights

Table 1. Descriptive statistics and correlations for survey variables ($N = 1020$).

| | | | | | | | | r | | | | | | |
Measure	M	SD	2	3	4	5	6	7	8	9	10	11	12	13
1. Civil Rights Issues	3.57	6.45												
2. Body Issues	-1.65	7.26	.75											
3. Age	46.02	16.71	-.08	-.13										
4. Church attendance	1.93	1.70	-.24	.33	.13									
5. Education	3.61	1.63	.16	.16	-.06	.03								
6. Female	0.51	0.50	.10	.09	-.06	.05	-.02							
7. LGBT	0.04	0.20	.17	.18	-.09	-.09	-.02	-.04						
8. Income	12.38	4.37	.10	.08	.03	-.03	.44	-.06	-.07					
9. White	0.73	0.44	-.01	-.01	.16	.02	.05	-.01	-.06	.17				
10. Ideology	4.16	1.53	-.48	-.53	.11	.32	-.06	-.08	-.13	-.01	.10			
11. Partisanship	4.11	2.06	.42	.44	-.07	-.29	.05	.05	.14	-.04	-.26	-.60		
12. Authoritarianism	2.17	1.31	-.31	-.39	.05	.22	-.32	.04	-.03	-.25	-.11	.28	-.19	
13. Disgust	3.33	2.57	-.17	-.21	-.10	.05	-.10	.12	-.02	-.14	-.21	.02	.03	.17

Table 2. Respondent attitudes on transgender rights statements.

Statement	Respondent attitudes (%)			Principal components analysis	
	Supportive	Neutral	Opposed	Civil rights dimension	Body-centric dimension
Transgender people deserve the same rights and protections as other Americans	63.53	27.84	8.63	0.77	0.22
Laws should protect transgender children from bullying in schools	61.27	28.04	10.69	0.79	0.05
Legal protections that apply to gay and lesbian people should also apply to transgender people	56.87	31.37	11.76	0.74	0.29
Laws to prevent employment discrimination against transgender people	50.59	30.88	18.53	0.67	0.37
Congress should pass laws to protect transgender people from job discrimination	47.65	33.92	18.43	0.77	0.33
Congress should pass laws to protect transgender people from discrimination in public accommodations like restaurants and movie theaters	45.1	33.82	21.08	0.77	0.33
Allowing transgender people to serve openly in the military	41.27	34.12	24.61	0.77	0.33
Allowing transgender people to change the sex listed on their driver's license or state ID card	37.94	33.43	28.63	0.52	0.66
Allowing transgender people to adopt children	37.26	35.29	27.45	0.57	0.63
Allowing transgender people to use public restrooms that are consistent with the way that they express their gender	32.65	31.86	35.49	0.51	0.66
Allowing students who have had a sex change to play college sports as a member of their current gender	31.66	33.63	34.71	0.42	0.67
Insurance companies should not be required to pay for medical treatment related to transgender health issues	29.61	33.14	37.25	0.26	0.67
Allowing Medicare to pay for a transgender person's hormone therapy	14.41	26.18	59.41	0.17	0.89
Allowing Medicare to pay for a transgender person's sex change surgery	12.25	24.71	63.04	0.13	0.89

statements are ordered from those where respondents express the most supportive positions to those where they are least supportive.

Respondents are divided in terms of which transgender rights positions they support in aggregate, though by at least a plurality the supportive position is the largest category for 9 of 14 statements. The sentiments generally garnering the most support cover many of the same civil rights questions that have been part of public dialogue around gays and lesbians. Majorities agree that "transgender people deserve the same rights and protections as other Americans" and that "legal protections that apply to gay and lesbian people should also apply to transgender people." Majorities also support specific policies on school bullying and employment discrimination. Pluralities support protection in public accommodations and open military service, plus adoption rights even though this issue also taps sentiments about proper gender roles[1] (Brewer 2008). A plurality also supports allowing transgender people to change the sex listed on their government-issued identity cards – an issue specific to some transgender persons.

Conversely, respondents on balance – excepting the identity card question – oppose policies that deal with the body, both how it is used to express gender and how some transgender people change it. Though opinion is closely divided, pluralities oppose two gender expression policies: allowing transgender people to use bathrooms of their choice and to play on sports teams consistent with their gender identities. This may reflect a discomfort among some for encountering transgender bodies in situations where sex and gender do not necessarily match, or even a more fundamental distaste for such mismatches. A plurality also agrees that "insurance companies should not be required to pay for medical treatment related to transgender health issues," a policy that may suggest body alteration to some given Tadlock's (2015) point on the prominence of transsexuals in public discourse about transgender people. Relatedly, majorities oppose allowing Medicare to pay for hormone therapy or sex change surgery, the two policies most clearly dealing with body alteration.

The disparity in support for particular transgender rights suggests that attitudes on these issues are multidimensional, a proposition unexamined in current published research. Rather than thinking of transgender rights questions monolithically, Americans may distinguish between policies that deal with long-contested civil rights questions versus policies that are more body-centric – both how gender is presented via the body and how the body is altered.

Table 2 also shows principal components analysis on the 14 transgender rights statements. Entries are rotated factor loadings. Shading indicates on which dimension each policy item predominantly loads. The analysis yields two dimensions with eigenvalues larger than the standard 1.00 cutoff.[2] The first dimension we term the "civil rights dimension." It encompasses most of the policy attitudes related to core questions of legal equality that have characterized the gay rights debate: public accommodations, bullying, employment non-discrimination, deserving the same rights as other Americans and gays and lesbians, and military service. The second dimension we term the "body-centric dimension." It covers the policy attitudes related more to body alteration and expressing gender through the body, including issues dealing with gender roles: Medicare payments, transgender health issues, restroom and sports team choice, sex listing on identity cards, and parenthood via adoption.

Given evidence of dimensionality, in subsequent hypothesis testing we use the additive scales described in the methods section as the dependent variables.[3] The means of the two dimensions show that in aggregate respondents score significantly lower on the body-centric dimension than the civil rights dimension [$t(1019) = 34.10$, $p = .00$]. The 3.57 mean on the civil rights scale indicates that the sample on balance is supportive of transgender rights on these questions, though not overwhelmingly so given the +14 maximum possible score. Conversely, the −1.65 mean on the body-centric dimension shows that respondents in aggregate hold attitudes somewhat opposed to policies relating to gender expression via the body and body alteration.

Disgust sensitivity and authoritarianism direct effects

Table 3 presents results for ordinary least squares (OLS) regression models testing H1–H3 regarding the effects of disgust sensitivity and authoritarianism, plus their interaction. Positive coefficients indicate that higher independent variable values predict supportive attitudes on transgender rights, whereas negative coefficients mean that higher predictor values are associated with opposition to those rights.

Model 1 under each dependent variable tests a basic model of demographics and political dispositions – roughly the extent of current academic knowledge of the correlates of transgender rights attitudes. For both issue dimensions, this basic model yields numerous

Table 3. Respondent placement on transgender policy scale dimensions.

	Civil rights dimension				Body-centric dimension			
	Model 1	Model 2		Model 3	Model 1	Model 2		Model 3
	β	β	b	β	β	β	b	β
Age	−0.01 (0.01)	−0.02 (0.01)	−0.04	−0.01 (0.01)	−0.03** (0.01)	−0.04** (0.01)	−0.09	−0.03** (0.01)
Church attendance	−0.03* (0.12)	−0.16 (0.12)	−0.04	−0.15 (0.12)	−0.67*** (0.13)	−0.50*** (0.12)	−0.12	−0.49*** (0.12)
Education	0.39** (0.12)	0.23+ (0.12)	0.06	0.24+ (0.12)	0.47*** (0.13)	0.21+ (0.13)	0.05	0.23+ (0.13)
Female	1.02** (0.37)	1.25*** (0.36)	0.10	1.24*** (0.36)	0.98* (0.39)	1.32** (0.37)	0.09	1.31*** (0.37)
LGBT	3.48*** (0.89)	3.27*** (0.82)	0.11	3.24*** (0.84)	3.22*** (1.13)	2.92** (1.09)	0.09	2.88** (1.09)
Income	0.13** (0.05)	0.09+ (0.05)	0.07	0.09+ (0.05)	0.07 (0.05)	0.01 (0.05)	0.01	0.01 (0.05)
White	1.21** (0.44)	0.61 (0.43)	0.05	0.63 (0.43)	1.60** (0.48)	0.80 (0.46)	0.05	0.72 (0.45)
Ideology	−1.23*** (0.14)	−1.09*** (0.14)	−0.26	−1.08*** (0.14)	−1.47*** (0.17)	−1.23*** (0.16)	−0.26	−1.22*** (0.16)
Partisanship	−0.62*** (0.11)	−0.63*** (0.11)	−0.20	−0.65*** (0.11)	−0.62*** (0.13)	−0.64*** (0.12)	−0.19	−0.66*** (0.12)
Authoritarianism	–	−0.66*** (0.15)	−0.14	−0.19 (0.21)	–	−1.13*** (0.16)	−0.21	−0.63*** (0.23)
Disgust	–	−0.36*** (0.07)	−0.15	−0.01 (0.14)	–	−0.45*** (0.08)	−0.19	−0.13 (0.16)
Authoritarianism × disgust	–	–	–	−0.14*** (0.05)	–	–	–	−0.15*** (0.06)
Constant	2.75* (1.29)	5.97*** (1.32)	–	4.66** (1.42)	0.34 (1.42)	5.34*** (1.34)	–	3.94** (1.45)
Adjusted R^2	0.28	0.315		0.32	0.33	0.40		0.41
F	45.02***	42.60***		39.58***	56.05***	69.89***		64.36***
N	1020	1020		1020	1020	1020		1020

Notes: β are weighted unstandardized OLS coefficients; b are standardized coefficients; SE in parentheses; models 1 and 2 were recomputed using weighted SUR OLS; statistically significant differences in row coefficients from SUR are underlined.

+$p < .1$.
*$p < .05$.
**$p < .01$.
***$p < .001$.

statistically significant effects, indicating substantial cleavages in opinion on transgender rights along demographic and political lines. Under the civil rights dimension, every predictor except age is significant. Attending religious services more frequently, being more conservative, and identifying as closer to the Republican Party all predict greater opposition to transgender rights on this dimension. Those with higher education and household income levels, women, LGBT identifiers, and whites are all more supportive of transgender civil rights. Model 1 under the body-centric scale produces similar results, except for income now being statistically insignificant and age becoming a significant predictor, with older respondents less supportive of transgender rights on this dimension.

Model 1 was then recalculated for both dependent variables using seemingly unrelated regression (SUR; not reported). SUR yielded neither substantially different coefficient sizes from regular OLS nor any changes in statistical significance from those reported in Table 3. However, SUR allowed easy testing for significant differences in the sizes of any one coefficient across dependent variables using chi-squared tests. Underlined entries indicate significant differences in row coefficients across both Model 1 columns. Age and church attendance have significantly larger effects on body-centric dimension attitudes than on civil rights attitudes, whereas income more strongly predicts the civil rights dimension. All other predictors have statistically similar effects comparing Model 1 under both policy dimensions.

This simple model adds to the scant empirical literature on transgender rights attitudes. The pattern of statistically significant demographic and political variables that we report resembles Flores (2015), though he found some of these predictors to have null effects in the 2011 PRRI survey. However, our model does not perfectly mimic his variables, so precise comparability is impossible. Additionally, we cannot ascertain whether new attitudinal cleavages emerged in American public opinion on transgender rights in the four years between the PRRI survey and ours. Nonetheless, Model 1 provides a baseline for assessing how incorporating more psychological variables into the model – disgust sensitivity and authoritarianism – adds explanatory power to our current limited knowledge of opinion dynamics on this topic.

Model 2 under each dimension adds disgust sensitivity and authoritarianism as independent variables. For the civil rights scale, both new predictors yield statistically significant effects. Compared to respondents scoring at the minimum value on authoritarianism, those at the maximum value are a predicted 2.63 units less supportive of transgender rights on this dimension. For disgust, those scoring at the maximum value are 3.20 units less supportive on the civil rights scale than respondents at the minimum.

However, the standardized coefficients under Model 2 for the civil rights dimension show that neither new predictor surpasses ideology or partisanship in substantive effects on the dependent variable per 1SD predictor value changes. Very conservative respondents place 6.52 units lower on the civil rights scale than the very liberal, whereas strong Republicans score 3.77 units lower than strong Democrats. Nonetheless, adding disgust sensitivity and authoritarianism as predictors improves the model fit for the civil rights dimension as the adjusted-R^2 in Model 2 increases 13.31% from Model 1.

Model 2 for the body-centric dimension produces similar results. Moving from the minimum to maximum values of authoritarianism and disgust sensitivity yields, respectively, 4.50 and 4.48 unit declines in support for transgender rights policies relating to the body. Per the Model 2 standardized coefficients under the body-centric dimension, ideology is again the predictor with the greatest substantive effect per 1SD change, though the partisanship effect approximates those of authoritarianism and disgust. And again, the model fit for this dimension improves substantially – 22.25% – by adding authoritarianism and disgust. Thus, the data support H1 and H2 that authoritarianism and disgust sensitivity positively predict opposition to transgender rights.

SUR chi-squared tests indicate that authoritarianism and disgust sensitivity have significantly larger effects on body-centric attitudes than civil rights attitudes. This pattern makes intuitive sense given research discussed earlier detailing how these two predispositions may be especially potent influences when body regulation is concerned. They predict opposition to civil rights for transgender persons, but that influence magnifies when body politics is primed.

Disgust sensitivity and authoritarianism interaction

H3 posits that authoritarianism and disgust sensitivity should moderate each other's effects on transgender rights attitudes. Specifically, we argue that those jointly expressing the highest levels of *both* predictors should be the least supportive of transgender rights, whereas those scoring lowest in *both* disgust sensitivity and authoritarianism should be the most supportive. Model 3 under each dependent variable tests H3 by interacting authoritarianism and disgust sensitivity. Both interactions prove statistically significant.

Figure 1 shows the substantive effects of these interactions. The lines show the effect of disgust sensitivity plotted against authoritarianism values along the x-axis. Scale values are the product of disgust and authoritarianism both held at their means and ±1SD. Panel A shows predicted civil rights dimension values. The negative effect of disgust sensitivity on civil rights dimension attitudes increases in strength as authoritarianism values also increase. Holding authoritarianism at –1SD from its mean, the net effect of a 2SD increase in disgust is to decrease civil rights support by –0.79 units, from predicted scores of 4.84 (95% CI: 4.77, 5.47) to 4.05 (95% CI: 3.34, 4.77). At the authoritarianism mean, the net decline in support for a 2SD shift in disgust is –1.70 units. At +1SD on authoritarianism, the same disgust effect grows to –2.61 units, decreasing predicted civil rights support from scores of 4.05 (95% CI: 2.13, 4.97) to 1.45 (95% CI: .77, 2.13). This represents a 330% increase in the net effect of a 2SD change in disgust across authoritarianism values.

Thus, while the lowest authoritarians are not immune to the negative effect of disgust sensitivity, they are less responsive to that disposition than higher authoritarians who prove more prone to translate disgust into lower support for transgender rights. Notably, given that all other predictors are conventionally held at their means in this calculation, even respondents who jointly report the highest disgust and authoritarianism values score on the supportive, positive side of the civil rights scale. However, the quarter of respondents on the negative, opposed side of the scale would additionally be characterized as male, heterosexual, more conservative, and closer to Republicans.

Panel B plots the interaction effect on predicted values of the body-centric policy scale, showing generally similar patterns. With authoritarianism at –1SD from its mean, a 2SD increase in disgust sensitivity reduces support for transgender rights policies on this dimension by –1.93 units, from predicted scores of 0.56 (95% CI: –0.14, 1.26) to –1.37 (95% CI: –2.10, –0.65). The decline associated with disgust increases to –2.96 units at

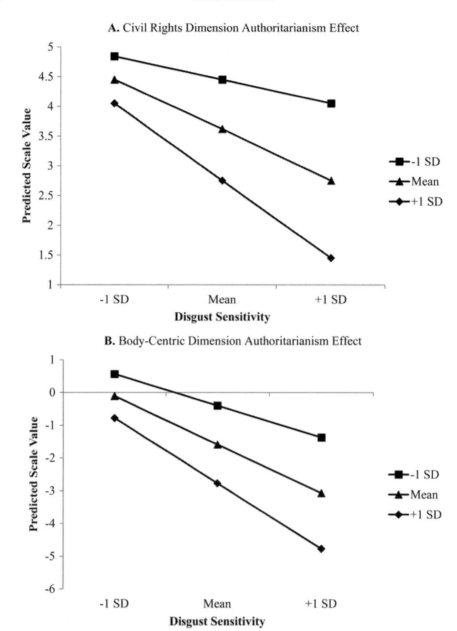

Figure 1. Transgender policy scale attitudes, authoritarianism effect by disgust sensitivity value. (a) Civil rights dimension authoritarianism effect. (b) Body-centric dimension authoritarianism effect.

the authoritarianism mean. Again, the greatest decline in policy support associated with disgust sensitivity occurs at +1SD on authoritarianism, diminishing support by −4.01 units from predicted scores of −0.76 (95% CI: −1.67, 0.11) to −4.77 (95% CI: −5.47, −4.07). This represents a 208% increase in the disgust effect across authoritarianism values. Thus, these moderated effects support H3 that declines in transgender rights support increase as values of disgust sensitivity and authoritarianism jointly increase.

Difference in dimension policy support

Respondents in aggregate are less supportive of transgender rights on the body-centric than the civil rights dimension, evidenced in the significant 5.22 unit difference in the scale means reported above. If Americans differentiate between the types of transgender rights policies they support, then what explains that distinction? Here, we model the difference between respondent support on the two dimensions, calculated as civil rights minus body-centric dimension values (scored ±28; $M = 5.22$, $SD = 4.89$). The two original scales are scored the same, so their raw difference is directly interpretable as difference in respondent support on the two dimensions. Positive scores indicate that respondents score higher on the civil rights than body-centric dimension, and vice versa for negative scores; 82.16% have positive difference scores.

Table 4 applies Model 2 from Table 3 to predict dimension difference values. Positive coefficients indicate that higher values on predictors increase the difference in respondent scores on the two policy scales, whereas negative values mean reduced differences. Given respondent patterns on the two scales, positive coefficients overwhelmingly mean that respondents score lower on the body-centric scale than average compared to the civil rights scale, thereby increasing their difference between scale support scores.

Though the disgust-authoritarianism interaction is statistically insignificant ($\beta = .01$, $p = .83$), both constituent items yield significant positive coefficients. Moving from the authoritarianism minimum to maximum increases the difference between scale scores by 1.87 units. The same move on disgust sensitivity increases that difference by 1.29 units. Respondents who are older, have higher household incomes, and who attend church more frequently also demonstrate greater scale differences, again largely being less supportive of body-centric policies than other respondents on average. Per the standardized coefficients, authoritarianism rivals church attendance in substantive heft for a 1SD predictor movement, with the other three significant predictors roughly equal in effect. Thus, the difference in support on the two policy dimensions is not a constant,

Table 4. Difference between respondent placement on transgender policy scale dimensions.

	β	b
Age	0.02* (0.01)	0.07
Church attendance	0.34** (0.11)	0.12
Education	0.012 (0.11)	0.01
Female	−0.07 (0.32)	−0.01
LGBT	0.35 (0.98)	0.02
Income	0.08* (0.04)	0.08
White	−0.09 (0.42)	−0.01
Ideology	0.14 (0.14)	0.04
Partisanship	0.01 (0.10)	0.00
Authoritarianism	0.47** (0.15)	0.12
Disgust	0.14* (0.07)	0.08
Constant	0.63 (1.15)	–
Adjusted R^2	0.06	
F	5.78***	
N	1020	

Note: β are weighted unstandardized OLS coefficients; b are standardized coefficients; SE in parentheses.
+$p < .1$.
*$p < .05$.
**$p < .01$.
***$p < .001$.

but rather a product of certain demographic and psychological orientations associated with relatively lower support on body-centric policies.

Discussion

This study expands our knowledge of opinion dynamics around transgender rights, a timely topic given changes in American popular discourse about transgender people and political developments around policies like HERO. Our research shows that Americans differentiate between transgender rights policies addressing traditional civil rights questions versus those that are more body-centric in nature, and that Americans are more supportive of the former. As hypothesized, disgust sensitivity and authoritarianism dampen support for transgender rights policies, and their effects moderate each other such that their strongest negative influence is among those scoring highly on *both*. Finally, we show that disgust and authoritarianism dispositions are significant factors behind the lower relative support for body-centric transgender rights policies. Thus, attitudes toward transgender rights involve body politics since the body structures those attitudes and brings certain political predispositions to bear on them.

Empirical work on transgender rights attitudes is nascent, and most current research explores little beyond simple demographic and political correlates. A key contribution of our work is showing that psychological factors influence transgender rights policy attitudes – a novel application to this issue area. Indeed, the effects illustrated here may inform broader research on LGBT attitudes. As scholars expand the literature on attitudes toward gays and lesbians, research may well incorporate not just more psychology, but also consider as we do how psychological dynamics interact.

Further development in LGBT rights literature may also address whether the attitudinal dynamics observed here are unique to transgender people, or also apply to gays and lesbians. Opponent messaging in the HERO campaign suggests that body-oriented messages may be effective in campaigning against LGBT rights if those messages can both be framed in terms of transgender people rather than gays and lesbians necessarily, and activate dispositions such as disgust sensitivity and authoritarianism among voters. Essentially, do Americans really lump the "T" with the "LGB" when they evaluate LGBT rights questions, or do they separate the groups? Given the differences in support for transgender rights policies traditionally associated with civil rights debates versus more body-centric policies, the answer might depend on the specific issue.

Relatedly, our research should encourage scholars not to discount the body politics aspect of group-centric politics, especially with transgender rights. For some in the general public, it may be considered taboo or offensive to discuss the bodily aspects of transgender individuals, especially when it involves transgender persons who alter their bodies via hormone therapy or surgery. But our study suggests that, regardless of what some might prefer, these bodily considerations are likely in the minds of average Americans as they think about transgender rights – and their comfort with the body politics of transgender persons will shape their support for transgender rights through psychological mechanisms such as disgust sensitivity and authoritarianism. At a minimum, the body politics of transgender Americans is part of our political dialogue over their rights, as the HERO opponents realized and strategically exploited. If scholars want to understand how the public engages with transgender issues and if real world political practitioners want to advocate those rights more effectively, then an appreciation of how transgender politics is inherently body politics is vital.

Notes

1. Our survey included a four-item gender role scale. It formed a separate dimension from authoritarianism in principal components analysis. It also exhibited statistically significant effects when included as a predictor in models presented here, but did not substantially attenuate the reported authoritarianism effects. Thus, though authoritarianism may relate to gender roles, it is conceptually and empirically distinct.
2. Given the .75 correlation between the civil rights and body issues scales (Table 1), transgender rights attitudes are multidimensional, but not orthogonal dimensions. The third eigenvalue was .42, and the two reported dimensions cumulatively explained 99% of data variance. Akaike's Information Criterion and Bayesian Information Criterion tests showed that the fit of a two-factor model was statistically better than one factor.
3. Factor scores for the policy dimensions are an alternative to additive scales as dependent variables. Additive scales assign items to dimensions based on loadings, whereas factor scores recognize that items may have non-trivial minority loadings on second dimensions (e.g., military service in Table 2). However, our analyses yield similar results using either additive scales or factor scores as dependent variables. Given the similarity in results, we report models using additive scales since they preserve the substantive interpretability of net transgender rights opinion.

Disclosure statement

No potential conflict of interest was reported by the authors.

Funding

This study was funded by the University of Toledo, University of Kansas, The Williams Institute, and Ohio University.

References

Adams, Thomas G., Patrick A. Stewart, and John C. Blanchar. 2014. "Disgust and the Politics of Sex: Exposure to a Disgusting Odorant Increases Politically Conservative Views on Sex and Decreases Support for Gay Marriage." *PLoS One* 9 (5): e95572.
Adorno, Theodor E., Else Frenkel-Brunswik, Daniel J. Levinson, and R. Nevitt Sanford. 1950. *The Authoritarian Personality*. New York: Harper and Row.
Altemeyer, Robert. 1981. *Right-Wing Authoritarianism*. Winnipeg: University of Manitoba Press.
Altemeyer, Robert. 1996. *The Authoritarian Specter*. Cambridge: Harvard University Press.
Barker, David C., and James D. Tinnick, III. 2006. "Competing Visions of Parental Roles and Ideological Constraint." *American Political Science Review* 100 (2): 249–263.
Brenner, Corinne J., and Yoel Inbar. 2015. "Disgust Sensitivity Predicts Political Ideology and Policy Attitudes in the Netherlands." *European Journal of Social Psychology* 45 (1): 27–38.
Brewer, Paul R. 2008. *Value War: Public Opinion and the Politics of Gay Rights*. Lanham: Rowman & Littlefield.
Casey, Logan. 2016. "Emotional Agendas: Disgust and the Dynamics of LGBT Politics." Ph.D. diss., University of Michigan.
Dasgupta, Nilanjana, David DeSteno, Lisa A. Williams, and Matthew Hunsinger. 2009. "Fanning the Flames of Prejudice: The Influence of Specific Incidental Emotions on Implicit Prejudice." *Emotion* 9 (4): 585–591.

Druschel, B. A., and Martin F. Sherman. 1999. "Disgust Sensitivity as a Function of the Big Five and Gender." *Personality and Individual Differences* 26 (4): 739–748.

Ellemers, Naomi, Russell Spears, and Bertjan Doosje. 1999. *Social Identity*. Malden: Blackwell.

Faulkner, Jason, Mark Schaller, Justin H. Park, and Lesley A. Duncan. 2004. "Evolved Disease-Avoidance Mechanisms and Contemporary Xenophobic Attitudes." *Group Processes & Intergroup Relations* 7 (4): 333–353.

Fausto-Sterling, Anne. 2012. *Sex/Gender: Biology in a Social World*. New York: Routledge.

Flores, Andrew R. 2015. "Attitudes Toward Transgender Rights: Perceived Knowledge and Secondary Interpersonal Contact." *Politics, Groups, and Identities* 3 (3): 398–416.

Haidt, Jonathan. 2001 "The Emotional Dog and Its Rational Tail: A Social Intuitionist Approach to Moral Judgment." *Psychology Review* 108 (4): 814–834.

Haidt, Jonathan, and Matthew A. Hersh. 2001. "Sexual Morality: The Cultures and Emotions of Conservatives and Liberals." *Journal of Applied Social Psychology* 31 (1): 191–221.

Haidt, Jonathan, Clark McCauley, and Paul Rozin. 1994. "Individual Differences in Sensitivity to Disgust: A Scale Sampling Seven Domains of Disgust Elicitors." *Personality and Individual Differences* 16 (5): 701–713.

Haidt, Jonathan, Paul Rozin, Clark McCauley, and Sumio Imada. 1997. "Body, Psyche, and Culture: The Relationship Between Disgust and Morality." *Psychology and Developing Societies* 9 (1): 107–131.

Hancock, Ange-Marie. 2004. *The Politics of Disgust: The Public Identity of the Welfare Queen*. New York: New York University Press.

Hetherington, Marc J., and Jonathan D. Weiler. 2009. *Authoritarianism & Polarization in American Politics*. Cambridge: Cambridge University Press.

Hodson, Gordon, Becky L. Choma, Jacqueline Boisvert, Carolyn L. Hafer, Cara C. MacInnis, and Kimberly Costello. 2013. "The Role of Intergroup Disgust in Predicting Negative Outgroup Evaluations." *Journal of Experimental Social Psychology* 49 (2): 195–205.

Hodson, Gordon, and Kimberly Costello. 2007. "Interpersonal Disgust, Ideological Orientations, and Dehumanization as Predictors of Intergroup Attitudes." *Psychological Science* 18 (8): 691–698.

Horberg, E. J., Christopher Oveis, Dacher Keltner, and Adam B. Cohen. 2009. "Disgust and the Moralization of Purity." *Journal of Personality and Social Psychology* 97 (6): 963–976.

Inbar, Yoel, David A. Pizarro, Joshua Knobe, and Paul Bloom. 2009. "Disgust Sensibility Predicts Intuitive Disapproval of Gays." *Emotion* 9 (3): 435–439.

Kelley, Kathryn. 1985. "Sex, Sex Guilt, and Authoritarianism: Differences in Responses to Explicit Heterosexual and Masturbatory Slides." *Journal of Sex Research* 21 (1): 68–85.

Larsen, Knud, and Ed Long. 1988. "Attitudes Toward Sex-Roles: Traditional or Egalitarian?" *Sex Roles* 19 (1): 1–12.

Laythe, Brian, Deborah Finkel, and Lee A. Kirkpatrick. 2001. "Predicting Prejudice from Religious Fundamentalism and Right-Wing Authoritarianism: A Multiple-Regression Approach." *Journal for the Scientific Study of Religion* 40 (1): 1–10.

Miller, William Ian. 1997. *The Anatomy of Disgust*. Cambridge: Harvard University Press.

Miller, Patrick R. 2011. "The Emotional Citizen: Emotion as a Function of Political Sophistication." *Political Psychology* 32 (4): 575–600.

Miller, Patrick R., and Pamela Johnston Conover. 2015. "Why Partisan Warriors Don't Listen: The Gendered Dynamics of Intergroup Anxiety and Partisan Conflict." *Politics, Groups, and Identities* 3 (1): 21–39.

Miller, Lisa R., and Eric Anthony Grollman. 2015. "The Social Costs of Gender Nonconformity for Transgender Adults: Implications for Discrimination and Health." *Sociological Forum* 30 (3): 809–831.

Morris, Mike, and Katherine Driessen. 2015. "'Fear' Aiming to Take HERO." http://www.houstonchronicle.com/news/houston-texas/houston/article/Fear-aiming-to-take-HERO-6589831.php.

Moyer, Justin. 2015. "Why Houston's Gay Rights Ordinance Failed: Fear of Men in Women's Bathrooms." https://www.washingtonpost.com/news/morning-mix/wp/2015/11/03/why-houstons-gay-rights-ordinance-failed-bathrooms/.

Navarette, Carlos David, and Daniel M. T. Fessler. 2006. "Disease Avoidance and Ethnocentrism: The Effects of Disease Vulnerability and Disgust Sensitivity on Intergroup Attitudes." *Evolution & Human Behavior* 27 (4): 270–282.

Norton, Aaron T., and Gregory M. Herek. 2013. "Heterosexuals' Attitudes Toward Transgender People: Findings from a National Probability Sample of U.S. Adults." *Sex Roles* 68 (11–12): 738–753.

Olatunji, Bunmi. 2008. "Disgust, Scrupolosity and Conservative Attitudes About Sex: Evidence for a Mediational Model of Homophobia." *Journal of Research in Personality* 42: 1364–1369.

Olatunji, Bunmi O., and Craig N. Sawchuk. 2005. "Disgust: Characteristic Features, Social Manifestations, and Clinical Implications." *Journal of Social and Clinical Psychology* 24 (7): 932–962.

Park, Justin H., Jason Faulkner, and Mark Schaller. 2003. "Evolved Disease-Avoidance Process and Contemporary Anti-Social Behavior: Prejudicial Attitudes and Avoidance of People with Physical Disabilities." *Journal of Nonverbal Behavior* 27 (2): 65–87.

Park, Justin H., Mark Schaller, and Christian S. Crandall. 2007. "Pathogen-Avoidance Mechanisms and the Stigmatization of Obese People." *Evolution and Human Behavior* 28: 410–414.

Peterson, Bill E., Richard M. Doty, and David G. Winter. 1993. "Authoritarianism and Attitudes Towards Contemporary Social Issues." *Personality and Social Psychology Bulletin* 19 (2): 174–184.

Public Religion Research Institute. 2011. "Strong Majorities Favor Rights and Legal Protections for Transgender People." Public Religion Research Institute. http://publicreligion.org/research/2011/11/american-attitudes-towards-transgender-people/#.Vr2ErvkrLZ4.

Raymond, Janice. 1979. *The Transsexual Empire: The Making of the She-Male*. Boston: Beacon.

Rios, Kimberly. 2013. "Right-Wing Authoritarianism Predicts Prejudice Against 'Homosexuals' but Not 'Gay Men and Lesbians.'" *Journal of Experimental Social Psychology* 49 (6): 1177–1183.

Rozin, Paul, Laura Lowery, and Rhonda Ebert. 1994. "Varieties of Disgust Faces and the Structure of Disgust." *Journal of Personality and Social Psychology* 66 (5): 870–881.

Sales, Stephen M. 1973. "Threat as a Factor in Authoritarianism: An Analysis of Archival Data." *Journal of Personality and Social Psychology* 28 (1): 44–57.

Schaller, Mark, and Lesley A. Duncan. 2007. "The Behavioral Immune System: Its Evolution and Social Psychological Implications." In *Evolution and the Social Mind: Evolutionary Psychology and Social Cognition*, edited by Joseph P. Forgas, Martie G. Haselton, and William von Hippel, 293–307. New York: Psychology Press.

Schirmer, Annett. 2013. "Sex Differences in Emotion." In *The Cambridge Handbook of Human Affective Neuroscience*, edited by Jorge Armony and Patrik Vuilleumier, 591–610. Cambridge: Cambridge University Press.

Smith, Kevin B., Douglas Oxley, Matthew V. Hibbing, John R. Alford, and John R. Hibbing. 2011. "Disgust Sensitivity and the Neurophysiology of Left–Right Political Orientations." *PLoS ONE* 6 (10): e25552.

Spielberger, Charles. 1972. *Anxiety: Current Trends in Theory and Research*. New York: Academic Press.

Stenner, Karen. 2005. *The Authoritarian Dynamic*. Cambridge: Cambridge University Press.

Tadlock, Barry. 2015. "Issue Framing and Transgender Politics: An Examination of Interest Group Websites and Media Coverage." In *Transgender Rights and Politics: Groups, Issue Framing, & Policy Adaptation*, edited by Jami K. Taylor and Donald P. Haider-Markel, 25–48. Ann Arbor: University of Michigan Press.

Terrizzi, John A. Jr., Natalie J. Shook, and W. Larry Ventis. 2010. "Disgust: A Predictor of Social Conservatism and Prejudicial Attitudes Toward Homosexuals." *Personality and Individual Differences* 49: 587–592.

Waylen, Georgina, Karen Celis, Johanna Kantola, and S. Laurel Weldon. 2013. *The Oxford Handbook of Gender and Politics*. Oxford: Oxford University Press.

Whitley, Bernard E. Jr., and Stefanía Aegisdóttir. 2000. "The Gender Belief System, Authoritarianism, Social Dominance Orientation, and Heterosexuals' Attitudes Toward Lesbians and Gay Men." *Sex Roles* 42 (11): 947–967.

Woody, Shelia R., and David F. Tolin. 2002. "The Relationship Between Disgust Sensitivity and Avoidant Behavior: Studies of Clinical and Nonclinical Samples." *Journal of Anxiety Disorders* 16 (5): 543–559.

Wright, John. 2015. "Houston Haters Launch Website, Release Disgusting Anti-LGBT Radio Ad." http://www.towleroad.com/2015/08/houston-hate/.

Naked transgressions: gendered symbolism in Ugandan land protests

Florence Ebila and Aili Mari Tripp

ABSTRACT

Studies of women's protest have adopted various social movement approaches that look at the mobilization of resources, the facilitating and constraining role of opportunity structures, and questions of framing and culture. This study looks at the role of symbolic resonance, a theme which is mostly absent from both feminist scholarship on women's movements, but also from social movement theory. This paper explores the symbolic meanings behind the public displays of the female naked body in the face of repressive authority in contemporary protest movements for peace, human rights and democracy in Africa, with a focus on the 2015 protests in Amuru District in Northern Uganda.

> I told them to leave us on our land but they were adamant and refused. I was overcome by anger and took off my clothes. I told them the first time you came, you assaulted my child, you undressed others and blindfolded them, you wanted to shoot them while they were naked … So now I am taking off my clothes so that you can shoot and kill me while I am naked. (Anek Karmella, Apaa, Uganda)

Studies of women's protest have adopted various social movement approaches that look at the mobilization of resources, the facilitating and constraining role of opportunity structures, and questions of framing and culture. This study looks at the role of symbolic resonance, a theme which is mostly absent from both feminist scholarship on women's movements, but also from social movement theory. This paper explores the symbolic meanings behind the public displays of the female naked body in the face of repressive authority in contemporary protest movements for peace, human rights and democracy in Africa, with a focus on the 2015 protests in Amuru District in Northern Uganda. It shows how the body symbolism of motherhood was successfully used as a resource for collective struggle to protect land rights, with broader implications for other African contexts, where female nakedness in protest is relatively common across Africa south of the Sahara.

In 2012 soldiers, police and the Uganda Wildlife Authority guards had evicted 6000 people from their homes in Apaa. The land had been sold to a South African investor who intended to turn the area into wildlife hunting grounds. When another team of surveyors appeared in 2015, local residents demonstrated, resulting in the injury of 82 demonstrators (Langol 2015). Then on 17 April 2015, Acholi women from Apaa in Amuru District, in northern Uganda launched another protest, undressing before two government ministers who had come to try to pacify the population and assure them that no one was to be displaced from their land. The women, some stark naked, others baring their breasts, wept and threw themselves on the ground, revealing their utter contempt, frustration and anger against the Uganda government's orchestrated evictions of families in Apaa. As the women engaged the government officials naked, other community members, including men, burst into a chorus of wailing, drawing on funereal tropes. Thus, both genders contravened culturally sanctioned gender roles, norms and expectations in their fight against a common enemy.[1]

Daudi Migereko, the Minister of Lands, broke down and was gushing tears, while the late Internal Affairs Minister Gen. Aronda Nyakairima appeared unshaken and stood still, looking in different directions to avoid eye contact with the naked women. He later announced that they had canceled the erection of the boundary mark stones and the demarcation exercise was, in fact, suspended. Later in January 2016 members of parliament Gilbert Olanya (Kilak County), and women's representative Lucy Akello went on their knees at a community event and Major General Julius Oketta (army representative to parliament) apologized. They said they regretted the evictions and said they must never occur again. However, not all were convinced that the problem was over and residents remained justifiably cautious about whether to trust these promises (Owich 2016).

The naked protests that took place in Apaa were as much symbolic as they were political, drawing on culturally resonant understandings of motherhood. Nakedness in Acholi culture is related to shame, but it has been one of the traditional means that Acholi women and men have used to express their anger. In our case study it is adopted as a political weapon women have used to express their deep seated anger against the government of Uganda for what it did to their sons and was now doing to the broader community. The female body, or more specifically the body of the mother, now stands at the center of political contestation over land. Rather than being a symbol of passivity and vulnerability, as some have portrayed motherhood in other parts of the world, the woman in this context is powerful and agentic because of her symbolic role as a mother and the vehemence of the mother's naked curse. Because the female is symbolically associated with the land, which receives the seed necessary for reproduction, protest by women around land rights is seen as all the more powerful. The paper points to the importance of understanding this women's protest not only in its literal dimension of a protest by women against political and economic marginalization and land grabbing, but it also speaks to the need to look at the deeper symbolic uses of the mother archetype that cannot be reduced to simply mothers protesting in the more literal sense that it is understood in most of the literature.

Women have used nakedness as a form of protest historically up to this day and they continue to do so worldwide, perhaps most famously in recent years by the Ukrainian organization FEMEN. One of the earliest well-documented accounts of such protest was that of Lady Godiva of Coventry in England, who loosened her hair and rode naked on a horse through the town of Coventry to free the city of servitude and taxation from her husband Earl Leofric on behalf of the Danish king in the mid-eleventh century (Davidson 1969). In Africa, these forms of protest go back to pre-colonial times and were marshaled in the struggle against colonialism in countries as diverse as Zambia (Geisler 2004), Guinea, (Schmidt 2005), Nigeria (Eames 1992) and Cameroon (Diduk 1989; Terretta 2007). Some of these protests have continued to this day in new contexts, from the democracy and human rights movement in Kenya in the 1990s (Maathai 2007; Tibbetts 1994), to protests around land rights among the Maasai in Tanzania, demonstrations against environmental degradation caused by oil companies in the Delta Region of Nigeria in the early 2000s (Anugwom and Anugwom 2009; Ikelegbe 2005; Laine 2015; Sokari 2009; Turner and Brownhill 2002), protests against housing evictions in South Africa in the 1990s, and struggles of Liberia's peace movement in the early 2000s (Gbowee and Lynn Mithers 2011).

Novelist Nuruddin Farah (1996) describes such a protest by women in the coastal city of Kismayo two years before Somalia collapsed into civil war. His account is eerily evocative of the Apaa protest:

> A few dozen women, defying the conviction that enjoins female sartorial modesty, bared their breasts in public in front of a crowd of men. Fists raised, voices harsh, they shouted "Rise, Rise!," challenging the men to action, reproaching them for their failure to confront the excesses of the dictatorship. By challenging the men in this manner, the women implied that they would not from then on defer to them as husbands, fathers, or figures of authority. There was a sense of public unease in Kismayo after this event, the haruspices interpreting the women's action as a transgression, a sign of worse things to come, a countdown to the total collapse of a centuries-old status quo. These harbingers of folly spoke of women preparing to take over the opposition, of the spread of AIDS, of families fragmenting. At stake was Somali culture itself, the death of which was now thought to be imminent. The discord at the hearth was seen as symbolic of discord at the national level. At the height of an autocrat's rule, especially towards the end of his reign, such people argued, the difference between the sexes is authority. Men become women, women men, the terms defining either rendered provisional. Thus the women gave politics a more intimate profile, bringing to the fore questions about the national crisis. It was the women, ironically, who took politics, confined by dictatorship to the privacy of the home, back into the public domain. (18)

Such naked protests have been used in other parts of the world, but with less frequency than one finds in parts of Africa today. In Imphal, Manipur in northeast India, in 2004 a group of Metei women staged a naked demonstration, protesting the torture, rape and murder of Thangjam Manorama, who had been in the custody of the Indian Army Assam Rifles Battalion. Although this form of protest is at odds with everyday norms of female modesty, it is rooted in a coherent repertoire of representation regarding women's nakedness found in theatre and in protest (Misri 2011). And although such naked protests have varied cultural meanings and resonance in different parts of the world, in general women have used such acts as a vehement curse or expression of revulsion against authorities and their actions, often as a last recourse. While we do not want to claim that the gender norms, values and expectations of Acholi or Ugandan women are the same for all African women, in general, one finds that norms regarding nakedness in Africa reflect a view that women's bodies are respected and their private parts are expected to be covered from the public gaze most of the time unless they are nursing or unless there is a deliberate ritual or ceremony that calls for removal of one's clothing. For example, among the neighboring Langi people, before Christianity took root, the clan held a ceremony where the newly married bride was stripped naked and rituals were performed in order to welcome her into her marital home. This ritual had a deeper liminal meaning of symbolic rebirth, ritually transforming a girl into a woman, of welcoming her into the husband's clan by stripping her of her natal clan identity, and of ensuring her fertility. Many such practices have fallen by the wayside, but the norm of modesty for women remains.

This paper explores the gendered nature of the protests as a product of marginalization of the poor and an effort to reclaim power. While it situates the study in the context of Uganda, it addresses broader questions about how and why women resort to nakedness in protest more generally. We begin with a discussion of the symbolic protest in the literature and the perceived limits of such forms of protest. We discuss the implications of the gendered symbolism of this form of social protest and what it means for women's mobilization more generally. We contextualize the event by showing how the women and men from Apaa used their bodies as symbolic tools of protest and continue with a discussion about the meaning of the body symbolism in this context. This paper builds on several literatures, which are brought together in exploring the relationship between the body and resistance. It draws on an interest in a part of the social movement literature on the use of political symbols in protest, but also on the anthropological insights of the relationship between the body and society, and finally, on the feminist literature on the social and cultural construction and meaning of the body.

The paper asks why did the women of Apaa resort to stripping naked before the government officials? What was the cultural and political imaginary from which this stripping emerged? How did the Acholi and the broader Ugandan citizenry interpret this transgression of the private into the public sphere? Did it resonate and how successful were these kinds of protests in advancing the cause of the women and the community of Apaa?

Social movements and symbolic protest

Some of the earliest work on social movements looked at the relationship between emotion and protest. For example, Gustave Le Bon's 1895 work on *The Crowd: A Study of the Popular Mind* argued that people fell into a near hypnotic state if they found themselves in a crowd, which could be characterized by "impulsiveness, irritability, incapacity to reason" among other states (cited in van Ginneken 1992). In the 1960s and 1970s sociologists and political scientists explained revolt by focusing on gaps between expectations and gratification and strains on the system and rapid socio- economic change led to "systemic frustration," which in turn brought about political violence (Feierabend and Feierabend 1972).

The literature on revolution that emerged partly in response to some of these studies, focused instead on states and structural change. Meanwhile, the social movement theories that replaced these earlier approaches in the global north veered in a completely different direction, focusing on theories of resource mobilization (including material, organizational and personnel resources), changes in political opportunity structures (such as elite configurations or alliances, state capacity, economic conditions), and frames or the extent to which social movement demands resonate with the public, media, elites and others.

More recently, a fourth area of concern, especially among those working on new social movements, has been a return to the role of emotions, moral protest and changing consciousness in the formation of social movements. James Jasper looked at post citizenship movements that included movements around animal rights, the environment, nuclear energy, peace, life style protections and alternative healing. As Polletta and Jasper (2001) argue, collective identity is a person's cognitive, moral and emotional connection with the community, or institution. It is a perception of a shared status formulation. A collective identity can be expressed through "names, narratives, symbols, virtual styles, rituals, clothing and so on" (Polletta and Jasper 2001, 285). Their interest is primarily in what collective identity is and how collective identities matter to social movements. Polletta and Jasper are interested in the interplay between individual and collective identity and they argue that collective identities are not the aggregate of individual identities. As useful as we find this approach, it is missing the symbolic view of the collective as a reflection of the self (in our case, represented as the body) and vice versa.

In fact, most theories of social movements and social protest do not look at symbolic action, mainly because the theories have been developed in the global north, where the symbolic element of protest has not been as pronounced or appreciated. This paper is interested not so much in the question of collective identity as it is in how people mobilize and draw on prexisting symbolic systems to give meaning to their protest. In that sense we agree with James Jasper that protest is a place where symbols are revived and reenacted, giving meaning to rights that have been violated, resources that have been misappropriated, and dignity that has been trampled on.

Political symbols

The literature on political symbols has been influenced by anthropologists like Clifford Geertz, who argued that political symbols can serve as an expression of solidarity and common feelings of identification. This could be with a particular event like a ceremony commemorating the death of a leader; or raising awareness around a particular issue (e.g., rubber bracelets for AIDS or cancer awareness); or it can mark a nationalistic identity (e.g., independence day celebration), or it can provide a cognitive roadmap or orientation with which to make sense of the world (Geertz 1973).

Symbols can legitimize the distribution of power. Rituals like elections, especially in authoritarian countries, can give the impression that those in power have legitimate claims to power. Thus symbols and their enactment can also be a means of domination and creating further divisions in society (Lukes 1975).

Some have seen symbols as expressions of the irrational workings of the mind and as disguised representations of the unconscious. For Theodor Adorno (Adorno et al. 1950), the political symbolism of Nazi Germany was a disguised latent desire of the unconscious. Similarly, political symbols can be a release for a social and psychic anxiety. Klatch (1988) gives the example of Martin Luther King as a symbolic leader as evoking hope and confidence for changing the status quo.

Harold Lasswell and Murray Edelman saw symbols as a way through which political elites defend their own interests and a way for the mass public to release anxiety. Symbols can reassure people and thus discourage resistance (Klatch 1988). They can also be way of unifying society and providing a way to mobilize people around a particular set of moral and psychological appeals. But they can also be used in divisive ways as the swastika was used by Nazis. For anthropologist Victor Turner (1982), symbols both reinforce structure but can also serve antistructural purposes and threaten social order by challenging the status quo.

Thus, symbols are seen as both giving meaning to politics, as an expression of political preferences, but also as a means of mobilizing interests. They are used by both the elite to maintain the status quo (Edelman 1967), but also by marginalized people to change society (Kowalewski 1980). They are not simply an ideational phenomenon and can represent real interests (Klatch 1988).

Body symbolism

Ultimately we are interested in this paper in body symbolism in the context of protest. Here we draw on two strands of research on the body. Numerous authors from Bordo (1993) to Crawford (1984) have depicted the body as conveying core social values as they relate to beauty, weight, eating disorders and other such phenomena. Another body of literature looks at the way that the body is agentic in the social world and acts on the world or what is referred to in the literature as "embodiment." In the political context, the body is not only a symbolic field for reproducing dominant values but also "a site for resistance to and transformation of those systems of meaning" (Crawford 1984, 95).

In this paper we also draw on work by Oldfield, Salo, and Schlyter (2009) for whom the body politics is conceptualized from a sociological and political point of view to explain how women and men use their bodies as tools of resistance. To Oldfield, Salo and Schlyter, body politics represents the negotiation of power via the body whether directly or through representation. As they explain: "We conceptualise 'body politics' as the negotiation of power via the body; processes that operate sometimes directly (for instance, violently), but also processes that work at a symbolic and representational scale" (2009, 3). It is this latter symbolic aspect we are especially interested in, which in general terms is akin to Carl Jung's notion of "collective unconscious." Once one looks at the gendered dimensions of protest in its symbolic context, the importance of the protest is not simply about individual women and men or groups of women and men protesting injustice, but rather, it is about what they represent in a deeper sense of the collective psyche. This then is less about women as literal mothers to the exclusion of women who are not mothers, and more about the mother archetype and harnessing it to curse those who have stolen land from local residents. The literal sense in which many social scientists try to read these protests profoundly misses their social significance, which is a form of communication at a symbolic level.

People draw on and manipulate the body for their own purposes, not always consciously (Comaroff and Comaroff 1992). The Comaroffs write about how nineteenth century British colonialism was interested in sanitizing African bodies, which were regarded as diseased and potentially contagious. The body was the site of the enactment of the colonial project, but it also was a site of contestation as well. There is a large literature that looks at these contestations in Africa over clothing in colonial Lesotho (Comaroff and Comaroff 1992), forcible fattening of girls among Azawagh Arabs in Niger (Popenoe 2004), female genital mutilation in Sudan, Kenya and Egypt during colonialism, and other such contested practices.

We build on the early recognition by Mary Douglas in her book *Natural Symbols* (1970) of the symbolic significance of the body. She argued that bodily symbols reflected the social and replicated the social situation and that the body symbolizes the social world.

Bodies can reveal core values of a society. In the case of the Amuru women, there are lines that can't be crossed and when they are crossed by the government, as in this case, the female body becomes one of the most powerful sources of resistance in society in general. The men play a role in weeping along with other women, but their role is secondary and it is a supporting role.

Judith Butler (1990) captures this dual role of body symbolism as both a reflection of society and its agency, arguing that various acts or series of repeated performances of gender create gender. Building on these ideas of Butler and Douglas, several scholars have looked at the connection between women's bodies and their position in society and the ways in which body based functions of women in bearing and nursing children are used to justify a social artifice which becomes the unchangeable order of things (Devisch 1985; Reischer and Koo 2004).

However, in our story, the same connections between women's bodies and their position in society become *the basis for resistance*, political action and agency in the public realm. Women's social roles are inscribed on their body, but not in a way that locks them into simply being birthing, nursing or nurturing mothers in a physical or literal sense. It is a source of authority that gives women, regardless of whether or not they have children, agency in the public realm. In using their bodies as a curse, women claim the ultimate moral authority that none can surpass in the societies in question. Everyone is born and everyone dies and so the symbolism of the woman's body as the creator of life, but also as one who can symbolically negate that life has a powerful resonance in Acholi and many other societies.

Limitations of naked protest

For all the power embedded in naked protest, there are also limits to this type of protest. Perhaps the most obvious failure is where there is a lack of resonance with the local culture. While nakedness is often associated with shame in most cultures, the subversive use of nakedness does not have the same resonance everywhere as means of shifting the shame from the protestor subject to the object of the protest. This was spectacularly evident in the 2013 FEMEN protests in Tunisia, which many Tunisian and other North African feminists eschewed, believing that this protest was culturally insensitive and inappropriate. Tunisian FEMEN activist Amina Sboui Tyler created a scandal in Tunisia when she posted topless pictures online in March 2013 in which she wrote "my body is my own and not your honour," on herself. She was charged and then acquitted for contempt and defamation for these actions but was also charged and jailed for desecrating a cemetery. Two French and a German member of FEMEN protested her arrest in Tunisia by exposing their breasts and were charged with public indecency and eventually released. FEMEN is a movement started in Ukraine and is based in Paris with the goal of protesting patriarchy using breasts as a weapon. Female nakedness is their symbolic response to the alienation of women from their bodies: As their website explains: "All functions of the female body are harshly controlled and regulated by patriarchy. Separated from the woman, her body is an object of monstrous patriarchal exploitation, animated by production of heirs, surplus profits, sexual pleasures and pornographic shows."[2] However, for many Tunisian feminists, the protest was regarded as setting back their cause rather than advancing it, even though they might have agreed with the overall goals of the movement. Thus cultural resonance is a major factor in gauging the success of such protests.

Another consideration is how the protest is framed. Some of these protests are framed within what Iris Marion Young called the "logic of masculinist protection." Misri recounts the protest of 22-year-old Pooja Chauhan in 2007 who walked in her underwear through the streets of Rajkot in India to protest emotional and physical abuse from her husband and in-laws over the payment of dowry by her family and her inability to produce a male child, as well as the lack of police response to her complaints. Out of desperation she launched her protest with a bunch of bangles and a red rose in one hand, and a baseball bat in the other. The baseball bat signified her need to take matters into her own hands and the bangles signified emasculation, that is, the failure of men to protect her as proof of their lack of manliness. The danger here, as Misri argues, is that such a protest can reinforce a form of idealized gender norms in which men are the protectors and women are vulnerable and in need of protection.

Judith Butler raises yet a third limitation, which has to do with the appropriation of the language and symbols of oppression by those who are oppressed by them. She refers to the term "queer" that has been transformed from a term that is a demeaning insult to one that is a positive self-affirmation. Naked protest might also fall into this same category of having the same kind of subversive effect, although one might argue that the female naked body does not categorically signify oppression in the same way that the term "queer" has signified. But Butler does raise an important question about the limits of such protest using these symbols and at what point do they resignify their opposite meaning, which is probably what happened with the FEMEN protests in Tunisia (Butler 1993).

Finally, a fourth limitation may be the focus on women as mothers. In the naked protests, but also in other protests, women take what is private about motherhood and place it in the public realm. Taylor (1994) shows this in her analysis of the Mothers of the Plaza de Mayo, who protested the disappearance of their children by the Argentinian junta starting in 1977 up to 2006. The women protestors redefined motherhood, the family and home in a patriarchal society, where the public roles of women were extremely limited and were reduced to the prostitute or madwoman and even nonmothers or antimothers. The mother in Argentinian society was one who stayed home with the children and was invisible. They modeled themselves on the Virgin Mary who transcended the public–private divide and marched as if they were in a religious procession with their heads covered and eyes looking upward, highlighting the acceptable feminine qualities of self-sacrifice, suffering and even irrationality as they demanded the return of their dead children. They took the symbols of the private realm and of childhood innocence and motherhood, (e.g., their white scarves, the baby shawl, the baby toy) and placed them in the public sphere of the repressive state, affirming life over death. One of their leaders, Hebé de Bonafini, even wore her bedroom slippers in demonstrations.

But some argue that this affirmed their passivity and powerlessness. Judith Butler would see this use of motherhood as separating the person I have been with the one who is performing motherhood, affirming the impossibility of stretching the role of motherhood, which is embedded with patriarchy (1993). However, Diana Taylor (1994) argues that the Mothers of Plaza de Mayo were, in fact, able to successfully redefine and politicize motherhood and were successful in influencing the way women were perceived as political actors in years to come. This was the precursor to many changes on the legislative front for women.

It seems that many of the critiques of the use of the motherhood trope come out of a particularly Western understanding of motherhood that sees only its limitations and sees it only as a source of weakness and vulnerability. Not all cultures see motherhood in this way and in many parts of Africa, motherhood is seen primarily as a source of strength and is often drawn on as a means of asserting political authority. This is true even of those authors like Ama Ata Aidoo, Tsitsi Dangarembga, Mariama Ba and Buchi Emecheta, who have challenged an uncritical view of an idealized motherhood by showing that women should be seen as more than mothers and wives. Moreover, in societies where women's roles are more limited, women out of necessity must find ways of expressing opposition within culturally comprehensible means. Thus, in the context of the Amuru protests, the form they took was extremely powerful.

In the Amuru case, women saw themselves as protesting the government officials, soldiers and others whom Apaa residents believed were behind the grabbing of their land. But at the same time, it was a very powerful collective appeal by women supported by men, who wailed as protest, but also because of men's perceived collective failure of leadership and inability to address the community concerns. The naked protest thus arises out of a patriarchal frame in which the roles ascribed to men are those of protector. This is clearly not a feminist inspired protest, but it is very much situated in the cultural and symbolic context of northern Uganda where these protests by women constitute a powerful form of collective political action.

These forms have become increasingly frequent in a country like Uganda. In 2014 naked women protested the government effort to grab their lands and give it to Soroti University for development.[3] There have been numerous reports of women engaging in naked protests of the land taken over by Chinese investors in Bukedea district in May 2015. These were not just rural protests, they were also carried out in urban areas by educated women. When Ingrid Turinawe, a female opposition political leader was arrested and stripped in 2012, women activists held a protest in Kampala removing their shirts.[4]

The April 2015 protests in Amuru were not the first time the women in northern Uganda used such tactics. In 2012 women in Lakang Amuru sub-county stripped before former Amuru Resident District Commissioner Milton Odong and a group of people who were planning on establishing a sugarcane plantation on their land. Also during the civil war in northern Uganda (1987–2006) over 1500 Acholi women in neighboring Gulu protested the war by baring their breasts. They wore mourning dresses, tied scarves around their heads, and carried baskets as they wept, chanted funeral songs and blew funeral horns (Tripp 2000).

Methods

Florence Ebila carried out a total of 17 in-depth interviews in February 2016 in Apaa village, Labala parish in Amuru District, where the women had staged the naked protest in April 2015. She interviewed in the Acholi language five women who undressed during the protest and four women who protested while dressed. She also interviewed eight men who wailed during the protest. Two focus group discussions were held with 11 children; 6 girls and 5 boys, all of them pupils of Apaa primary school. The interviews were analyzed using a version of the five-step process developed by Grant McCracken for qualitative in-depth interviews (1998).

Four out of five of those who undressed were widows who had lost their husbands either to the Lord's Resistance Army (LRA) war or as a result of the war. Widowhood is very significant to the Acholi and also to other African cultures because widows symbolize people who are in need of help. The widowed bodies were considered much more sacred vehicles to deliver the naked curse because their bodies were considered to have been sanctified by suffering since they had already experienced death of a loved one. Their bodies were beyond shame since there would be no husband to complain about them having exposed what is considered private to their men only, that is, their naked bodies. In terms of seniority, these were also very old women who had acquired status because of their age. They were protecting orphans so they took upon themselves the whole burden and shame of the community by accepting to be the channel through which to voice the protest on that day. These were women who were ready to die for their land.

In terms of age, two of the women interviewed were in their early thirties, three in their forties, one in her fifties, one in her sixties and the last one in her nineties. The oldest respondent, who was in her nineties, was a traditional healer who had invaluable insights into Acholi culture. In terms of responsibilities held in the community, two of the women were leaders within the community with one serving as Local Council one Chairperson in charge of women affairs and the other was the head teacher of Apaa Primary school, while one was a nurse. The fact that women of such high status in a rural community would have participated in such a protest, is quite remarkable, suggesting once again how the government actions had pushed women to the brink. One of the women had become very active in the politics of her village and was campaigning for the position of Chairperson of the Local Council 1 besides being the campaign agent of one of the candidates who stood for the position of Member of Parliament for Kilak North. The fifth and youngest among those who undressed, is a widowed businesswoman who sells produce and also sells food in a small eatery in Apaa trading center.

Out of the four women who were interviewed and who did not undress, two were present at the scene of the protest. One sat among the people who wailed and another was among those who were praying. The 90-year-old woman who was interviewed was not present at the scene of protest because she had gone to the hospital. The fourth woman, who had become disabled from the brutal beatings of the soldiers at earlier protests, did not go to the junction on that day.

According to her, those who were sickly like her had been advised the day before to remain at home.

All the nine men who were interviewed were at the scene of the protest. While six were among the group who wailed, one prayed and the other two combined their crying with providing leadership and guidance to the protestors. Three of the men were interviewed in their capacities as leaders within the Apaa community. These were politicians, including the then aspiring Member of Parliament Kilak North, Anthony Akol (who won the seat and is now representing Kilak North in Parliament), the Local Council 1 leader from Apaa, Abola Maryan, and Lony Francis Ojok, Local Council 3 candidate for Pabbo. Two elders were interviewed who were authorities in Acholi oral history and culture. One represented the category of the religious leadership in Apaa.

The case of Apaa: origins of conflict

What then happened in Apaa to lead to the mass protests that included transgressing moralities and gendered expectations? What was the cultural and political imaginary from which the stripping emerged? In order to understand what happened in Apaa, there is a need to historicize the events that led to the protest to help contextualize the political contestations that have been at play in this land crisis of Apaa.

Most of the respondents trace the origin of the conflict between the government of Uganda and the people of Apaa to the year 2007 and the end of the more than 20-year-old war between the government and the LRA. When the people of Apaa returned to their homes from the camps where the government had resettled them temporarily to protect them from the LRA war, they were ordered to move away from Apaa because they were told it was a game reserve. The land was said to belong to the East Madi reserve and workers from Uganda Wildlife Authority were sent to Apaa to evict the villagers out of the place in 2010.

In yet another version of the story, the origin of the conflict can be traced to the pre-colonial and colonial periods when Acholi and Madi used to fight over hunting grounds. According to oral tradition, there was a dispute over the strip of land bordering two groups, the Madi and the Acholi. In 1926 there was a big conflict between the Madi and the Acholi and one local chief called Doli was killed during one of the fights. After he was killed in 1927, a meeting was held in Gondokoro in Nimule in present day South Sudan. That was the headquarters of the British where the local court could take place. That is where the conflict was resolved and thereafter the Acholi and Madi began to live in harmony. At that time the British decided that the boundary between the Madi and the Acholi should be the river between the two ethnic groups and it was named *Juka,* which in Acholi means "stop the conflict" and which the Madi apparently call *Zoka.* This is one version of the story as reported by the Acholi whom we interviewed for this research.

Some Acholi claim that in actual fact, their land extended beyond Juka into Tirikwa. Tirikwa is a corruption of two Acholi words *Teri Kwar,* which literally translates as "your red arse." In Acholi, reference to the opponent's private parts is meant to be an insult. The naming of the village Tirikwa, was to the Acholi therefore meant to be a permanent symbolic gesture of abuse to their neighbors, which ended when the British signed the 1927 agreement in Gondokoro that established the ethnic boundaries. According to Nancy Rydberg,[5] such naming of places is not uncommon. The Acholi have similarly descriptive and sometimes offensive names for other places: *Olayilong Junction* is the junction where one urinates in his pants, *Lakwat Omee* is where the pastor got drunk and *Cet Kana* is donkey shit. The symbolic insult through reference to the private parts of the body became a permanent marker of place and memory for the Acholi. It was the place they had to give up for the sake of peace during the colonial era.

After independence from the British in 1962, the currently disputed land of Apaa was deserted because of an attack of tsetse flies that caused sleeping sickness among the occupants. It was in fact during the Idi Amin regime in the 1970s that the Acholi were encouraged by Amin to go back and settle on the disputed land. The people occupied the land until they moved to or were placed in government-run camps for the internally displaced around the mid-1990s because of the LRA war. The land boundary question resurfaced again after the Acholi went back to settle on the land after the end of the LRA war in 2007. So when officials from the Uganda Wildlife Authority came and ordered the residents of Apaa to move away from the area because it was gazetted as a game reserve, Apaa residents disputed their claim and referred the rangers back to history: to the living waters of Juka that had been used to separate the Acholi from the Madi.

It is unclear what designs the government had for the land because they were not transparent. It also appeared that the government and military were being used to advance private interests of various kinds. Beyond the swirl of rumors, observers who had investigated the situation carefully noted that there appeared to be foul play on the part of the government. Divinity Union Ltd., a company owned by the president's brother, Gen. Salim Saleh, produced a report in 1998/1999 that revealed that it was interested in transforming Acholiland into a breadbasket for Africa by uprooting the Acholi from land ownership and having them work as cheap labor on commercial farms under the Ministry of Defense. The plan was debated by the sixth parliament and was rejected by the Inter-faith groups and by the member of parliament from Gulu, Norbert Mao (also Democratic Party president). It later came to light that the report had deliberately hidden the fact that Amuru district is the location of large oil deposits. Meanwhile the government earmarked 40,000 hectares of Amuru land for the Madhvani sugar cane plantation while part of the land was to be used to create a wildlife preserve owned by a white South African businessman (Refugee Law Project 2012; Serwajja 2009). When Apaa women decided to protest naked on 17 April 2015, it was a well-planned response that emanated from the deep rooted feeling of helplessness in the face of what appeared to be several land grabbing schemes carried out by the state. In pushing them off their land, the state was violently trampling their livelihood, their bodies and blatantly violating their rights.

Apaa residents interviewed wanted instead a dialogue between the government and the people of Apaa in order to solve the problem of ownership amicably. They continue to question and reject the use of stones to demarcate their land. They argue that no other district in Uganda has been demarcated using such stones and therefore there is no need for this to be done in Apaa. They have demand that the government stop relocating them to Adjumani since their ancestors have always lived in the area and had been part of Acholiland for generations. They have rejected the government's plan to evict them to bring "development" to the area and have asked whether wildlife is more important than people. They have demanded the right to have a say regarding their land.

Symbolism of naked protest by women

The symbolic act of undressing and mourning is interpreted in many different but related ways by the Apaa residents. There had been several protests prior to the one of 17 April 2015.

During such protests the women and men of Apaa had sat in the sun and protested peacefully against the impending eviction. According to respondents, the soldiers would come and burn their huts, beat them up and force them to move, but they refused to move. The particular action that sparked rage was when the soldiers came and arrested some young men from the community, undressed and blindfolded them, and tortured them naked. As one of the women protestors explained:

During this conflict over land, the army has been arresting the young men and taking them to Madi (Adjumani), and while on their way, they are tortured. They are made to lie on the ground and then the army men walk all over them, stepping on their bodies, right from the top of their heads to their feet. One of the young men's testicles was crushed like that and now he is unable to have children. Even the young men who were arrested recently when they came and fired tear gas at us, suffered the same torture. This had been a big problem. They have also mutilated the hands of two young men. They cut their hands off.

The above brutality angered the mothers, who regarded the state to be a monster that was out to destroy their children and emasculate their men. They asked the questions: "Why were our sons tortured naked?" "Is it the habit of government to kill people while they are naked?" They explained to us that, "The naked torture was one of the motivations for the naked protest by the women of Apaa." This has parallels with the use of rape of men during the war as another form of emasculation. An ACORD report (2001) cited a medical superintendent at the Lacor hospital as saying that male rape was "Used by the government soldiers as a weapon. The anger goes very deep. It is the women who bring it up. Male rape is a major cause of people's anger at the army." The same ACORD report cites one of the workshop participants who talked about how "when a man is raped, it takes away his manhood and he fails to act to bring change." In the Apaa protest, this emasculation and feeling of powerlessness by the men caused a role reversal and women took up the "masculine" role of protecting the place after men had been diminished in this way. According to the women who protested naked, they wanted to make it easier for the soldiers by undressing ahead of time as they awaited their murders. The naked protesters were ready to die naked, while mocking the state.

However, the naked protest was also a tool used by the residents of Apaa to curse and wish their enemies the worst fate possible. According to one of the widows who protested naked, undressing is a curse that can lead to the death of the person with whom one is angry, especially if the one who is undressing is wronged and undresses deliberately to prove her point. In order to avert the ill-fated consequences of the curse, the one who did wrong has to sacrifice to the ancestors, repent wholeheartedly and ask for forgiveness from the person whom he/she has wronged. The women used their naked bodies to express several things: anger, frustration and bitterness against the alleged land grabbers. According to one of the women, the naked protest in Amuru sent two messages: The first message was directed to the men from their community, to tell them that they had failed in their roles as protectors of women and children. The second message was to curse the government officials, soldiers and all the other people whom Apaa residents suspected were behind the grabbing of their land.

To fully appreciate the meaning behind the use of nakedness as a form of protest, one has to refer back to Acholi culture and understand the meaning behind the act. What does protesting naked mean in Acholi culture? How has it been used in the past? According to the respondents who were interviewed for this research, when someone undresses it means they are very angry. It means that there has been great provocation from the other party and the one who undresses has borne it for too long and can no longer bear it. It also means that the one who undresses is innocent or has not done anything wrong to deserve such provocation. Because of the constant provocation, the one who undresses expresses their frustration and anger through the act of undressing. This is where the body becomes a tool of communication. It fulfills what Wendy Harcourt (2009) refers to in her analysis of body politics as counterculture by making visible what had not been visible in the relationship between the two factions. The body becomes an "important way of knowing," because it succeeds in defining the parameters of the disagreement.

Naked exposure was also used as a tool for cursing. It was one thing to undress and remain naked, but it was another to somersault and expose the birth canal in the process of protesting. It was also terrible for a woman to slap her vagina while cursing. A woman's nakedness symbolized a return to the origin, a rebirth. The body of a woman is considered sacred in Acholi culture and cannot be exposed in any way. It is believed that a woman's private parts symbolize the source of life. A child is expected to respect and revere this place which is responsible for its own creation and existence. One could not, out of respect for motherhood, see his or her mother's vagina because that would be the most abominable thing to do. If a mother got angry and undressed before her child, that was a curse that could kill the child or bring bad luck to the child forever.

Symbolically, the vagina has the power to produce life and to swallow it back if it is not happy. Conception is done during happy moments as part of the union between man and woman that produces life. Culturally, even the process of conception among the Acholi involves sexual intercourse, which is supposed to be done in the dark when the man did not see the wife's nakedness. One of the male respondents explained the privacy surrounding sex in this manner:

> Acholi culture is not like other cultures where people bare themselves often in public [kima-sulo[6]]. Even speaking about sex openly is taboo. In fact, while growing up you do not know some of the names of your body parts, they are not even spoken out loud. So by the time that happens [referring to the naked protests] you must know that every solution has failed and if you relate it to what happened in this case, everything has failed, the leaders have failed, the elders have failed, the religious leaders tried and they all failed so that was the only option and that actually helped because from that point we started having dialogue to see how best this thing could be resolved.

In other words, the widowed protestors symbolically represented the source of life and their protest was a curse that threatened social death to the authorities. The nakedness symbolized the pain of birth a woman goes through before she produces a child. This was the pain that the women felt for their land as mothers of the community. According to another male respondent:

> Traditionally it is believed that since it is the woman who births children, if she undresses and reveals to you her private parts from which you came, some misfortune will befall you. That part of the body should not be seen when one is sorrowful, it should only be seen at a time of joy. We believe that that part of her body responds to her sorrow towards you to cause you to suffer a misfortune or some form of curse. To avert the curse, the offender must come and apologise and ask for the forgiveness of the aggrieved party.

To re-enact that pain of loss for the sake of their land, the naked protestors meant to show that their land was very important to them and any attempt to grab it brought to them such pain like that one which a woman experiences during child labor. This is implied in the rhetorical question that respondents asked over and again: "These people are chasing us away from our land; where do they expect us to go?" And that is a question that the government failed to answer. Faced with nakedness, the government officials folded their files, averted their eyes from the shame and left Apaa at least for a while.

The Apaa protests drew on traditional Acholi means of bodily expression for women. If a mother had a son or daughter who constantly offended her, she would try all means to solve all the problems with them. If, for example, the son was an alcoholic who came back home and abused his mother, she could decide to first take the case to the clan. If the son did not listen to the clan, then they would call his uncles and discuss the problem with them. If he still continued misbehaving and abusing the mother, then she could undress to express her deepest regret and frustration. It was only a mother's nakedness that could curse because mothers are very important in Acholi society. Mothers are the source of life and it is believed that they can either give life or take it away by virtue of the sacredness of their bodies.

There are, however, rules about who and when one can use nakedness as a means of protest. Undressing is regarded as the last option, when all other options of protest have failed. It is also considered a tactic for those who have no other recourse. In April 2016, Dr. Stella Nyanzi, a female researcher at Makerere Institute of Social Research at Makerere University, stripped to her underwear to protest against being locked out of her office in a dispute over her employment contract.[7] Nyanzi's naked protest, unlike the Apaa protest, sparked a debate on radio, newspapers and social media especially around the question of agency. Many questioned whether a woman of her status did not have other avenues at her disposal, without having to resort to what others have labeled a "weapon of the weak." Nyanzi, who had her defenders, argued that she was indeed using a "weapon of the weak" because she felt that she was fighting a battle that was too big for her.

Nyanzi's actions revealed some of the boundaries of what many Ugandans consider acceptable when it comes to using this form of protest both in terms of who can legitimately use this mode of protest and in what context.

Other ways of protesting include using the breast as a means of cursing. A woman can lift up her naked breasts, even if she has not undressed completely and pronounce a curse upon a stubborn child saying, for example; "You who do not listen to me, did I not feed you from my breast? If not, you can continue to ignore my advice." Such a pronunciation brings a curse upon that child.

In order to avert the curse, sacrifices have to be made otherwise the child can become mad or "redundant." It is very difficult to undo a curse. A mother can also hit her vagina while cursing. Another way of cursing is when one raises one's foot and hits the sole of the foot on the ground while lamenting and saying: "It is these feet that took care of you. I dug and fed you. Why do you not listen when I talk? If you know that I did these things for you then you should listen." Such a pronouncement is a curse in itself to the child to whom it is targeted.

If a husband and a wife quarrel and disagree, the wife will first use other options to express her anger before using the option of undressing. She may lock the house and refuse to open for the husband to express her displeasure. She may do something provocative like refusing to breastfeed the baby, if she has a baby, or refusing to cook food, all with the aim of sparking a quarrel and a discussion and resolution of the problem. If, however, the husband continues his bad habits and does not change, the wife can deny him sex. This had treacherous consequences because ritual sacrifices have to be made before the two can engage in sexual relations together again. If they ignore the curse and go back to having sex without performing the required ritual, it is believed that one of them can die. Thus, the body has been used in several ways culturally as a means of protest, as a means of expressing happiness or anger depending on the circumstance among the Acholi and it provides the context for the protests we have witnessed in the region.

Symbolism of male wailing

As mentioned earlier, men wailed throughout the protest and, the tears symbolized helplessness in the face of an adversary. Traditionally, Acholi people were warriors who would fight to defend their honor against invasion. The Lamogi rebellion of 1911 took place within the current Amuru district. The Acholi took up arms and fought the British invaders, killing three British soldiers. Many Acholi fighters died of gas suffocation and currently the site of the war has been turned into a tourist site in memory of the gallant fighters who defended their land and the family honor with their blood. Defending the land against foreign invasion with their lives has historically therefore been a male responsibility. For Acholi men of Apaa to sit down and cry in 2015 instead of engaging in a fight to protect their land was indeed a demonstration of a high level of powerlessness not seen in recent memory. They felt that the circumstances had reduced them to being like children. There were therefore a series of responses to explain why men cried together with women and children in Apaa on that day.

> Men cry in the most extreme circumstances. If you see a man cry, you know that he is deeply hurt by something. We do not have anything else. All we have is this land to take care of our children, to feed them, we farm and then send our children to school. If they remove us from here and take us to live in a camp like we used to live, we will not have any way to survive and that is what saddens us the most. How will we live?

Another man explained:

> The men had to cry, because they were angry and sad but did not have any strength or ability to fight back. The situation called for them to do something obscene. Because if you see your wife helpless and undressing, you feel like you should really do something obscene. But we decided that people should not be violent. We cannot be violent. Imagine that day if some people tried to beat up a soldier or police officer and kill him, how many people would have lost their lives? We said people cannot see our mother's naked and we are just sitting here, so we cried.

A woman also explained:

> The reason why men chose to protest by crying ... when you look at this land issue we are faced with, they [meaning government soldiers] have and rely on guns. We do not have guns. So as a man, what tools are you left with? Your tears, you have to cry like a woman. You do not otherwise have a way to fight against someone who has a gun. But when it is your land, your home, you must do something. You must put up a fight. So that even as a woman if you are chased off your land you know your husband struggled for you.

One man explained: "There was nothing I could do otherwise if it was not for the guns they were holding, we would fight physically." And another: "We cried because we had nothing to do. I wished I could jump on someone and fight but the gunmen were also there waiting for such reactions."

These are explanations we got from the residents of Apaa, which represent the community's general perception about the meaning associated with male tears as a sign of protest. Male tears symbolized helplessness and anger because their tormentors had weapons, which left them with no recourse. According to Patrick Otim[8], male tears were also a reaction by men to the violation of their manhood by the state. The traditional role that men had in the society as protectors of families and communities had been subverted and there was nothing they could do about it except to cry.

Most respondents agreed that male nakedness did not bear a curse in the same way as it did for the women. A man can undress to express his anger but it will not carry a curse like the nakedness of a woman. According to one of our informants, in the past when men went hunting and encountered a fierce buffalo, they would take off their clothes and fight it while naked in order to enhance their power. In the Apaa protest, a man from Fuudyang was among those who undressed and protested naked. He removed his trousers and wore only a green T-shirt during the protest.

If we take the Fuudyang man's undressing and understand it in the context of the responses from the male audience who cried and also in the context of what one of the respondents said about how fighting a wild beast required undressing, the single male naked body during that protest could be interpreted to have represented a war cry. The soldiers and the government officials symbolized the fierce buffalo that had to be fought while naked. This was clearly a different signification from the women's naked protest. However, because the soldiers had guns, the fight between the Acholi men and the soldiers did not take place physically but rather was implied at the symbolic level. One of the respondents reasoned this way: "The way these people have been coming here is not the way you should approach civilians who do not have any weapons and have not done anything wrong. Even when Kony [the Acholi leader of the rebel LRA] was in the bush, they did not come at him with all their military might the way they are doing with us." The men were sending a signal that they were ready to fight to defend that which was theirs if worst came to worst.

During the war with the LRA, Sverker Finnström (2006) and Chris Dolan (2011) describe a prominent elder in Gulu as ritually displaying his penis in condemnation of the LRA rebels while his wife bared her breasts during the war in northern Uganda. The elder said "If these children originate from my penis, I curse them." According to p'Bitek (1971) the naked curse involving pointing ones private parts at someone is the gravest curse. It is as powerful as the blessing for war and cannot easily be retracted. The blessings and the curse are two sides of the same coin. The curse is as if to say, why are you turning against your parents, who gave you life. Thus, according to Finnström, the reason this curse is considered so powerful is because it symbolically represents kinship and being a mother or father. Finnström and P'Bitek seem to imply therefore that even the naked male body could produce as much of a curse as the female body contrary to what the respondents interviewed in this study thought.

Conclusions

In this confrontation, the state became the aggressor, violating rather than defending the rights of citizens. Their guns become a symbol of power that was seen as emasculating the men by terrorizing and intimidating the citizenry. This resulted in both a physical confrontation between the community and the military, but also a symbolic one in which a reversal of traditional gender roles was used to express the strongest of curses and resistance on the state and military. Women defended their land through their bodies, while men defended it through tears. This is symbolic gender politics informing body politics, which are, as Schlyter puts it "real bodies of flesh and blood that experience hunger and cold, that work and become tired, that live and move around in homes, cities and physical landscapes" (Schlyter 2009, 13).

For the women and men of Apaa, the violation of male bodies by the state is not just a physical act, it is also a psychic and cultural attack by the masculinized nation state. The gun, the phallic symbol of power, reduces the men to crying like women and children. The protest helps us better appreciate the traditional gender roles and expectations of Acholi men and women, but also to see that these roles are not static and neither are they dominated by discourses of inferiority and superiority attached to the female or male body. The symbolic aspect of the protest transcends such gendered expectations and allows for the types of "transgressions" witnessed in Amuru.

What then are we to make of these types of protests and how do they fit into the broader repertoire of women's protest and goals of women's empowerment? On the one hand, they appear to reinforce traditional gender norms and operate very much within the complimentarity model of male and female spheres that is commonly found throughout Africa (Tripp 2015). Traditionally in Acholi society, a woman was respected for being a mother and homemaker, a man was expected to provide for the family and protect the honor of his family and these were their respective sources of authority. The charge by the Apaa residents that the state has emasculated men and that women become agentic because the men have failed as protectors seems to reinforce existing gender relations and expectations, as Misri (2011) would argue.

On the other hand, the protest revealed how Acholi society was at the same time flexible in playing with, manipulating, changing and redefining gender roles and expectations through symbolic means in responding to a provocation. It reveals the ways in which people draw on the repertoire of protest tactics available to them. Apaa women's nakedness, the men's tears, and the children's wails resulted in the state officials' promise to desist from landgrabbing and it shows just how powerful and resonant such symbolic protests can be. The symbolic association of women with the land made their revolt all the more powerful. The reproductive connotation of motherhood became the basis and justification for political action rather than a symbol of passivity, as it is often regarded in Western societies. This is a dimension of protest that deserves greater scholarly recognition, not just in societies where people are limited in their means of protest by a lack of education, communication and other resources with which to engage the state, but also in post-industrialized societies, where social movements draw on symbols but do not always recognize the powerful role of this dimension of protest. Such subversions and inversions of the social order are able to accomplish at a symbolic level what does not always seem possible in everyday life, but they point to the possibilities and to the capacity of society to create new realities, roles and power relations between the genders.

Notes

1. http://www.ntv.co.ug/news/local/17/apr/2015/amuru-women-strip-ministers-protest-over-land- 5564#sthash.cuM1O3Ub.dpbs Amuru women strip before ministers in protest over land. NTV. April 17, 2015. Accessed March 25, 2016.
2. http://femen.org/about-us/ Accessed March 23, 2016.
3. https://tuko.co.ke/9721-why-women-in-uganda-strip-naked-to-protest-land-grabbing.html
4. http://www.ibtimes.co.uk/uganda-women-protesters-strip-protest-ingrid-turinawe-332439
5. Correspondence with authors by Nancy Rydberg, a doctoral student at the University of Wisconsin-Madison, March 24, 2016.
6. Kimansulo is a kind of nude dancing that has captivated some Ugandan night clubs where women and young girls strip and dance naked for payment. It is the equivalent of strip clubs in the Western world.
7. https://www.youtube.com/watch?v=CQ6cmz9AzIo; https://www.youtube.com/watch?v=xMjr6GlRznc. Accessed 7 December 2016.
8. Correspondence between authors and Patrick Otim, 25 March 2016.

Disclosure statement

No potential conflict of interest was reported by the authors.

Funding

This work was supported by Makerere Institute for Social Research.

References

ACORD. 2001. *Research Report of Internally Displaced Persons (IDPs), Gulu District*: ACORD.
Adorno, Theodor, Else Frenkel-Brunswik, Daniel Levinson, and Nevitt Sanford. 1950. *The Authoritarian Personality*. New York: Harper and Brothers.
Anugwom, Edlyne Ezenongaya, and Kenechukwu N. Anugwom. 2009. "The Other Side of Civil Society Story: Women, Oil and the Niger Delta Environmental Struggle in Nigeria." *GeoJournal* 74 (4): 333–346.
Bordo, Susan. 1993. *Unbearable Weight: Feminism, Western Culture, and the Body*. Berkeley: University of California Press.
Butler, Judith. 1990. *Gender Trouble: Feminism and the Subversion of Identity*. New York: Routledge.
Butler, Judith. 1993. *Bodies That Matter: On the Discursive Limits of "Sex"*. New York: Routledge. 121–140.
Comaroff, Jean, and John Comaroff. 1992. *Ethnography and the Historical Imagination*. Boulder, CO: Westview Press.
Crawford, R. 1984. "A Cultural Account of "Health": Control, Release, and the Social Body." In *Issues in the Political Economy of Health Care*, edited by J. B. McKinlay, 60–103, New York: Tavistock.
Davidson, H. R. Ellis. 1969. "The Legend of Lady Godiva." *Folklore* 80 (2): 107–121.
Devisch, R. 1985. "Approaches to Symbol and Symptom in Bodily Space-Time." *International Journal of Psychology* 20: 389–415.

Diduk, Susan. 1989. "Women's Agricultural Production and Political Action in the Cameroon Grassfields." *Africa* 59 (3): 338–355.

Dolan, Chris. 2011. *Social Torture: The Case of Northern Uganda, 1986–2006*. Oxford: Berghahn Books.

Eames, Elizabeth. 1992. *Ija Obinrin Ondo-the Ondo Women's War. The Politics of Women's Wealth in Yoruba Town*. Cambridge: Harvard University Press.

Edelman, Murray. 1967. *The Symbolic Uses of Politics*. Urbana: University of Illinois Press.

Farah, Nuruddin. 1996. "The Women of Kismayo." *The Times Literary Supplement*, November 15.

Feierabend, Ivo K., and Rosalind L. Feierabend. 1972. "Systematic Conditions of Political Aggression: An Application of Frustration-Aggression Theory." In *Anger, Violence and Politics*, edited by Ivo K. Feierabend, Rosalind L. Feierabend, and Ted Robert Gurr, 136–183. Englewood Cliffs, NJ: Prentice-Hall.

Finnström, Sverker. 2006. "Wars of the Past and War in the Present: The Lord's Resistance Movement/Army in Uganda." *Africa* 76 (2): 200–220.

Gbowee, Leymah, and Carol Lynn Mithers. 2011. *Mighty Be Our Powers: How Sisterhood, Prayer, and Sex Changed a Nation at War: A Memoir*. New York: Beast.

Geertz, Clifford. 1973. *The Interpretation of Cultures: Selected Essays*. New York: Basic Books.

Geisler, Gisela. 2004. *Women and the Remaking of Politics in Southern Africa: Negotiating Autonomy, Incorporation and Representation*. Uppsala: Nordiska Afrikainstitutet.

van Ginneken, Jaap. 1992. *Crowds, Psychology, and Politics, 1871–1899*. Cambridge Studies in the History of Psychology. New York, NY: Cambridge University Press.

Harcourt, Wendy. 2009. *Body Politics in Development: Critical Debates in Gender and Development by Wendy*. London: Zed Books.

Ikelegbe, Augustine. 2005. "Engendering Civil Society: Oil, Women Groups and Resource Conflicts in the Niger Delta Region of Nigeria." *Journal of Modern African Studies* 43 (2): 241–270.

Klatch, Rebecca E. 1988. "Of Meanings & Masters: Political Symbolism & Symbolic Action." *Polity* 21 (1): 137–154.

Kowalewski, David. 1980. "The Protest Uses of Symbolic Politics: The Mobilzation Functions of Protestor Symbolic Resources." *Social Science Quarterly* 61 (June): 93–113.

Laine, Strutton. 2015. *The New Mobilization from Below: Women's Oil Protests in the Niger Delta, Nigeria*. New York: New York University Press.

Langol, Okumu. 2015. "Uganda Land Grab: Women Protestors, Facing Armed Soldiers, Unleash Secret Weapon – Nudity." *Black Star News*, April 20.

Lukes, Steven. 1975. "Political Ritual and Social Integration." *Sociolgy* 19 (May): 289–308.

Maathai, Wangari. 2007. *Unbowed: A Memoir*. New York: Anchor Books.

Mary, Douglas. 1970. *Natural Symbols: Explorations in Cosmology*. New York: Pantheon Books.

McCracken, G. 1998. *The Long Interview*. Newbury Park, CA: Sage Publication.

Misri, Deepti. 2011. "'Are You a Man?' Performing Naked Protest in India." *Signs* 36 (3): 603–625.

Oldfield, Sophie, Elaine Salo, and Ann Schlyter. 2009. "Body Politics and Citizenship." *Feminist Africa*, 13.

Owich, James. 2016. "Mps Apologise to Amuru Voters." *The Monitor*, January 5.

p'Bitek, Okot. 1971. *Religion of the Central Luo*. Nairobi: East African Literature Bureau.

Polletta, Francesca, and James M. Jasper. 2001. "Collective Identity and Social Movements." *Annual Review of Sociology* 27: 283–305.

Popenoe, R. 2004. *Feeding Desire: Fatness, Beauty, and Sexuality among a Saharan People*. London: Routledge.

Refugee Law Project. 2012. *Border or Ownership Question: The Apaa Land Dispute. Advisory Consortium on Conflict Sensitivity (ACCS): Refugee Law Project, School of Law*. Kampala: Makerere University.

Reischer, Erica, and Kathryn S. Koo. 2004. "The Body Beautiful: Symbolism and Agency in the Social World." *Annual Review of Anthropology* 33: 297–317.

Schlyter, Ann. 2009. *Body Politics and Women Citizens: African Experiences*. Sida Studies No. 242009.

Schmidt, Elizabeth. 2005. "Top Down or Bottom Up? Nationalist Mobilization Reconsidered, with Special Reference to Guinea (French West Africa)." *American Historical Review* 110 (4): 975–1014.

Serwajja, Eria. T. 2009. "The Quest for Development through Dispossession: Examining Amuru Sugar Works in Lakang-Amuru District of Northern Uganda." A paper presented at the International Conference on Global Land Grabbing II, Cornell University, Ithaca, NY.

Sokari, Ekine. 2009. "Women's Responses to State Violence in the Niger Delta: Violence as Instruments of Governance." *Pambazuka*, 420. Accessed January 5, 2016. http://www.pambazuka.org/gender-minorities/women%E2%80%99s-responses-state-violence-niger-delta.

Taylor, Diana. 1994. "Performing Gender: Las Madres De La Plaza De Mayo." In *Negotiating Performance: Gender, Sexuality, and Theatricality in Latin/O America*, edited by Diana Taylor, 275–305. Durham, NC: Duke University Press.

Terretta, Meredith. 2007. "A Miscarriage of Nation: Cameroonian Women and Revolution, 1949–1971." *Stichproben: Vienna Journal of African Studies* 12: 61–90. Special issue on Fracturing Binarisms: Gender and Colonialisms in Africa.

Tibbetts, Alexandra. 1994. "Mamas Fighting for Freedom in Kenya." *Africa Today* 41 (1): 27–48.

Tripp, Aili Mari. 2000. *Women & Politics in Uganda*. Madison: University of Wisconsin Press; James Currey and Fountain Publishers.

Tripp, Aili Mari. 2015. *Women and Power in Post-Conflict Africa*. New York: Cambridge University Press.

Turner, Victor. 1982. *From Ritual to Theatre: The Human Seriousness of Play*. New York: Performing Arts Journal Publications.

Turner, Terisa E., and Leigh S. Brownhill. 2002. "Women's Oil Wars in Nigeria." *Labour, Capital and Society / Travail, capital et société* 35 (1): 132–164.

"Female athlete" politic: Title IX and the naturalization of sex difference in public policy

Elizabeth A. Sharrow ⓘ

ABSTRACT
How did the passage of Title IX of the Education Amendments of 1972 politically define the "female athlete?" Since the mid-1970s, debates over the application of policy to athletic domains have been profoundly contentious. In this paper, I trace the policy deliberations concerning equity in athletics throughout the 1970s and explore the implications for our political understandings of what makes certain bodies "athletes" versus "female athletes" in contemporary sports and politics. I draw upon literatures from political science, sport sociology, and gender studies, and rely on archival methods to trace the process through which policymakers wed biological sex to policy implementation. I argue that Title IX unexpectedly became a central site for the construction of binary sex difference through three specific means: (1) conflict over the *understandings* of the role that biological sex should play in congressional debate before Title IX's passage, (2) conflict over *application* of sex to policy design in light of perceived capacities of women's bodies, and (3) *naturalization* of sex-segregated policy design which defines the relationship between sex and the physical body. The intersectional implications of Title IX's history demonstrate that policy has not yet fully ameliorated the raced, classed, and heterosexist inequities haunting institutions of American education.

"These are the bodies that Yale is exploiting": protest and bodies in Title IX

When the Yale University Women's Crew team entered the office of their Director of Women's Athletics in March of 1976 they were stripped naked to the waist. Written across their chests and backs was the text: "Title IX" (Yale Women Strip To Protest a Lack Of Crew's Showers 1976). The text referenced the sex equity provision of the Education Amendments of 1972 which secures women equal treatment to men in American educational institutions. The rowers were protesting the conditions under which they trained. Yale's boathouse was located miles from campus and although it contained showers and a locker room for men, the women's team lacked access to a comparable facility. Rowing left the athletes soaked, both from the sweat of their efforts and the splash off their oars. Without a locker room, the women were made to wait on the unheated bus for their ride back to campus after practice until the men completed their warm, post-practice showers. Several women fell seriously ill during the New England winter as a result of their training conditions; their protest was designed to highlight the consequence of their unequal treatment. They read aloud a statement written by team captain Chris Ernst which began, "These are bodies that Yale is exploiting ... " (Gilder 2015, 54).

The Yale women centered their political critique on the embodied concerns of unequal treatment, mobilizing Title IX as evidence that they deserved a healthier athletic training environment. It was the physical body required of athletic pursuits to which, they claimed, Title IX offered particular protections. They were athletes, *female athletes*, contending that their university was treating them as though they were unworthy of the same support received by their male colleagues. This, they argued, constituted sex discrimination; the athletes' protest made national news in the *New York Times*, claiming their bodies for Title IX (Yale Women Strip to Protest a Lack of Crew's Showers 1976).

Since the mid-1970s the policy's applications to sports have been the most profoundly contentious, more so than provisions regarding graduate and public university admissions, or sex equity in college classrooms (e.g., Hanson, Guilfoy, and Pillai 2009; Hogshead-Makar and Zimbalist 2007; Rosenthal 2008). But how has a law designed to protect against sex discrimination and differential treatment in educational institutions come to foreground bodies as an element of politics? And with what consequence for political identity has the "body" emerged as a central category of Title IX? In this paper, I trace the implications of debates over policy design for our political understandings of what makes certain bodies "athletes" – and others "female athletes" – in contemporary sports and politics.

I argue that Title IX unexpectedly became a foremost site for the construction of bodily difference through policy design and implementation via three political processes: (1) conflict over the *understandings* of the role that biological sex should play in congressional debate before Title IX was passed, (2) conflict over *application* of sex to athletic policy in light of perceived capacities of women's bodies, and (3) *naturalization* of sex-segregated policy design which defines the relationship between sex and the physical body. My argument engages multiple literatures on policy feedback, the construction of political identity, sociology of sport, and gender studies which have yet to consider this politicization of the "female athlete" identity, nor the implications of US civil rights policy approaches to sex non-discrimination more generally. I draw on archival sources to trace the process through which policymakers wed purportedly embodied, biological sex to policy design.

"Female athletes": sex and public policy[1]

Key to understanding the relationships among policy, sex, and sports are the political debates over sex discrimination in education from 1970 to 1979. During these years, policymakers designated *women* as a target population of non-discrimination policy. Women *athletes*, in contrast, were targeted by policy only when policymakers designated athletic programs of American schools and colleges within Title IX's domain (Edwards 2010). *Women athletes* became central figures in Title IX's implementation because they had to claim a right to sport (on proliferating numbers of "women's" teams) only by also claiming their "female" bodies. This unambiguously distinguished them from their "male" counterparts under Title IX's policy regime. Policy draws this distinction by endorsing *sex-segregated* sports, and women-specific athletic teams, long established as hallmarks of policy design (McDonagh and Pappano 2007). Consequently, "female athletes" have become a fulcrum for embodied government regulation.

Implicitly, however, Title IX's "female athletes" are thus constituted outside the androcentric category of "athlete." In 1979, the Office for Civil Rights (OCR) published Title IX's "Policy Interpretation on Intercollegiate Athletics" which has, in the majority of contexts, instructed schools to create "women's" teams where they had been historically lacking, ensuring that women compete in separate competitive venues from men on "men's teams" (OCR 1979). Our colloquial understandings of Title IX rarely problematize the policy's more complicated legacies, including the promotion of sex-conscious approaches to athletic competition through sex-segregated teams, nor the resulting codification of embodied sex difference in policy design (see, as exceptions, McDonagh and Pappano 2007; Milner and Braddock 2016). Rather than liberating women from antiquated notions of their physical limitations, policy design has subtly played a role in legitimizing outmoded understandings of male physical hegemony.

This article excavates policy history in order to explicate the methods of political identity formation turning first to several streams of scholarship that inform my approach to analyzing Title IX. Next, I use archival evidence to illustrate the three sequential processes that linked the body to policy and identity. Finally, I offer some implications of reifying the sex binary for our evaluation of policy.

Policy, identity, and the sporting body: multiple streams of scholarship

In this section, I bring into conversation cross-disciplinary literatures on the history of Title IX and sex non-discrimination policy with political science literature on the formation of political identity. My interest in the embodied politics of the "female athlete" requires additional engagement with scholarship on the sociology of sport and feminist scholarship on gender and the body. Reading across these literatures renders open questions about politicized identity and the "female" body within public policy.

Policy history literature and the dominant narrative of Title IX's success

First, it is essential to articulate the ubiquitous narrative that defines our shared sense of Title IX's meaning both within and beyond scholarly literature. The 1972 passage of Title IX expanded US civil rights law to protect women in education from entrenched practices of discrimination (Costain 1979; Rose 2015). Lawmakers modeled the text of the law around Titles VI and VII of the Civil Rights Act of 1964, calling for non-discrimination policy in federally funded educational institutions "on the basis of sex." Although the congressional text did not reference athletic programs, debates over subsequent policy design swiftly coalesced around the application of the law to sports (Edwards 2010; Fishel and Pottker 1977; Gelb and Palley 1982). Over the ensuing 44 years, the implementation of public policy has dramatically re-shaped American athletics at both the high school and college levels (Acosta and Carpenter 2014; Stevenson 2007).

Policy design, which instructs colleges and universities to create equitable opportunities for both sexes in order to reverse practices of women's exclusion, has engendered first- and second-order implementation effects. Both interest groups and scholars argue that Title

IX's implementation generated the primary, intended effects of increasing women's athletic participation and access to scholarships and resources of college sports (Brake 2010; Kane and Ladda 2012; NCWGE 2012; NWLC 2012; White House 2012).[2] Women and men now partake in organized athletics in far greater numbers than they did in the early 1970s (NCAA 2016).[3]

This proliferation in formal athletic participation has run parallel to (and, to some extent, fueled) an intense cultural interest in sports, as well as increased educational expenditures directed at athletics (Clotfelter 2011). Since 1972, women's college athletic participation has expanded 12-fold, an evolution facilitated by the structural growth of thousands of new teams for American girls and women (Acosta and Carpenter 2014; NCAA 2016). Similarly, girls' high school athletic participation has increased substantially. Half of girls graduating from American high schools now have considerable athletic experience (NFSHSA 2016; Stevenson 2007) as compared to only one of 12 girls in 1971 (NFSHSA 2015).

In addition to these direct consequences, sociologists, economists, and many feminist interest groups suggest second-order, spillover effects of policy implementation. Girls with athletic backgrounds are likely to enroll in college (Shifrer et al. 2015), participate in the workforce as adults (Stevenson 2007, 2010), and enjoy better, long-term health (e.g., Kaestner and Xu 2010; Staurowsky et al. 2015). The implementation of policy changed educational and sporting institutions; over time, the girls and women who inhabit these altered institutions are themselves transformed.[4]

"Feedback" literature and the making of policy constituencies

Despite the evidence regarding Title IX's transformative *social* effects, the *political* effects of Title IX, including the emergence of protests like that at Yale, remain under-explored.[5] In other policy domains, scholars of American politics concerned with identifying how public policy makes politics focus increasing attention on the relationships among policy, social groups, and political identity. Schattschneider (1935), Lowi (1964) and Wilson (1974) famously argue that public policies of various types generate distinctive patterns of political mobilization. Their studies inspired a generation of scholars investigating questions of how policy "feeds back" into the political arena, reshaping ensuing policymaking and constituent mobilization (e.g., Campbell 2012; Mettler and Soss 2004; Skocpol 1992).

Policy and legal scholars argue that legal regimes, policy design, and processes of group identification intersect to cultivate feedback effects for political identity among policy recipients (e.g., Bruch, Ferree, and Soss 2010; Soss 1999). Following Althusser's (1970) contention that law "hails" groups into being, scholars show that policy can engender group identification among previously inchoate or apolitical social groups, shaping the "social construction of target populations" (Schneider and Ingram 1993, 1997).[6] Policy, in other words, may have political effects that can reshape future politics at both the institutional and mass levels, inspiring changes to individual and group consciousness (Béland 2010; Campbell 2012; Mettler and Soss 2004; Pierson 1993). Additionally, policies can, "set political agendas and shape identities and constituent interests. They can influence beliefs about what is possible, desirable, and normal" (Soss and Schram 2007, 113). Political identity can be a key element in understanding how political change occurs (Strach 2013).

Myriad applications of this "policy feedback" approach demonstrate that public policies across the spectrum can reshape their specific, intended constituencies (Campbell 2012). Retired Americans are politicized through Social Security (Campbell 2003), post-war education benefits conferred by the G.I. Bill shape the activism and civic engagement of World War II veterans (Mettler 2005), and encounters with the welfare state confer perceived status, informing recipient population opinions on the nature of government (Soss 1999). Although public policy does not invariably lead to positive feedback effects (Patashnik 2008; Patashnik and Zelizer 2013), there is ample evidence that policy design and implementation frequently re-make constituent political interests.

Anecdotally, scholars hypothesize Title IX's function as a catalyst for "female athlete" political identity formation. Mettler and Soss (2004) reference Title IX as an example of public policy which educated women on their expanding set of political rights. Anne Norton conjectures that "decisions on equal protection and Title [IX] have encouraged, and in some cases created, populations of female athletes and have given more salience to that identity" (Norton 2004, 58). John Skrentny argues that policy "helped create hundreds of thousands of women athletes" (Skrentny 2002, 231). But these examples are merely suggestive; no scholarship to date has formally analyzed the relationships among civil rights policy, athletes, and politics.

Sociology of sport and the literature on cultural gender politics

Instead of a scholarly emphasis on analyzing politics, the evolving cultural status of the "female athlete" has emerged as a focal point for investigation. Scholars investigating social change in light of Title IX conclude that policy produced certain uneven outcomes (see one review of the literature in Knoppers and McDonald 2010). On the one hand, "female athletes" can now, more than ever, participate in sports historically reserved for men (NCAA 2016). However, these teams are rarely sex integrated and often reinforce norms of male physical superiority, even imposing rules that penalize physical contact between players when women play sports such as hockey and lacrosse while celebrating such aggression in the men's game (Theberge 2000). Sociological approaches highlight that sex-segregated sporting practice can reify false notions of women's physical inferiority compared to men's "natural" strength (Fields 2004; Ring 2009).

Concurrently, women athletes must negotiate paradoxical gender expectations and often face pressure to downplay their muscled strength in service of more normatively gendered femininity (Krane et al. 2004; Theberge 2000). Sociologists of sport identify diverging struggles for men and women athletes, most pronounced in sporting settings where gender expectations pressure athletes to conform to either feminine or masculine ideals. Women's ice hockey (Theberge 2000) and men's figure skating (Adams 2011) each challenge the naturalized association of masculinity to athleticism. Although these sports may hold a key to decoupling the associations between physical strength and male supremacy, oppressive gender expectations continue to limit both women and men, even in light of policy-driven change. This literature focuses on the root of this paradox as cultural or social rather than political (Lorber 1994).

The spotlight on culture indicates that the purported "revolution" in women's sports produced contradictory outcomes. Although policy has conditionally improved women's access to sport, it has made limited durable modification to the long-standing double-standards for "female athletes'" compulsory heterosexuality (Wright and Clarke 1999) and semi-obligatory adherence to traditional gender norms (Cooky 2009; Dworkin and Messner 1999; Messner 1988). Women athletes continue to suffer from a dearth of media coverage as well (Cooky, Messner, and Musto 2015). Not only do women's sports consistently receive a dismal share of the total media attention, their lack of coverage remains largely unchanged over time despite the significant increase in their athletic participation. The absence of routine media coverage sends a troubling message that women's athletics are less exciting, less competitive, and less worthy of resources than their male counterparts (Cooky, Messner, and Hextrum 2013).[7] Conse-quently, we now hold competing narratives of both transformation and stagnation in Title IX's social and cultural legacies.

This literature also makes clear that "female athlete" *bodies* are a part of what consti-tutes the fraught cultural politics of gender in sport (Dworkin and Messner 1999; Heywood and Dworkin 2003). Women's bodies perceived to be suspiciously strong can be sex-tested at the Olympic level (Karkazis et al. 2012; Pieper 2016), and the pervasive, homophobic anxiety regarding lesbianism leads many women athletes to "apologize" for confounding traditional femininity by performing hyper-heterosexuality while in the public domain (Festle 1996; Griffin 1998). These sociological studies map rocky terrain for the role of athletics in reshaping gender roles and expectations while also hinting at a fundamental disconnect between the methods of policy design and implementation, and the full achievement of equity promised under Title IX. Again, the role public policy played in constituting these cultural politics remains under-analyzed.[8] This scholar-ship suggests the need to engage policy studies with the cultural scaffolding that reinforces our associations among gender, women, and the body. I turn next to the expansive, fem-inist stream of literature on this topic.

Feminist scholarship on the body

Bodies, and women's bodies in particular, have been a significant concern in feminist scholarship for decades (e.g., Fausto-Sterling 2000; Young 1980, 2002). Disentangling the notion of binary sex from the body has been a central aim of feminist theory since DeBeauvoir (1953) famously argued that one is "not born a woman," theorizing the relationship between bodies and the gendered self. This conversation also thrives in Black feminist thought, where intellectuals have long articulated the relationships among systems of domination, embodiment, race, and sex (e.g., Cohen 1999; Collins 2000; Hancock 2016). Feminists consistently call for greater attention to the ways in which culture, science, politics, and art shape the body itself (e.g., Bordo 1993; Dietz 2003; Moi 1999; Price and Shildrick 1999).

Work on the relationship between public policy and bodies suggests that direct and indirect regulation of bodies is a principal concern in the politics of reproduction (Luker 1985; Roberts 1997), birth control policy (Gordon 1990), sex education (Irvine 2002), disability policy (Stone 1984), and medical science (Fausto-Sterling 2000). Although the body is fundamental to the sporting experience, we do not yet understand how Title IX, a civil rights policy originally aimed at ending sex discrimination in edu-cation, came to shape a set of embodied politics wherein "female athletes" could claim their bodies for Title IX.[9]

Methodological approach to studying Title IX's history

In order to address these gaps and conundrums in research, I focus on the 1970s, particularly the congressional debates preceding the passage of the Education Amendments of 1972 through the finalization of the 1979 policy interpretation (OCR 1979). During this period, stakeholders within the US Congress and the federal bureaucracy debated the methods for policy interpretation and design. I draw on primary and secondary historical data sources from the archives of the US federal government (including congressional hearings and floor transcripts, papers at the Richard Nixon Presidential Library, the Gerald R. Ford Presidential Library, and the Jimmy Carter Presidential Library), the private papers of the National Collegiate Athletic Association (Indianapolis, IN), as well as the women's history papers in the Sophia Smith Collection (at Smith College), and the Schlesinger Library on the History of Women in America (at the Radcliffe Institute for Advanced Study). Taken as a whole, these sources reveal an unlikely history.

Although others have detailed the political battles over creating policy implementation guidelines in the 1970s (Edwards 2010; Rose 2015; Skrentny 2002; Suggs 2005; Ware 2011), my work explores the under-appreciated implications of these political battles, particularly as they pertained to the question of sex integration. I aim to join the conversation started by other scholars about the consequences of segregation (McDonagh and Pappano 2007; Milner and Braddock 2016), focusing herein on the history of policy debates between policymakers and activists. By examining disputes over the implementation of segregationist policy in athletics, I argue that political conflict created an interlocking relationship among biological sex, physical capacity, and political identity. These conflictual political processes have unexpectedly cemented the body as a central category of Title IX. Next, I present my original findings from this archival research, periodizing the events of the 1970s in order to illustrate three means through which policymakers constructed bodily difference through: *understandings* of sex as a biologic binary, the *application* of these beliefs to policy debates, and the *naturalization* of binary sex into policy design.

Conflict over *understanding* biological sex in policy creation: 1970–1972

When congressional debate on the topic of sex discrimination in education brought the question of women's unequal treatment in education to the national stage, sports were neither dominant, nor wholly absent as Congress considered the formal legislation that would become Title IX.[10] Senator Birch Bayh (D-IN) and Representative Edith Green (D-OR), together with a small cadre of elite feminist activists,[11] carefully assembled a "stealth" (Rose 2015, 167) coalition which aimed to incorporate sex non-discrimination language in a legislative amendment to the Civil Rights Act of 1964.[12] Dr Bernice Sandler, a pre-eminent activist in developing Title IX, recalled that Green intentionally attached the law to an omnibus education bill, noting she "thought that if the bill drew attention, it would be saddled with amendments, or worse, killed altogether" (Wulf 2012). Deliberation in the Senate signaled the political struggle over interpretation and implementation that would follow.

Central to the limited debate that transpired before Title IX's passage were concerns about sex integration. At issue was how sex non-discrimination law might require men and women to be treated, particularly within the historically androcentric domains of military institutions and athletic programs. Senator Peter Dominick (R-CO) raised pointed questions about whether policy might obviate sex-segregated locker rooms, showers, or athletic teams, while Senator Strom Thurmond (R-SC) voiced concerns over the repercussions of potential sex integration. Their statements forced Bayh to go on record to moderate their concerns:[13]

> These regulations would allow enforcing agencies to permit differential treatment by sex only [sic] – very unusual cases where such treatment is absolutely necessary to the success of the program – such as in classes for pregnant girls or emotionally disturbed students, in sports facilities or other instances where privacy must be preserved (118 U.S. Congressional Record 5807, 28 February 1972).

Senator Bayh assumed that sports – like pregnancy – invoked the female body in unique ways when he coupled anxieties over sports with concerns over pregnancy. Bayh implied, and assured fellow lawmakers, that the prevailing logic embedded in the realm of athletics is that of sex "difference." He subtly reified the sex binary during these foundational debates, suggesting that biologic difference was relevant for policy-makers puzzling over incorporating women into male enclaves. The coupling of "females" in sports with pregnant female bodies suggested the belief that women's bodies are not only different from men's, they are also capable of fundamentally distinctive things (including giving birth) by virtue of biology.

By collapsing the capacities of pregnant female bodies onto proposed legislation for "*female* athletes," Bayh posited sex as a marker for *female* bodies as those who require "special treatment" and a designated space separate from the men. Men remained marked as the natural heirs to athletic domains. This approach managed to silence the critiques of lawmakers hoping to use the threat of sex-integrated spaces to kill the promise of Title IX, but it simultaneously established a fraught legislative history which conceptualized and incorporated strict ideas about fundamental sex difference into the archive of policy.

Title IX's feminist proponents, comparative outsiders in congressional lawmaking with the intended strategy to remain under the radar on this issue in the early 1970s, worked to downplay concerns about sex-integrated teams and locker rooms, neither affirming nor disputing Bayh's protectionist logics during recorded debate.[14] Although Sandler and her small cohort of activists anticipated that sex non-discrimination policy would be a thorny matter, their primary aim was to ensure that the law passed.[15] The recorded debate around athletics indicated that the few lawmakers who were publicly debating the sex non-discrimination provision shared an *understanding* about binary sex difference which they inscribed in the legislative record. Opponents of sex equity provisions invoked the threat of integration as proof that the means of achieving sports equity were sufficiently preposterous to negate the need for any legislation at all. Proponents, publicly lead by Senator Bayh, called these threats a bluff, suggesting that the mechanisms for equity did not require the denial of sex difference. When President Nixon signed the Education Amendments into law on June 23, 1972, these limited conversations constituted the full trail of congressional intent for interpreting the sex non-discrimination provision in the realm of athletics.[16] However, the content of discussions around athletics foreshadowed the debates about the *application* of sex to policy design that were to come.

Conflict over the *application* of biology to the capacity of "female" bodies: 1972–1975

This meager legislative discussion of Title IX's application to athletics came to be highly consequential when the OCR in the Department of Health, Education, and Welfare (DHEW) took up the task of writing implementation guidelines in the summer of 1972.[17] Without a robust trail of legislative intent on the means for implementation, OCR's initial policy guidelines gave institutions little direction on the specific question of how to ensure equal athletic opportunities for girls and women.[18] DHEW Secretary Caspar Weinberger suggested in a July 1973 memo addressed to OCR that women should be allowed a tryout for existing men's "noncontact" teams, but women's failure to make the existing "men's team" did not also necessitate that schools establish a separate "women's team" to meet women's needs (Fishel and Pottker 1977, 109).[19]

There were several consequences of this working interpretation. First, the back-and-forth between OCR and Weinberger in the years following Title IX's passage further demonstrates the application of a binary understanding of sex in bureaucratic debates. The debates increasingly employed the idea that women and men were "different" in terms of the way sex non-discrimination policy ought to engage their rights to sport on "men's" versus "women's" teams.[20] In the mid-1970s, bureaucrats invoked the congressional *understanding* of sex difference into policy *application*.

Importantly, the second-wave feminist movement was not yet a highly structured and institutionalized lobbying force on educational issues, neither embedded with state bureaucrats who might provide key information, nor (yet) capable of mounting a sweeping response to the bureaucratic debate on topics of athletics (Banaszak 2009; Goss 2012). In the months before and after Title IX's passage the debate was largely restricted to within elite circles.[21] Sandler and Margaret Dunkle, operating under the Project on the Status and Education of Women (PSEW), authored an important policy document on the topic of athletic equity in 1974.[22] The paper, titled "What Constitutes Equality for Women in Sport?", argued for Title IX's strict enforcement without explicitly taking a stand on "mixed teams."[23] Even as PSEW delineated the strengths and weaknesses of segregated sports, their logic throughout was premised on the understanding that women and men were *different* types of athletes. Even while conceding that segregated sports may better serve the "average female" than the "superior woman athlete," the paper invoked language that reified embodied sex difference.

The debate among feminists invoked this difference-based approach. Even the National Organization for Women (NOW), the most pro-integration feminist group, feared that women's abrupt incorporation into sporting spaces would require them to meet the long-standing, ostensibly gender-neutral standards for team try-outs and physical strength. Women, denied training opportunities by sex discrimination and dissuaded from pursuing muscled strength by restrictive gender norms, were thought to be incapable of competing with men.[24] Even as medical scientists published reports that women were no more susceptible to athletic injury than were men (Haycock and Gillette 1976), policy debates proceeded under the presumption of male superiority and greater physical invincibility. The PSEW paper referenced a number of sex-based studies of women and men's physical capacities, simultaneously conceding that the "average female" is smaller than the "average male," even as the authors also questioned whether looking to averages may itself engage in improper, sexist logic.

Women's rights advocates struggled to disprove many sexist assumptions. They were fearful that full integration might confirm women's weakness and forego alternatives which could secure women greater numbers of competitive opportunities on their own teams. Furthermore, women's historic exclusion from athletics left activists with limited information about women's actual physical capacities. In this sense, even feminists were hobbled in their vision for future policy by the same discrimination they aimed to combat. Locked as they were in a logic of binary sex difference and a history of women's exclusion from physical training and competition, feminist activists struggled to unify around a clear, anti-sexist alternative.

The long-standing practice of women's exclusion from "men's" athletic teams proved a difficult problem to solve. Abruptly treating women "the same" as men in policy design by way of offering them the opportunity to try out for "men's" athletic teams could not automatically solve historic discrimination against women-as-athletes. Thus, even the most active women's groups, like NOW, PSEW, and the National Coalition for Girls and Women in Education (NCGWE) found themselves advocating for a "difference-based" approach to creating athletic opportunities for women.

Not all groups favored the same version of regulation. NOW, in particular, only supported segregation in the short-term. In a 1974 "Legislative Alert," they wrote, "NOW is opposed to any regulation which precludes eventual integration. Regulations that 'protect' girls and/or women are against NOW goals and are contradictory to our stand on the ERA."[25] Yet their main concern was for securing athletic opportunity for the "average female" who had never been allowed access to sport. Women's past exclusion from athletic training, coaching, and youth sports meant that the "average female" was unprepared to join athletic teams populated by men advantaged through years of preparation.

In the mid-1970s, it was less politically costly for feminist activists to adapt and expand existing institutional structures rather than articulate a vision for integrated sports that would require major modifications to men's sporting enclaves. Even NOW struggled to articulate a demand for full integration as a first stage of implementation. Advocating for restructuring sports altogether would have required that activists confront entrenched male interests, including the coaches and athletic directors who were already mobilizing against Title IX's more modest implementation.[26] Assenting to sex-segregated sports, which *applied* logics of sex difference rather than questioning them, helped women's rights advocates win the battle against exclusion and discrimination, if not the war against misogyny.

"Separate but equal" and the *naturalization* of sex difference: 1975–1979

With biology firmly under-girding the debate over non-discrimination policy, policymakers worked to craft the specifics of policy design. Between 1975, when OCR circulated guidelines articulating plans for the "elimination of sex discrimination in athletic programs" (OCR 1975), and 1979, policymakers considered the specifics of how to apply issues of sex difference to athletic teams. Football coaches emerged as increasingly verbal advocates for the male-dominated status quo.[27]

Policymakers, including both feminists and men's athletics advocates, acknowledged that there were two separate issues: participation opportunities (including athletic scholarships) and resource allocation. Women's groups, increasingly committed to pursuing a "separate but equal" strategy that would ensure a transformation from the historic practices of women's exclusion, found themselves in discussions framed largely by the fears of men's coaches. Entrenched men's interests were overwhelmingly concerned with finding a policy design that would minimally disrupt the status quo, guided as they were by the fear of being required to fund women's new opportunities. In time, policymakers struck a deal: men's teams would neither be obliged to accept women on their "men's" rosters, nor would they be required to equally allocate the athletic budget between the sexes. Instead, the 1979 guidelines instructed schools to create *separate* opportunities for women where they had been lacking without a strict mandate for equal funding. Separate teams based on the *naturalized* premise of two distinct sexes became the desired policy solution, even for the women's rights advocates (namely NOW) who preferred them as merely a short-term intervention to a complex problem.

This *naturalization* also resulted from policy design that adopted rather than challenged the segregationist status quo. Activists were unprepared, perhaps unwilling, but surely too preoccupied by battling with entrenched male athletic interests in the late 1970s to take up several questions which haunt sporting structures. What fundamentally defines "women?" Is biology destiny? Did women require the protections against male competition that they had been historically afforded? Such questions were set aside, rather than openly debated in the second half of the decade.

The processes of *understanding, applying,* and *naturalizing* produced certain complications. In a deep irony of second-wave feminist politics, the response of activists whose political mobilization had aimed to undermine women's differential treatment came to *support* a segregated model for equity in sports that assented to a difference-based approach by the end of the 1970s. The consequence of women's historical exclusion from athletic training required activists to swallow the idea of women's physical inferiority in order to protect a potential future filled with enduring opportunities for the next generation. As such, rather than fundamentally undermining biologic approaches to women's inclusion into sports, policymakers and feminists relied upon them to interrupt the processes of women's exclusion. A binary understanding of embodied biology thus became the enduring legacy for women's inclusion into sports.

Discussion and conclusions

The implications of this legacy bear upon the policy feedback effects of Title IX including the construction of political identity, the reification of supposedly binary sex, and our shared meanings of what women "are." Since the 1970s, women's ability to re-articulate the meanings of femininity through physical pursuits has been fraught with normative expectations attached to embodied sex and operationalized through public policy. The particular modes of policy design that produce primarily sex-segregated sports teams are both good *and* problematic. To a great extent, Title IX's implementation has done what previously seemed impossible: it has remade high school and college athletics in a new form which values and secures opportunities for "women's" bodies. Despite being beholden to the system of sex-segregated sports, women athletes now have opportunities to contest the grounds of their marginalization, ending their wholesale exclusion from sporting domains. As the Yale rowers illustrate, the "female athlete" is now an effective mobilizing identity of embodied rights-claiming. The construction of a policy constituency has enabled women to engage more fruitfully in political protest at the same time as it has expanded the terrain of opportunity available to women athletes as a group. However, protest and opportunity, tied as they are to troubled embodied politics, mean that women (and both transgender and intersex athletes) are limited by their need to protest as "female athletes," rather than be incorporated fully into the category of "athlete" itself.

By generating policy implementation mechanisms that relied on biologic understandings of sex, institutions of American politics constituted the political identity of the "female athlete." Although many women played sports on women's teams before Title IX, sports were not a foremost issue on the feminist agenda before the passage of Title IX and there is very limited evidence of women mobilizing to make political claims around the identity of a "female athlete" until after 1972 (Ware 2011). Through the categorical definition of sex as a characteristic of bodies, policy distinguished this identity. Since policy only conceives of individual identities through the category of sex, the defining feature of the "female athlete" in this sense is not her athleticism, but instead her presumed identity as female. She is politically cast not as an athlete who happens to be female, but as a female who happens to be, in some sense, athletic. Neither is she merely an athlete. She exists in the modified category of "female athlete," defined by her embodied sex, while the category of athlete remains marked as inherently male.

Thinking intersectionally, other complications emerge. Title IX's collegiate "female athlete" is requisitely able-bodied and capable of being admitted into colleges and universities in order to claim her "right" to sport. As such, she is predominately racialized as a white woman, middle or upper economic class. To this day, white women are overrepresented in college athletics when compared both to their proportion among college women and among the general population of women (Pickett, Dawkins, and Braddock. 2012). As such, by codifying rights to sports through educational institutions, the federal government dictated that Title IX would largely replicate and not fully ameliorate the other raced and classed inequalities haunting institutions of American education.

Yet primarily, and most insidiously, the "female athlete" is explicitly sexed by the effectuation of the very law that aimed to end the use of sex as a legal marker of access to education and sports. The "female athlete" is unambiguously and unavoidably biologically female. Bodies that defy such sex-based classification (including transgender and intersex athletes) do not easily find protections from discrimination under standing policy design.[28] In this sense, the political category of sex as applied to bodies in sporting settings generated an antiquated, rather than liberated category of gender, haunted by legacies that exclude individuals whose gender-identity may not align with characteristics of their physical body. Furthermore, even cisgender "female athletes," through their myriad acts of aggressive play, unrelenting power and speed, unapologetic perspiration, and competitive zeal, inherently flaunt, exceed, and collapse long-standing definitions of femininity. The ways in which purportedly "female" bodies commandingly embrace conventionally masculine traits of muscled strength inherently challenge the sex-based binary distinction upon which Title IX was built.

Thus, the "female athlete" represents not merely a figure of progress, but also a figure imbued with deep tensions. Women who fail to conform to feminine expectations while

competing often face social denigration of their athletic performances as excessively masculine and inappropriate for women's bodies.[29] Women's bodies thought to be suspiciously strong, unnervingly fast, or too masculine, not only stretch gendered
understandings of physicality, they defiantly undermine the male/female binary assumptions that constitute the political category of sex inherent to Title IX (Butler 1998). Yet
contradictorily, the better and more competent the athlete, the greater the countervailing
pressure to balance these physical feats by performing femaleness in gender normative
ways. Sociologists demonstrate that gender policing of female athletes remains a factor
on sports teams across the country and in media portrayals of women in sport (Cooky,
Messner, and Musto 2015; Schultz 2014). Women athletes must now, politically and culturally, continue to perform a certain brand of femaleness (always already in juxtaposition
to male bodies under Title IX) even as they compete in sports. In a perverse consequence
of history, the price to pay for shifting understandings of women's physicality is borne by
the very bodies Title IX aims to empower.

Perhaps two of the most important methods for evaluating any civil rights policy hinge
on the extent to which it effectively curtails discrimination or circumvents potential discrimination by another name. Here, Title IX – and our shared understanding of it as a
model of policy success – falls short, at least in part. Beyond the domain of sports, the naturalized practice of segregating women and men contributes to the difficulty in addressing
continued and often pernicious discrimination against cisgender women, as well as transgender and intersex people. So long as we fail to acknowledge the fraught legacy of accepting purported sex difference at the core of policy design, we also remain haunted by
attempts to renaturalize this false dichotomy in other policy applications (see also Davis
2014). The resurgence of bathrooms as a contested domain for transgender students
and the problematic demands by conservative political groups that students adhere to
bathrooms which serve their "real" sex underscore this point (see also Westbrook and
Schilt 2014). Instead of ensuring students' equal treatment regardless of whether their
physical body matches their gender identity, Title IX's reliance on the body as a fundamental category in education means that both trans- and cisgender students potentially
face the requirement that they declare their embodied sex in order to be protected from
discrimination on its basis. So long as Title IX continues to rely on policy design that
invokes binary sex as a category in athletics, public policy will fail to afford non-discrimination protections to some of the most vulnerable populations in terms of gender-identity,
race, economic class, and physical ability within educational institutions more broadly.

Ultimately, this history of policy development demonstrates that current policy guidelines continue to undermine women's full liberation from the antiquated notion that their
bodies are always second-class. This gendered hierarchy that continues to favor men (as
athletes and elsewhere) is ubiquitous across multiple domains in American society and
remains a pernicious element of American culture (see also MacKenzie 2015). At the
same time, turning to history reminds us that *understanding, applying,* and *naturalizing*
binary sex in policy resulted from political processes, not a natural order. In the face of
evolving social and political arrangements around the meanings of gender and women's
demonstrable physical accomplishments, institutions of American politics – indeed activists claiming the identity of "female athletes" themselves – have as much potential as
ever to evolve and address the current limitations of public policy.

Notes

1. I will refer to women athletes under Title IX as "female athletes" throughout the article in order to underscore my argument that policy design is constitutive of our gendered understanding of Title IX's athletes in the binary "male/female" sense. I retain the use of quotations throughout in order to denaturalize the use of this gendered term.

2. Of course, many women were athletes long before Title IX (e.g., Cahn 1995; Guttmann 1991). Even still, policy generated significant growth in participation since 1972.

3. Although girls' and women's athletic participation initially expanded more rapidly than did boys' and men's, it is under-recognized that boys and men have also seen an overall growth, rather than the threatened decline, in sporting opportunities since 1972 (NCAA 2016; NFSHSA 2016).

4. Importantly, scholars increasingly acknowledge that these benefits are not equally available to all women. Girls enrolled in urban schools are less likely than girls in suburban schools to have access to athletic teams (Sabo and Veliz 2012), as are women enrolled at community colleges versus 4-year baccalaureate programs (Castañeda, Katsinas, and Hardy 2008). Girls and women of color, many of whom are also disproportionally represented in urban high schools and community colleges, are less likely to reap the benefits of policy implementation (NWLC and PRRAC 2015; Pickett, Dawkins, and Braddock. 2012). Women and girls with disabilities are unlikely to have sporting opportunities at any level (Duncan 2013), and both transgender and intersex athletes' participation opportunities remain beholden to the shifting matrix of rules that govern the conditions of their inclusion in sport (Griffin 2012; Karkazis et al. 2012). Thinking "intersectionally" (e.g., Cohen 1999; Collins 2000; Crenshaw 1989; Hancock 2008, 2016; Strolovitch 2007), it is clear that Title IX's implementation has been unevenly transformative for various subpopulations of women.

5. This absences is noted elsewhere, specifically among historians who call for a focus on "the role of sports advocacy in feminist politics" (Cahn 2014).

6. For example, most elderly Americans now identify as "retirees," free from the requirement of full-time employment as a result of status conferred through Social Security (Campbell 2003).

7. A significant body of research also points to the consequences of sexualized coverage of women athletes which focuses on their physical attractiveness, appearance, and non-sporting activities instead of their athletic accomplishments (e.g., Kane 1996). The absence of routine coverage of strong women athletes precludes opportunities to reframe how both girls and boys think about women's strength (Daniels 2012; Daniels and Wartena 2011).

8. Though the role of culture is often also set aside by scholars of policy development, doing so obscures important factors particularly for scholarship concerned with gender (Strach 2013).

9. Notably, the invocation of sex difference inherent to Title IX's policy design also allows men to claim *their* bodies for policy. Although the preponderance of policy advocacy has coalesced around women's opportunities, men too have mobilized their status as "male athletes" to assert gendered rights under Title IX (Messner and Solomon 2007; Rosenthal 2008; Walton and Helstein 2008).

10. As Malkiel (2016) demonstrates, the struggle for coeducation in elite American colleges and universities was ongoing in the late 1960s and early 1970s. However, formal federal policy discussions on the issues of women's exclusion from educational institutions writ large did not begin until 1970.

11. In the early 1970s, the feminist coalition targeting educational domains was small, led primarily by the Women's Equity Action League (WEAL). WEAL was founded in 1968 by feminists who objected to the National Organization for Women's (NOW) support of abortion rights, and NOW's activist tactics. Although WEAL's advisory board included several Members of Congress who became very active on Title IX (including Representatives Edith Green (D-OR), Shirley Chisholm (D-NY), Patsy Mink (D-HI), and Martha Griffiths (D-MI)), Dr Bernice Sandler lodged the first sex discrimination complaints under Executive Order 11246. She was politicized after being denied a faculty appointment for coming on "too strong for a woman" (Sandler 2000).

12. The group attempted to downplay open discussion of the sex-based provision by asking interest groups to abstain from lobbying (Costain 1979; Fishel and Pottker 1977; Skrentny 2002).

13. Discussion transpired in both the House and the Senate in 1971. On August 6, the Senate considered the notion of coed football teams. Senator Bayh argued that the proposed legislation would neither "mandate the desegregation of football fields" nor men's locker rooms. Revealing the undercurrents of male entitlement and sexism, Senator Dominick replied, "If I may say so, I would have had much more fun playing college football if it had been integrated."

14. In the 1970 congressional hearings on sex discrimination in education, feminist experts neither mentioned discrimination in athletics, nor women athletes as key stakeholders in the unfolding discussion.

15. Sandler noted during a 1981 interview, "We knew it was going to cover athletics; it was not a surprise. We just didn't tell many people" (Millsap 1988, 32).

16. The complete histories of congressional debate over university undergraduate admissions policies, the inclusion of military academies under the purview of Title IX, and single-sex educational activities (like beauty pageants and father–daughter dances) are reviewed in both primary (Fishel and Pottker 1977) and secondary sources (Rose 2015). Skrentny (2002) also details the contingent debates around racial desegregation which helped distract from the sex equity provisions.

17. The trail of initial bureaucratic conversations is found primarily in the Margaret Dunkle Papers at the Schlesinger Library, the Richard Nixon Presidential Library, and in Fishel and Pottker (1977).

18. The first memo circulated to colleges and universities regarding implementation made no mention of the application of law to athletics. Margaret Dunkle Papers, 1957–1993; "Memorandum to Presidents of Institutions of Higher Education Participating in Federal Assistance Programs," August 1972. MC 530, Box 1, Folder 11. Schlesinger Library, Radcliffe Institute, Harvard University. It was not until October of 1972 that a concerted conversation about athletics began.

19. The "contact sports" distinction continues to be highly contentious (Fields 2004).

20. These discussions foreshadowed how this model of difference manifests itself today. "Men's" versus "women's" teams are often defined by different rules, different equipment, and gendered expectations (see, for example, McElwain 2004; Ring 2012; Theberge 1997). Since this model became policy, the promotion of segregated teams has become increasingly impactful in the means of how we consume, spectate, and value "men's" versus "women's" games.

21. Although Sandler was among the 50 representatives of women's education, athletic, and student groups invited by OCR to discuss initial responses to the legislation in August 1972, OCR later reported that these meetings were a "disappointment" (Fishel and Pottker 1977, 106). Dunkle Papers; "Letter to Sandler from DHEW", July 27, 1972. Box 1, Folder 11. Schlesinger Library.

22. Sandler operated as the Executive Director at PSEW for 20 years. The Schlesinger collection holds the PSEW files.

23. The draft history of the paper is located in the Dunkle Papers at the Schlesinger, Box 29, Folders 1–4. The final draft can be found in the PSEW Records, MC 557, Box 8, Folder 5. Schlesinger Library.

24. The PSEW paper attributed women's historical exclusion from sports as a key cause of this belief. Here again, advocates erred toward public policy that required institutions to increase opportunity for women on "women's teams" as the initial intervention.

25. National Organization for Women Records, 1959–2002; MC 496, box 55, folder 24. Schlesinger Library.

26. The full record of this organization exists across files at the Gerald Ford Presidential Library and the private papers of the National Collegiate Athletic Association. Article-length considerations require me to elaborate these dynamics in other work.

27. White House Central Files, Education; Box 9. Gerald Ford Presidential Library, Ann Arbor, MI.

28. Both transgender and intersex people continue to face difficulties in achieving full access to sport under a sex-segregated regime (Buzuvis 2011).
29. The ways in which "female athletes" stretch the definitions of femininity also have complicated implications for the perceived threat of lesbianism and homophobia in sports (Cahn 1995; Griffin 1998).

Acknowledgements

I would like to thank Dara Strolovitch, Regina Kunzel, Kathryn Pearson, Joe Soss, Mara Toone, and the American Politics Faculty Workgroup at UMass Amherst for their support in developing this work. I appreciate comments from Nadia Brown and Sarah Gershon, as well as those from anonymous reviewers for helping me improve the manuscript and contribute to this special issue.

Funding

I acknowledge research support from the American Academy of University Women, the Gerald Ford Presidential Foundation, the Social Science Research Council, the Myra Sadker Foundation, the New England Regional Fellowship Consortium, and the National Collegiate Athletic Association.

ORCID

Elizabeth A. Sharrow ⓘ http://orcid.org/0000-0001-5880-7905

References

Acosta, Vivian, and Linda Carpenter. 2014. "Women in Intercollegiate Sport: A Longitudinal, National Study, Thirty Seven Year Update, 1977–2014." Accessed March 8 2016. http://www.acostacarpenter.org/

Adams, Mary Louise. 2011. *Artistic Impressions: Figure Skating, Masculinity, and the Limits of Sport*. Toronto, Ontario: University of Toronto Press.

Althusser, Louis. 1970. "Ideology and Ideological State Apparatuses." In *Lenin and Philosophy and other Essays*, 121–176, Translated by Ben Brewster. New York: Monthly Review.

Banaszak, Lee Ann. 2009. "Moving Feminist Activists Inside the American State: The Rise of a State-Movement Intersection and Its Effects on State Policy." In *The Unsustainable American State*, edited by Lawrence Jacobs, and Desmond King, 223–254. New York: Oxford University Press.

Béland, Daniel. 2010. "Reconsidering Policy Feedback: How Policies Affect Politics." *Administration & Society* 42 (5): 568–590.

Bordo, Susan. 1993. *Unbearable Weight: Feminism, Western Culture, and the Body*. Berkeley: University of California Press.

Brake, Deborah. 2010. *Getting in the Game: Title IX and the Women's Sports Revolution*. New York: NYU Press.

Bruch, Sarah K., Myra Marx Ferree, and Joe Soss. 2010. "From Policy to Polity: Democracy, Paternalism, and the Incorporation of Disadvantaged Citizens." *American Sociological Review* 75 (2): 205–226.

Butler, Judith. 1998. "Athletic Genders: Hyperbolic Instance And/or the Overcoming of Sexual Binarism." *Stanford Humanities Review* 6 (2): 103–111. http://www.stanford.edu/group/SHR/6-2/html/butler.html

Buzuvis, Erin. 2011. "Transgender Student-Athletes and Sex-Segregated Sport: Developing Policies of Inclusion for Intercollegiate and Interscholastic Athletics." *Seton Hall Journal of Sports & Entertainment Law* 21 (11): 1–59.

Cahn, Susan K. 1995. *Coming on Strong: Gender and Sexuality in Twentieth-Century Women's Sport.* Cambridge, MA: Harvard University Press.

Cahn, Susan K. 2014. "Turn, Turn, Turn: There Is a Reason (for Sports History)." *Journal of American History* 101 (1): 181–183.

Campbell, Andrea Louise. 2003. *How Policies Make Citizens: Senior Political Activism and the American Welfare State.* Princeton, NJ: Princeton University Press.

Campbell, Andrea Louise. 2012. "Policy Makes Mass Politics." *Annual Review of Political Science* 15 (1): 333–351.

Castañeda, Cindy, Stephen G. Katsinas, and David E. Hardy. 2008. "Meeting the Challenge of Gender Equity in Community College Athletics." *New Directions for Community Colleges* 142: 93–105.

Clotfelter, Charles T. 2011. *Big-Time Sports in American Universities.* New York: Cambridge University Press.

Cohen, Cathy J. 1999. *The Boundaries of Blackness: AIDS and the Breakdown of Black Politics.* Chicago, IL: University of Chicago Press.

Collins, Patricia Hill. 2000. *Black Feminist Thought: Knowledge, Consciousness, and the Politics of Empowerment.* New York: Routledge.

Cooky, Cheryl. 2009. "'Girls Just Aren't Interested': The Social Construction of Interest in Girls' Sport." *Sociological Perspectives* 52 (2): 259–283.

Cooky, Cheryl, Michael A. Messner, and Robin Hextrum. 2013. "Women Play Sport, But Not on TV: A Longitudinal Study of Televised News Media." *Communication & Sport* 1 (3): 203–230.

Cooky, Cheryl, Michael A. Messner, and Michela Musto. 2015. "'It's Dude Time!': A Quarter Century of Excluding Women's Sports in Televised News and Highlight Shows." *Communication & Sport* 3 (3): 261–287.

Costain, Anne. 1979. "Eliminating Sex Discrimination in Education: Lobbying for Implementation of Title IX." In *Race, Sex, and Policy Problems*, edited by Marian Lief, and Michael B. Preston Palley, 3–26. Lexington, MA: Lexington Books.

Crenshaw, Kimberle. 1989. "Demarginalizing the Intersection of Race and Sex: A Black Feminist Critique of Antidiscirmination Doctrine, Feminist Theory and Antiracist Politics." *The University of Chicago Legal Forum* 39: 139–168.

Daniels, Elizabeth A. 2012. "Sexy versus Strong: What Girls and Women Think of Female Athletes." *Journal of Applied Developmental Psychology* 33 (2): 79–90.

Daniels, Elizabeth A., and Heidi Wartena. 2011. "Athlete or Sex Symbol: What Boys Think of Media Representations of Female Athletes." *Sex Roles* 65 (7): 566–579.

Davis, Heath Fogg. 2014. "Sex-Classification Policies as Transgender Discrimination: An Intersectional Critique." *Perspectives on Politics* 12 (1): 45–60.

DeBeauvoir, Simone. 1953. *The Second Sex.* London: Second Cape.

Dietz, Mary G. 2003. "Current Controversies in Feminist Theory." *Annual Review of Political Science* 6 (1): 399–431.

Duncan, Arne. 2013. "We Must Provide Equal Opportunity in Sports to Students with Disabilities." *U.S. Department of Education Blog.* Accessed 1 September 2016. http://www.ed.gov/blog/2013/01/we-must-provide-equal-opportunity-in-sports-to-students-with-disabilities

Dworkin, Shari, and Michael Messner. 1999. "Just Do … What?: Sports, Bodies, Gender." In *Revisioning Gender*, edited by Beth B. Hess Myra Marx Ferree, and Judith Lorber, 341–356. Lanham, MD: Rowman Altamira.

Edwards, Amanda Ross. 2010. "Why Sport? The Development of Sport as a Policy Issue in Title IX of the Education Amendments of 1972." *Journal of Policy History* 22 (3): 300–336.

Fausto-Sterling, Anne. 2000. *Sexing the Body: Gender Politics and the Construction of Sexuality.* New York: Basic Books.

Festle, Mary Jo. 1996. *Playing Nice: Politics and Apologies in Women's Sports.* New York: Columbia University Press.

Fields, Sarah. 2004. *Female Gladiators: Gender, Law, and Contact Sport in America.* Champaign: University of Illinois Press.

Fishel, Andrew, and Janice Pottker. 1977. *National Politics and Sex Discrimination in Education.* Lexington, MA: Lexington Books.

Gelb, Joyce, and Marian Lief Palley. 1982. "Title IX: The Politics of Sex Discrimination." In *Women and Public Policies*, 95–124. Princeton, NJ: Princeton University Press.

Gilder, Ginny. 2015. *Course Correction: A Story of Rowing and Resilience in the Wake of Title IX.* Boston, MA: Beacon Press.

Gordon, Linda. 1990. *Woman's Body, Woman's Right: Birth Control in America.* New York: Penguin Books.

Goss, Kristin A. 2012. *The Paradox of Gender Equality.* Ann Arbor: University of Michigan Press.

Griffin, Pat. 1998. *Strong Women, Deep Closets: Lesbians and Homophobia in Sport.* Champaign, IL: Human Kinetics.

Griffin, Pat. 2012. "'Ain't I a Woman?' Transgender and Intersex Student Athletes in Women's Collegiate Sports." In *Transfeminist Perspectives: In and Beyond Transgender and Gender Studies*, edited by Anne Enke, 98–111. Philadelphia, PA: Temple University Press.

Guttmann, Allen. 1991. *Women's Sports: A History.* New York: Columbia University Press.

Hancock, Ange-Marie. 2008. "Black Female Athletes." In *African-Americans and Popular Culture, Volume 2: Sports*, edited by Todd Boyd, 1–10. Westport, CT: Praeger Publishers.

Hancock, Ange-Marie. 2016. *Intersectionality: An Intellectual History.* New York: Oxford University Press.

Hanson, Katherine, Vivian Guilfoy, and Sarita Pillai. 2009. *More Than Title IX: How Equity in Education Has Shaped the Nation.* Lanham, MD: Rowman & Littlefield.

Haycock, Christine E., and Joan V. Gillette. 1976. "Susceptibility of Women Athletes to Injury: Myths vs. Reality." *Journal of American Medicine* 236 (2): 163–165.

Heywood, Leslie, and Shari Dworkin. 2003. *Built to Win: The Female Athlete As Cultural Icon.* Minneapolis: University of Minnesota Press.

Hogshead-Makar, Nancy, and Andrew Zimbalist. 2007. *Equal Play: Title IX and Social Change.* Philadelphia, PA: Temple University Press.

Irvine, Janice M. 2002. *Talk About Sex: The Battles Over Sex Education in the United States.* Berkeley: University of California Press.

Kaestner, Robert, and Xin Xu. 2010. "Title IX, Girls' Sports Participation, and Adult Female Physical Activity and Weight." *Evaluation Review* 34 (1): 52–78.

Kane, Mary Jo. 1996. "Media Coverage of the Post Title IX Female Athlete: A Feminist Analysis of Sport, Gender, and Power." *Duke Journal of Gender Law & Policy* 3 (1): 95–127.

Kane, Mary Jo, and Shawn Ladda. 2012. *Research Digest: 40th Anniversary of Title IX.* Rockville, MD: President's Council on Fitness, Sports, and Nutrition.

Karkazis, Katrina, Rebecca Jordan-Young, Georgiann Davis, and Silvia Camporesi. 2012. "Out of Bounds? A Critique of the New Policies on Hyperandrogenism in Elite Female Athletes." *The American Journal of Bioethics* 12 (7): 3–16.

Knoppers, Annelies, and Mary G. McDonald. 2010. "Scholarship on Gender and Sport in Sex Roles and Beyond." *Sex Roles* 63 (5/6): 311–323.

Krane, Vikki, Precilla Y. L. Choi, Shannon M. Baird, Christine M. Aimar, and Kerrie J. Kauer. 2004. "Living the Paradox : Female Athletes Negotiate Femininity and Muscularity." *Sex Roles* 50 (5/6): 315–329.

Lorber, Judith. 1994. *Paradoxes of Gender.* New Haven, CT: Yale University Press.

Lowi, Theodore J. 1964. "American Business, Public Policy, Case Studies, and Political Theory." *World Politics* 16 (4): 677–715.

Luker, Kristin. 1985. *Abortion and the Politics of Motherhood.* Berkeley, CA: University of California Press.

MacKenzie, Megan. 2015. *Beyond the Band of Brothers: The US Military and the Myth That Women Can't Fight.* New York: Cambridge University Press.

Malkiel, Nancy Weiss. 2016. *"Keep the Damned Women Out": The Struggle for Coeducation.* Princeton, NJ: Princeton University Press.

McDonagh, Eileen, and Laura Pappano. 2007. *Playing With the Boys: Why Separate Is Not Equal in Sports.* New York: Oxford University Press.

McElwain, Max. 2004. *The Only Dance in Iowa: A History of Six-Player Girls' Basketball*. Lincoln: University of Nebraska Press.

Messner, Michael A. 1988. "Sports and Male Domination: The Female Athlete as Contested Ideological Terrain." *Sociology of Sport Journal* 5: 197–211.

Messner, Michael A., and Nancy Solomon. 2007. "Social Justice and Men's Interests: The Case of Title IX." *Journal of Sport & Social Issues* 31 (2): 162–178.

Mettler, Suzanne. 2005. *Soldiers to Citizens: The G.I. Bill and the Making of the Greatest Generation*. New York: Oxford University Press.

Mettler, Suzanne, and Joe Soss. 2004. "The Consequences of Public Policy for Democratic Citizenship: Bridging Policy Studies and Mass Politics." *Perspectives on Politics* 2 (1): 55–73.

Millsap, Mary Ann. 1988. "Advocates for Sex Equity in Federal Education Law: The National Coalition for Girls and Women in Education." Ed. D. Dissertation, Harvard University.

Milner, Adrienne N., and Jomills Henry Braddock. 2016. *Sex Segregation in Sports: Why Separate Is Not Equal*. New York: Praeger.

Moi, Toril. 1999. *What Is a Woman? And Other Essays*. Oxford: Oxford University Press.

NCAA (National Collegiate Athletic Association). 2016. *NCAA Sports Sponsorship and Participation Rates Report, 1981–82-2015–16*. Indianapolis, IN: NCAA.

NCWGE (National Coalition for Women and Girls in Education). 2012. *Title IX at 40: Working to Ensure Gender Equity in Education*. Washington, DC: NCWGE.

NFSHSA (National Federation of State High School Associations). 2015. *1969–2014 High School Athletics Participation Survey Results*. Indianapolis, IN: National Federation of State High School Associations. Accessed 8 March 2016. http://www.nfhs.org/ParticipationStatics/PDF/Participation%20Survey%20History%20Book.pdf

NFSHSA (National Federation of State High School Associations). 2016. *2015–16 High School Athletics Participation Survey*. Indianapolis, IN: National Federation of State High School Associations. Accessed 8 March 2016. http://www.nfhs.org/ParticipationStatistics/PDF/2015-16_Sports_Participation_Survey.pdf

Norton, Anne. 2004. *Ninety-Five Theses on Politics, Culture, and Method*. New Haven, CT: Yale University Press.

NWLC (National Women's Law Center). 2012. *Title IX: 40 Years and Counting*. Washington, DC: NWLC.

NWLC (National Women's Law Center), and (Poverty & Race Research Action Council) PRRAC. 2015. *Finishing Last: Girls of Color and School Sports Opportunities*. Washington, DC: NWLC.

OCR (Office for Civil Rights in the U.S. Department Health, Education, and Welfare). 1975. *Memorandum: Elimination of Sex Discrimination in Athletic Programs*. Washington, DC: Office for Civil Rights, Department of Health, Education and Welfare. Accessed 8 March 2016. http://eric.ed.gov/?id=ED119583

OCR (Office for Civil Rights in the U.S. Department of Education). 1979. "A Policy Interpretation: Title IX and Intercollegiate Athletics." *Federal Register, Vol. 44, No. 239*. Accessed 8 March 2016. http://www2.ed.gov/about/offices/list/ocr/docs/t9interp.html

Patashnik, Eric. 2008. *Reforms at Risk: What Happens after Major Policy Changes Are Enacted*. Princeton, NJ: Princeton University Press.

Patashnik, Eric, and Julian E. Zelizer. 2013. "The Struggle to Remake Politics: Liberal Reform and the Limits of Policy Feedback in the Contemporary American State." *Perspectives on Politics* 11 (4): 1071–1087.

Pickett, Moneque Walker, Marvin P. Dawkins, and Jomills Henry Braddock. 2012. "Race and Gender Equity in Sports: Have White and African American Females Benefited Equally From Title IX?" *American Behavioral Scientist* 56 (11): 1581–1603.

Pieper, Lindsay Parks. 2016. *Sex Testing: Gender Policing in Women's Sports*. Urbana-Champagne: University of Illinois Press.

Pierson, Paul. 1993. "When Effect Becomes Cause: Policy Feedback and Political Change." *World Politics* 45 (4): 595–628.

Price, Janet, and Margrit Shildrick, eds. 1999. *Feminist Theory and the Body: A Reader*. Edinburgh: Edinburgh University Press.

Ring, Jennifer. 2009. *Stolen Bases: Why American Girls Don't Play Baseball*. Champaign: University of Illinois Press.

Ring, Jennifer. 2012. "Invisible Women in America's National Pastime … or, 'She's Good. It's History, Man'." *Journal of Sport & Social Issues* 37 (1): 57–77.

Roberts, Dorothy E. 1997. *Killing the Black Body: Race, Reproduction, and the Meaning of Liberty*. New York. Pantheon Books.

Rose, Deondra. 2015. "Regulating Opportunity: Title IX and the Birth of Gender-Conscious Higher Education Policy." *Journal of Policy History* 27 (1): 157–183.

Rosenthal, Cindy Simon. 2008. "Sports Talk: How Gender Shapes Discursive Framing of Title IX." *Politics & Gender* 4 (1): 65–92.

Sabo, Don, and Phil Veliz. 2012. *The Decade of Decline: Gender Equity in High School Sports*. Ann Arbor, MI: SHARP Center for Women and Girls.

Sandler, Bernice R. 2000. "'Too Strong for a Woman'—The Five Words That Created Title IX." *Equity & Excellence in Education* 33 (1): 9–13.

Schattschneider, Elmer Eric. 1935. *Politics, Pressures and the Tariff: A Study of Free Private Enterprise in Pressure Politics, as Shown in the 1929–1930 Revision of the Tariff*. New York: Prentice-Hall.

Schneider, Anne L., and Helen M. Ingram. 1993. "Social Construction of Target Populations: Implications for Politics and Policy." *American Political Science Review* 87 (2): 334–347.

Schneider, Anne L., and Helen M. Ingram. 1997. *Policy Design for Democracy*. Lawrence: University of Kansas Press.

Schultz, Jaime. 2014. *Qualifying Times: Points of Change in U.S. Women's Sport*. Champaign: University of Illinois Press.

Shifrer, Dara, Jennifer Pearson, Chandra Muller, and Lindsey Wilkinson. 2015. "College-Going Benefits of High School Sports Participation: Race and Gender Differences over Three Decades." *Youth & Society* 47 (3): 295–318.

Skocpol, Theda. 1992. *Protecting Soldiers and Mothers: The Political Origins of Social Policy in United States*. Cambridge, MA: Harvard University Press.

Skrentny, John David. 2002. *The Minority Rights Revolution*. Cambridge, MA: Harvard University Press.

Soss, Joe. 1999. "Lessons of Welfare: Policy Design, Political Learning, and Political Action." *American Political Science Review* 93 (2): 363–380.

Soss, Joe, and Sanford F. Schram. 2007. "A Public Transformed? Welfare Reform as Policy Feedback." *American Political Science Review* 101 (1): 111–127.

Staurowsky, Ellen J., *et al.* 2015. *Her Life Depends on it III: Sport, Physical Activity, and the Health and Well-Being of American Girls and Women*. East Meadow, NY: Women's Sports Foundation.

Stevenson, Betsey. 2007. "Title IX and the Evolution of High School Sports." *Contemporary Economic Policy* 25 (4): 486–505.

Stevenson, Betsey. 2010. "Beyond the Classroom: Using Title IX to Measure the Return to High School Sports." *The Review of Economics and Statistics* 92 (2): 284–301.

Stone, Deborah. 1984. *The Disabled State*. Philadelphia, PA: Temple University Press.

Strach, Patricia. 2013. "Gender Practice as Political Practice: Cancer, Culture, and Identity." *Politics, Groups, and Identities* 1 (2): 247–250.

Strolovitch, Dara Z. 2007. *Affirmative Advocacy: Race, Class, and Gender in Interest Group Politics*. Chicago, IL: University of Chicago Press.

Suggs, Welch. 2005. *A Place on the Team: The Triumph and Tragedy of Title IX*. Princeton, NJ: Princeton University Press.

Theberge, Nancy. 1997. "'It's Part of the Game': Physicality and the Production of Gender in Women's Hockey." *Gender & Society* 11 (1): 69–87.

Theberge, Nancy. 2000. *Higher Goals: Women's Ice Hockey and the Politics of Gender*. Albany, NY: SUNY Press.

Walton, Theresa, and Michelle Helstein. 2008. "Triumph of Backlash : Wrestling Community and the 'Problem' of Title IX." *Sociology of Sport Journal* 25: 369–386.

Ware, Susan. 2011. *Game, Set, Match: Billie Jean King and the Revolution in Women's Sports*. Chapel Hill: University of North Carolina Press.

Westbrook, Laurel, and Kristen Schilt. 2014. "Doing Gender, Determining Gender: Transgender People, Gender Panics, and the Maintenance of the Sex/Gender/Sexuality System." *Gender & Society* 28 (1): 32–57.

WhiteHouse, Office of the Press Secretary. 2012. "Obama Administration Commemorates 40 Years of Increasing Equality and Opportunity for Women in Education and Athletics." *WhiteHouse.gov.* Accessed 1 September 2016. http://www.whitehouse.gov/the-press-office/2012/06/20/obama-administration-commemorates-40-years-increasing-equality-and-oppor

Wilson, James Q. 1974. *Political Organizations*. Princeton, NJ: Princeton University Press.

Wright, Jan, and Gill Clarke. 1999. "Sport, the Media and the Construction of Compulsory Heterosexuality: A Case Study of Women's Rugby Union." *International Review for the Sociology of Sport* 34 (3): 227–243.

Wulf, Steve. 2012. "Title IX: 37 Words That Changed Everything." *ESPN-W Online.* Accessed 1 September 2016. http://espn.go.com/espnw/title-ix/article/7722632/37-words-changed-everything

Yale Women Strip to Protest a Lack of Crew's Showers. 1976. *New York Times*, March 4.

Young, Iris Marion. 1980. "Throwing like a Girl: A Phenomenology of Feminine Body Comportment Motility and Spatiality." *Human Studies* 3 (1): 137–156.

Young, Iris Marion. 2002. "Lived Body vs Gender: Reflections on Social Structure and Subjectivity." *Ratio* 15 (4): 410–428.

Disability and the meaning of reproductive liberty

Amber Knight

ABSTRACT
This article brings together three literatures: political theories of liberty, feminist theories on reproductive rights, and the disability studies literature on ableism. I engage with these debates to consider the meaning of a core political concept – liberty – by examining women with disabilities' reproductive experiences and interests. In light of the dynamics of gender inequality and ableism, I seek to problematize the notion that reproductive freedom is synonymous with the negative right to privacy. Although governmental noninterference has allowed many women to gain control of their bodies and reproductive fates, the narrow focus on privacy – and the attendant issues of contraception and abortion – overlooks important dimensions of reproduction that are more likely to affect women with disabilities, including the structural factors that discourage disabled women from having children at all. The article concludes that feminist theorists should embrace a conception of positive liberty committed to actively dismantling ableist barriers to motherhood, including: inadequate access to assisted reproductive technologies; a lack of financial support for social welfare programs; and discriminatory attitudes that assume that disabled women are not "mother material." Until these structural obstacles to "choice" are eradicated, genuine reproductive liberty will remain an elusive goal for many women with disabilities.

Introduction

A central tenet of feminist theory is that women's reproductive capacities have been controlled and regulated within a male-dominated society. Subsequently, feminists contend that reproductive liberty is at the heart of women's emancipation. Women must be able to choose whether and when they will conceive, and how many children they will have, in order to freely participate in social, economic, and political life. The widely adopted feminist mantra that "my body belongs to me" expresses the notion that women – not men or the state – should have decision-making power in matters that affect their own reproductive lives. While early feminist scholarship importantly analyzed women's bodies as sites of political struggle, the mainstream literature did not adequately acknowledge diversity among women as a group. However, over the last few decades, intersectional research has drawn our attention to the fact that reproductive liberty is a matter of degree:

some women's reproductive decisions are more freely chosen than others. One of the wider implications of intersectional research is that an individual woman's ability to exercise choice varies based on her standing within social hierarchies of race, class, and sexuality (Price 2011).[1]

Although the field of feminist theory has widely embraced contextualized and intersectional research on reproduction, as evidenced by the burgeoning literature on women of color (Roberts 1997; Smith 2005; Price 2010) and lesbians (Lewin 1993; Mamo 2007), less has been said about disabled women's reproductive experiences and interests.[2] The relative lack of attention devoted to disability-related reproductive issues can be partly explained by the mainstream pro-choice movement's narrow focus on the legal right to privacy and the attendant issues of contraception and abortion. Consequently, important dimensions of reproduction that are more likely to affect women with disabilities have gone overlooked, including the various factors that discourage disabled women from having children at all. While nondisabled feminists have largely struggled for the right to assume roles other than mothers, many women with disabilities demand the opposite, equating reproductive rights with the right to motherhood. Until mainstream pro-choice feminist discourse champions the right to bear and raise children to the same degree that it emphasizes a woman's right to prevent or terminate a pregnancy, women with disabilities will remain marginalized. This persistent marginalization undermines solidarity within the women's movement and also leaves the causes and consequences of ableism unexamined.

In recent years, a growing body of pathbreaking feminist literature has taken up issues surrounding disability and reproduction (Kafer 2013; Piepmeier 2013; Jarman 2015). These authors contend that a "reproductive justice" framework can better account for the role of ableism in reproductive regulation than a "pro-choice" framework. This article contributes to this discussion in an attempt to offer some conceptual clarity to the conversation. All too frequently, the terms justice, liberty, and equality are used without adequate precision or sufficient attention to their distinct significance. I argue that blurring the boundaries of individual liberty and assimilating it to other goods, like justice, risks losing the peculiar importance of each distinctive political virtue.[3] Hence, at the most general level, this article aims to provide conceptual clarity in order to help feminists critically reflect on what our goals should be and how to best pursue them. In my view, examining the precise meaning of reproductive liberty is not simply an academic exercise. Rather, it is normatively important. As Dimova-Cookson (2004) explains, "Because freedom can come to represent opposite values (for example, lack of political obligation on the one hand, and voluntary embracing of duties, on the other), it is important to specify what kind of freedom we defend" (555).

Drawing from the canon of political thought, I begin by discussing the difference between justice and liberty, arguing that feminist theorists should focus more on the struggle for liberty instead of turning to the concept of justice when thinking about reproduction. Next, I answer the question posed by Mills (2011) – "what is reproductive freedom, or in other words, what kind of freedom is it?" (38) – by considering the unique experiences of women with disabilities. The article ultimately argues that positive liberty theory offers a more expansive and comprehensive definition of "choice" that can better incorporate the reproductive concerns of women with disabilities because it: (1) expands the definition of an external barrier to encompass socioeconomic constraints, including financial hurdles restricting access to assisted reproductive technologies

(ARTs) and inadequately funded social programs to support mothers with disabilities as they raise their children and (2) addresses internal barriers to free choice, including ableist mechanisms of socialization that discourage women with disabilities from thinking about themselves as "mother material." The article ultimately suggests that genuine reproductive liberty will remain an elusive goal for many women with disabilities until both external and internal barriers to free choice are eradicated.

Before I proceed, however, any theoretical account of disability must begin with the acknowledgment of diversity within the group with respect to capacities, lived experiences, and interests. The term "women with disabilities" encapsulates individuals with a range of physical, mental, and psychological impairments as diverse as autism, blindness, Down syndrome, and bipolar disorder. In addition, disability and gender intersect with other salient dimensions of identity, including one's racial, class, and religious background. Obviously, women with disabilities are not one monolithic entity with identical reproductive experiences or interests. That said, historically many women with disabilities have been dissuaded and coercively prevented from becoming mothers through various means, including: pervasive stereotypes that cast disabled women as unfit for motherhood (Campion 1995); forced abortions and involuntary sterilizations (Nielsen 2012); the loss of the custody of their children (Breeden, Olkin, and Taube 2008); and discrimination in the adoption process (DeVries 2009). Given this history, this article aims is to identify and examine structural obstacles to becoming a mother, while at the same time recognizing that many disabled women value the right to privacy, demand access to contraception, and support the continued legalization of abortion.

Reclaiming and reconceptualizing liberty

As a concept, liberty has fallen out of favor with many contemporary feminist theorists.[4] As early as the 1980s, MacKinnon (1987) argued that "anyone with an ounce of political analysis should know that freedom before equality, freedom before justice, will only further liberate the power of the powerful and will never free what is most in need of expression" (15). According to MacKinnon, a liberal formulation of freedom – as being synonymous with governmental noninterference – benefits socially privileged individuals by licensing their choices to perpetuate oppressive relations. For instance, "free enterprise" enables capital to exploit the working class, and "sexual liberation" defends the right of men to view pornography by exploiting women's bodies. In addition, this ideal privileges the choices of those who have the means to realize them. If a person's socioeconomic needs are met and they stand in relations of equality or even privilege to others, then it makes sense for them to want government to simply stay out of their way as they make decisions about the kind of life they want to lead. Therefore, when liberty is tantamount to governmental noninterference, it is hardly surprising that many feminists are willing to concede the ideal to libertarians, many of whom conceive of it as little more than individual consumer choice within a free marketplace.

Much of the recent literature on reproductive rights also prefers the language of justice.[5] Piepmeier (2013) explains why, writing,

> Reproductive justice is a scholarly and activist framework that expands conversations around a host of questions relating to reproduction. Rather than framing the central issue as "choice,"

which is unrealistically and unproductively individualized, reproductive justice demands that we recognize how social context shapes reproduction and how community opens and closes particular possibilities … (176)

In her view, justice has a wider lens, so to speak, because it addresses the full range of pro-creative activities – including the ability to bear and raise a child – and acknowledges that we make reproductive decisions within a broader social context, including inequalities of wealth, respect, and power across lines of (dis)ability. Ultimately, Piepmeier persuasively urges scholars to think about reproduction as something that extends far beyond individual decision-making. In doing so, she displaces the language of free choice in favor of justice.

Although reproductive liberty cannot be defined by an individualized notion of choice that ignores the broader societal contexts that shape reproduction and parenting, as Piepmeier argues, liberty should continue to animate our conversations about reproductive rights. "Liberty" and "justice" are distinct political values, and although they may be interrelated they are not interchangeable. In Berlin's ([1958] 1969, 125) words, "Everything is what it is: liberty is liberty, not equality, or fairness, or justice … " . The significance of these concepts is a matter of endless theoretical dispute, and political theorists have mapped out long genealogies of these ideals by tracing their multiple meanings throughout different historical contexts (Skinner 1998; Solomon and Murphy 2000). Rather than rehash these genealogies here, I argue that feminist disability theorists should reclaim liberty as a core political concept and analytic prism, especially in the domain of reproduction.

Why should liberty take center stage? Feminist political theorist Nancy Hirschmann provides a useful starting point. Even though she does not explicitly address the issue of reproduction, her insights about the pitfalls of a justice framework for disability rights are relevant to the issue at hand. In "Disability Rights, Social Rights, and Freedom" (2015), Hirschmann argues that an emancipatory disability politics would be more efficacious if it focused more on the struggle for liberty instead of justice for two reasons. First, Hirschmann notes that justice is interrelated to the notion of "desert," which binds justice to responsibility and individuality rather than our basic humanity or species membership. When someone makes a claim based on desert, he or she is arguing that someone *deserves* something from someone on some basis.[6] This is a problem, according to Hirschmann, because the link between desert and justice buys into the "medical model" of disability, which seeks compensatory mechanisms for impairment.[7] The idea here is that if justice requires society to help redistribute resources in such a way that people do not undeservingly suffer from personal misfortune, disability will inevitably be considered an undeserved tragedy to be eligible for compensation. From a disability perspective, the idea that disability is an undeserved misfortune, rather than a socially induced condition, is deeply problematic. According to Hirschmann,

Ever since Aristotle, justice has been tied to the notion of "desert." There is a tacit underlying assumption that in a just world people get what they deserve, and such assumptions shape our conclusions about just entitlements. And because we hold prejudicial attitudes about the inferiority of disability— something to be feared and hated, a reminder of the fragility of our own bodies— the demand for justice unavoidably replicates and depends on the able-bodied view of the disabled as "injured," diminished, lacking, less. (2015, 8)

Second, according to Hirschmann, a problem with taking justice as the central focus for disability politics is that it is concentrated on the past since it "is always a remedy for injury." Justice is inevitably backward looking and locks the justice seeker into Nietzsche's ressentiment (2015, 8).[8] Simply put, the focus on justice prompts a focus on victimhood and powerlessness. Instead of spending time seeking redress for past injury, Hirschmann argues that a renewed focus on freedom divorces us from the conceptual and political baggage of the past and moves us forward in a new direction.

Feminist disability theorists should take Hirschmann's argument into serious consideration. Because freedom is forward looking and untethered to desert, it is easier to make claims to resources and social change by virtue of our basic humanity. It would be a mistake to overstate Hirschmann's point, however, by giving the impression that justice does not matter, or that liberty and justice are necessarily in tension with one another. Rather, she suggests that "justice needs to be subordinate to freedom when we think about disability rights" because what actually makes something unjust is the inhibition of people's liberty and the "unequal distribution of freedom" that results from unequal concentrations of the means to make individual choices (i.e., money, resources, and power) (2015, 10–13). Accordingly, she suggests that liberty is actually the purpose or end-point of justice, and that emancipatory political movements should ultimately strive to allow all people to live lives of their own choosing (2015, 10). If we apply Hirschmann's critique to disabled women's reproductive rights, it means that feminist disability theorists should start our analyses from the perspective of liberty. Because exercising choice is the hallmark of freedom, choice should rightfully remain the central focus of feminist discourse and analysis. The wider implication is that we should not abandon a choice framework – we simply need to amend and expand it.

How can we better understand reproductive choice? A traditional negative liberty view of reproductive freedom is a necessary but insufficient step. Why? What do I mean by negative liberty?[9] Political theorists generally contend that negative liberty involves not being restricted by others from doing what you want to do. It is "negative" in the sense that it requires the absence of something, namely external obstacles or barriers. A basic feature of negative liberty is the idea that barriers come from outside the self. From this perspective, a person is unfree when something or someone prevents them from doing what they want or forces them to do what they do not want to do. In order to promote negative freedom, governmental restraint is key.

Positive liberty, on the other hand, is the possibility of acting in such a way as to take control of one's life and realize one's fundamental purposes. It is "positive" in the sense that it requires the presence of something, such as minimal threshold of economic security or education. Oftentimes, proponents of positive freedom suggest that barriers to freedom can be internal, due to ignorance, irrational desires, and illusions. In this way, autonomy is often considered to be a component of positive liberty. Although there are many definitions, political theorists generally characterize autonomy as the capacity for self-government.[10] It refers to a person's ability to guide her life from her own perspective rather than be manipulated by others or forced into a choice. In order to promote positive freedom, one must secure the provision of the conditions necessary to make autonomous decisions and take advantage of negative liberties. On this view, the state is not always an impediment to freedom. Rather, it can be a resource that protects against the worst abuses of capitalism and other structures of social inequality that diminish opportunities to make authentic choices.[11]

When applied to reproduction, much of the discussion about reproductive liberty – within mainstream pro-choice feminist discourse, and normative liberal political theory – emphasizes the importance of defending individual choice against state coercion, including laws limiting access to contraception and abortion. Indeed, some theorists argue that reproductive liberty should be solely understood as a negative right to noninterference, insofar as citizens are not obliged to actively foster others' capacities for the exercise of reproductive choice (Robertson 1996; Harris 2007). In contrast to this view, I argue that the right to unimpeded choice is a necessary but insufficient step toward achieving reproductive liberty. Although it is important to protect an individual woman's decision to prevent or terminate a pregnancy free from unwarranted government interference, the lived experience of physical and mental impairment reveals how choice cannot be effectively exercised in practice by simply defending a woman's freedom to be left alone.

Embedding individual choice in external context

Positive liberty theory enriches our understanding of reproductive liberty in two important ways.[12] First, it embraces a more contextualized and socially embedded view of the individual by focusing on the provision of the conditions necessary to take advantage of negative liberties. Freedom is a pipe dream if a person does not have the means to realize her choices. Hence, if a woman with a mobility impairment cannot receive adequate obstetric care because her physician's office does not have equipment to accommodate her, or she cannot afford contraception because she lives in poverty, the right to privacy is more of an empty gesture than a substantive right.[13] Because individual choice is not exercised in a vacuum, proponents of positive liberty insist that the wider political community, often through the vehicle of the state, must help secure the external conditions necessary for one's choices to be realized.[14] A serious commitment to positive liberty means that the government will have to at least partially subsidize and secure the medical and social facilities necessary to prevent and assist pregnancy and also develop mechanisms for distributing wealth and income more equitably so that individuals can really choose between courses of action in family planning.

Politically, feminists will need to confront the question, "what are the limits of positive freedom?" A positive liberty approach maintains that the political community provide women with the means to fulfill their reproductive decisions, and this position obviously demands a range of comprehensive changes in social, political, and economic arrangements, including some degree of public funding for contraception, abortion, ARTs, adoption, and childcare.[15] Yet, few would go so far as to say that women should have a right to any or all resources they require to either have or not have children. This would simply not be sustainable. Therefore, matters pertaining to individual freedom, even in the realm of reproduction, must be raised in conjunction with other compelling considerations about what is required for a just society. In democratic deliberations about public resource allocation, feminists championing reproductive rights will have to consider the extent of existing concentrations of wealth, budget constraints, the bargaining power of various political and economic stakeholders, and other factors as they strategize how to fairly equalize public resources so that women are not disadvantaged in their reproductive prospects.

In sum, positive liberty theory offers an approach for thinking about questions of resource allocation rather than proposing definitive answers or fixed guidelines to them. It points our attention toward the policy decisions that allow some doors to be opened while others are shut, as well as the cultural narratives that justify and perpetuate the current provision of public resources.

With respect to the unique experiences of women with disabilities, feminists should demand that public resources are used to equalize access to ARTs and various social welfare programs that assist mothers and their children. To begin, evidence suggests that inadequate access to ARTs prevents many women with disabilities from realizing their reproductive decisions to become mothers. ARTs comprise a variety of procedures designed to achieve pregnancy without sexual intercourse. The Centers for Disease Control and Prevention (CDC) generally defines ARTs to include "all fertility treatments in which both eggs and sperm are handled." Assisted insemination, assisted ovulation, surrogacy, and in vitro fertilization (IVF) are among the most commonly used ARTs in the US. These new technologies have successfully enabled thousands of people who would otherwise be unable to procreate to do so. In the US, approximately one in every hundred babies born is now conceived through ART (Liu and Adashi 2013, 53). They are especially instrumental in enabling women experiencing infertility, lesbian couples, and single women to conceive.

While reproductive technologies provide some disabled women their only opportunity to have biological children, the reality is that it is often out of reach for many prospective mothers. One of the biggest barriers is the high cost. For instance, a single IVF cycle ranges from 12,000 to 15,000 dollars. High costs disproportionately impact women with disabilities as a group, as they are more likely to live in poverty than their nondisabled counterparts, largely due to job discrimination and meager redistributive measures (DeNavas, Proctor, and Smith 2011). Moreover, the costs of ARTs are generally paid directly by patients because the majority of private insurance plans do not compensate infertility treatments, and Medicaid – which covers nearly *half* of all women with disabilities – does not provide coverage (Liu and Adashi 2013). The growing cost of treatment combined with limited health insurance coverage means that individual clinics and providers are largely responsible for determining who is allowed to receive and pay for ART. Hence, even though ARTs expand the range of women's reproductive choices in theory, they are difficult to utilize in practice because many disabled women cannot afford to pay for the services out of pocket. If one of the leading factors limiting access is the lack of insurance coverage, the government should mandate the extension of health care coverage to encompass ART. As of 2013, 15 states have adopted legislative mandates to cover infertility treatments to varying degrees, but there is no national policy on ART eligibility (Liu and Adashi 2013).

In addition to equalizing access to ARTs to broaden women's options regarding conception, the state also needs to invest in publically subsidized social programs that assist mothers with disabilities as they raise their children. In an era of neoliberal welfare reform, the state has drastically slashed social programs. As a result, many women who need public assistance caring for their children are left to fend for themselves. Cuts to public assistance hit mothers with disabilities especially hard since disability and poverty are highly correlated. Mothers with disabilities and their families depend heavily on public benefits, so they are disproportionately impacted by reductions to the

Supplemental Nutrition Assistance Program (SNAP), Temporary Assistance for Needy Families (TANF), Head Start, and various childcare subsidies.

It should also be noted that some governmental policies are designed to disincentivize recipients of public assistance from having children. A recent survey revealed that 52% of parents with disabilities receive Supplemental Security Income (SSI) (NCD 2012, 250). However, according to the Social Security Administration, marriage between 2 SSI recipients results in an automatic 25% reduction in total benefits. The National Council on Disability refers to this policy as a "marriage penalty" (NCD 2012). Even though SSI recipients who want to have kids do not necessarily have to get married to fulfill their reproductive desires, the marriage penalty poses a conundrum for disabled individuals who have religious or social objections to bearing and raising children outside of the institution of marriage.

Another factor to consider is that many women with disabilities unfairly experience greater costs of daily living because our society is designed with an able-bodied person's needs in mind. Significant portions of their income have to be put toward things like arranging adequate transportation and finding or creating accessible housing. This is also true of the adaptive parenting equipment and other home modifications that are essential to the provision of childcare. Cureton (2016), who is a parent with a visual impairment, explains how environments often have to be retrofitted to accommodate parents with disabilities:

> Visually impaired people ... use magnifiers, label readers, our other senses and help from others in order to navigate public transportation systems with our children, buy and prepare food for our families, organise and wash clothes, practice good hygiene and ensure that we and our children are safe and secure ... [We] have installed security alarms on doors, bookcases and cupboards that alert us when our children may be in danger. Some of us require our children to wear squeaky shoes so that we can keep track of their movements. We can use labeling tape around the house and medicine plungers of different sizes that make parenting tasks easier for us. And we often use assistive devices that are specifically designed for disabled parents, such as accessible changing tables, bathtubs and cribs that incorporate monitoring devices of various kinds. (32)

Yet many disabled parents may not be able to afford the expensive assistive devices and equipment necessary to perform the activities of daily living (ADLs) with babies and children. Also, parenting responsibilities are not covered as personal attendant services under Medicaid. Unfortunately, there are few opportunities to receive public assistance for devices and services that would go a long way toward supporting disabled parents.

With respect to solutions, it would obviously be impossible to provide an exhaustive list of policy reforms here, but it should be clear that the state has a prominent role in creating and funding public assistance programs that support disabled mothers and their children. The first step involves getting rid of marriage penalties. People who want to start a family should not be unfairly forced to decide between marriage and a critical source of income to provide for themselves and their children. In addition, there should be public resources available for home modifications and assistive technologies that facilitate childcare. Finally, Medicare and Medicaid should expand the definition of ADLs to include parenting activities so that some tasks are covered as personal assistant services during times when disabled mothers face challenges fulfilling these duties independently. Again, the reforms mentioned here are not intended as a comprehensive recipe for success.

Rather, these suggestions are meant to engage readers in thinking about some specific socioeconomic changes and policy reforms that could make the choice to become a disabled mother a more attainable decision.

Enhancing autonomy by confronting internal barriers to choice

Second, positive liberty theory concerns itself with internal, or psychological, barriers to freedom. Thus, if a woman with a disability chooses not to become a parent because "the training against motherhood begins when a woman is diagnosed as disabled and continues throughout her childbearing years," as O'toole (2002) explains, then we cannot be sure that her choice is genuinely free (82). To be clear, I am not suggesting that all women with disabilities who do not want to have children are suffering from false consciousness or that they are suppressing their "real" desires in the face of cultural attitudes. Many disabled women sincerely do not want to become mothers. My point is simply that our desires are variable. Preferences are at least partly the byproduct of social and environmental influences. Because disabled women's desires are shaped in a specifically ableist context that actively dissuades them from reproducing, it is simply impossible to know what kind of choice a women with a disability would have made if she had lived in a more welcoming environment. The focus on internal barriers is important because women with disabilities might limit their own reproductive behavior. The state does not need to interfere for liberty to be limited if disabled women are complicit in restricting their own choices because they have been socialized to forgo motherhood. Hence, feminist theorists need to think through the ways in which stereotypes and other mechanisms of socialization shape disabled women's reproductive desires and impede autonomous decision-making.

With respect to stereotypes, disabled women are commonly considered unfit as sexual partners and as mothers. They are consistently presumed to be *asexual, incapable of parenting,* and *breeders of defective offspring.* First, while nondisabled women are routinely sexually objectified, women with disabilities are widely assumed to be asexual. In particular, people with mental impairments are considered childlike, and the general public assumes that they are not sexual beings.[16] These cultural assumptions about "appropriate" sexual behavior inform policies and practices. Disability studies scholars have documented how parents, doctors, and social workers have systematically repressed disabled people's sexuality (McRuer and Mollow 2012). For example, Block (2002) analyzes how many parents angelicize their adolescent and adult cognitively disabled children, seeing them as lacking erotic desire and unable to face the dangers that accompany sexuality. Accordingly, many parents monitor and supervise their children's sex lives. In addition, people with disabilities often report how group homes and long-term care facilities purposely destroy opportunities for them to engage in sexual activity, and how those residing in institutions are especially subject to intense surveillance from physicians and social workers due to a lack of privacy (Adams 2015). Because disabled women are discouraged from forging sexual partnerships, it can be especially challenging for many of them to conceive.

Next, women with disabilities are often assumed to be innately incapable of caring for their children, regardless of their actual or potential capabilities.[17] They are often assumed to lack the requisite capacities to bathe and diaper babies, prepare food, provide discipline, and make responsible decisions regarding children's welfare and safety, among other responsibilities. The perception that a woman with a disability cannot fulfill the expectations of motherhood is especially common when she has her own need for assistance. Due to the widespread presumption of parental unfitness, disabled women report discrimination in adopting, being permitted to provide foster care, and in winning child custody after divorce. For instance, The National Council on Disability reports that impairment may be considered in determining the best interest of a child for purposes of a custody determination in family court in every state, noting that two-thirds of dependency statutes allow the court to reach the determination that a parent is unfit on the basis of their disability alone (NCD 2012, 14). Because an impairment in-and-of-itself can be used as the grounds for the termination of parental rights, parents with disabilities are more likely to lose custody of their children after divorce (Kirshbaum, Taube, and Lasian Baer 2003).

Finally, many people assume and fear that women with disabilities will produce "defective" offspring that are financially burdensome to society. This fear has fueled concentrated efforts at preventing pregnancy, and people with genetic conditions are especially discouraged from passing on their genes. Consider the public condemnation that Bree Walker experienced. Walker is a former television news anchor in Los Angeles with a rare congenital impairment called ectrodactylism, a genetic condition that results in the fusing together of fingers and toes. When Walker and her husband decided to have a baby knowing that there was a high likelihood that their child would inherit the condition, a radio host in Southern California questioned Walker's reproductive decision on air:

> She has a genetic deformity and there's a 50–50 chance that her baby will in fact have the deformity, so is this an appropriate thing to do? Is it fair to the kid to bring him into the world with one strike against him? (quoted in Campion 1995, 137)

Several listeners who weighed in on the radio show denounced Walker for knowingly "inflicting" her condition onto her offspring.

Hence, disabled women make reproductive decisions in a context of heightened public scrutiny where they are bombarded with the message that they are not "mother material." Friends, relatives, physicians, and geneticists draw on all of these stereotypes to advise prospective mothers with disabilities against having children. Moreover, women who ignore these cultural messages are often portrayed as unrealistic, irresponsible, or selfish if they choose to become mothers. Under these conditions, it is hardly surprising that many disabled women see motherhood as an occupation that is out of reach.

The remedy to these internal barriers is cultural or symbolic and could involve a number of strategies to transform social norms so that "disabled mother" is no longer a contradiction in terms. To begin, images of disabled people engaging in sexually satisfying relationships (for reproductive and non-reproductive purposes) are scarce in the mainstream media.[18] Disability rights activists and their allies have challenged the relative silence around sexuality in recent years. We need to continue to support current efforts to assert disabled individual's sexual agency through art, poetry, and websites like Dating4Disabled.com.[19] Furthermore, in order to challenge the presumption of parental unfitness, all people need to be exposed to images and cultural representations – in films, television, and printed media – of mothers with disabilities leading their ordinary lives: breastfeeding, picking their children up from school, and playing together at the park. In addition, we need to flip the dominant script and discuss some of the advantages of having a disabled parent. As Cureton (2016) argues, having a disability can often improve, rather than diminish, a person's ability to care for and raise their children:

> Our [disabled parents'] strategies for meeting our child's basic needs ... often require us to be especially attentive to our children, maintain a close proximity to them, and spend substantial time and effort with them and thinking about them. This heightened sensitivity can lead to a stronger bond between us and our child, alert us to their needs and interests, lead us to learn about our child's habits, routines and concerns and develop greater trust and communication with them. (33)

Finally, eugenic rhetoric needs to be challenged. While we no longer embrace the eugenic policies of the early twentieth century, rhetoric about "defective" offspring persists. Rather than limiting certain kinds of people from reproducing in order to solve social problems, our aim should be to fix the environment to accommodate the widest possible range of human form and function so that people with a range of capacities can flourish.

That said, it is important to consider how positive liberty theory's concern with the internal psychological dimensions of decision-making poses a unique challenge in the case of cognitive impairment. Certain capacities, including the ability to reason and independently execute one's choice as a political agent, are usually viewed as essential prerequisites for autonomy.[20] Yet women with cognitive impairments often encounter difficulties in rationally forming preferences and independently pursuing developed plans. Indeed, US courts have denied women with cognitive disabilities their reproductive rights – and justified practices like forced sterilization – on the grounds that their incompetence renders them incapable of giving consent and making their own informed decisions.[21] Hence, if the capacities to reason and independently execute decisions are prerequisites for autonomy, as many proponents of positive liberty maintain, should women with cognitive disabilities be considered subjects of freedom?

Although this is a difficult question that warrants a deeper investigation than the brief treatment provided here, feminist theories of relational autonomy might serve as a useful entry point into a discussion about cognitive impairment and reproductive liberty. As Mackenzie and Stoljar (2000) explain, the phrase "relational autonomy" does not represent a single perspective, but instead designates a loosely related collection of views that share an emphasis on the social embeddedness of the self and on the social structures and relations that make autonomy possible (4). In the context of reproduction, relational autonomy demands a theoretical shift. Rather than fixating on the question, "does a women with a cognitive impairment have, or not have, a minimal threshold of rational competency to exercise reproductive autonomy?" we become more invested in knowing, "what types of relational supports are required for a cognitively impaired woman to exercise autonomous agency in matters pertaining to reproduction to the greatest degree possible?" Hence, it shifts our focus from an assessment of individual competencies toward the constitutive role that social institutions and interpersonal relationships play in developing an individual women's potential for reproductive choice.

As a matter of practice, disability activists have developed "supported decision-making" as a means to provide the relational supports necessary for assisted choice.[22] Although there is no "one-size-fits all" model, supported decision-making generally occurs when people with cognitive disabilities use one or more trusted family members, friends, social workers, or legal advocates to help them understand the situations they face so that they may make their own choices. Legally, a "supporter" may assist a woman with a cognitive disability make reproductive decisions by helping her: understand options, responsibilities, and consequences of life decisions, including decisions about contraception, abortion, pregnancy, and/or childrearing; access, collect, and obtain medical and financial records; and communicate her decision to appropriate persons. By honoring interdependency, supported decision-making challenges the liberal presumption that full rationality and independence are prerequisites for autonomy. This type of an arrangement suggests that choice does not have to be radically individuated, but can be undertaken in a collaborative manner. Hence, even though some women with cognitive impairments may need assistance making reproductive choices, it does not follow that they are necessarily unfree.

In sum, women with disabilities may choose to forgo motherhood because they have been bombarded with the social message that they are not "mother material." If we take the internal barriers to free choice seriously, it follows that the community is obligated to actively combat degrading stereotypes that portray women with disabilities as asexual, incapable of parenting, and breeders of defective offspring. Also, even though positive liberty theory's preoccupation with autonomy seems to pose a unique challenge in the case of the reproductive rights of women with cognitive disabilities, feminist scholarship on relational autonomy opens the possibility that women with cognitive disabilities may be able to effectively make autonomous reproductive decisions with some degree of collaborative assistance.

Conclusion

Feminists have long contested the usurpation of women's decision-making power, especially in matters regarding their own bodies. "Pro-choice" feminists have fought long and hard to secure a legal zone of privacy where women can exercise reproductive choices to the greatest degree possible, free from excessive governmental overreach. However, in recent years, the "pro-choice" label has lost popularity, and many feminists prefer to speak of reproductive justice instead (Calmes 2014). The widespread disenchantment with the rhetoric of choice is understandable because it is often used as a shorthand for governmental noninterference. While many affluent, white, able-bodied women may be content with the privacy rights that have been secured under *Griswold v. Connecticut* (1965) and *Roe v. Wade* (1973), women of color, poor women, and women with disabilities have not enjoyed these gains to the same degree because many reproductive choices remain unavailable to them in practice.

Yet, this article contributes to the broader literature on body politics and reproductive rights by suggesting that the retreat away from individual choice is somewhat misguided. Rather than abandon a choice framework altogether, I argue that feminists should amend and expand the meaning of choice by reconceptualizing liberty and reconsidering the affirmative role that the state can play in creating the background conditions necessary for autonomous decision-making. Ultimately, I hope to have shown that positive liberty theory – which focuses on the public provision of the conditions necessary to take advantage of negative liberties, and also concerns itself with actively dismantling internal barriers to freedom – offers a more expansive and comprehensive definition of "choice" that can better incorporate the concerns of women with disabilities who may want to have a child, but have systematically been denied that right.

Notes

1. Roberts (2009) refers to what she calls a "reproductive caste system," wherein the reproductive capacities of healthy and wealthy married white women are valued more than those of poor women, women of color, and women with disabilities (784).
2. That said, it is important to acknowledge early feminist champions of the reproductive rights of women with disabilities, including Finger (1985) and Asch and Fine (1988).
3. As this article will hopefully make clear, the fundamental question of what the term liberty means is a central point of contention among political theorists, but most definitions put the ability of the individual to make choices and act on them front and center. Hence, I consider a "pro-choice" framework to be primarily concerned with individual liberty.
4. I use the terms "liberty" and "freedom" synonymously. Attempts have been made to distinguish between them (see Pitkin 1988), but the distinction has not been widely adopted.
5. For a lengthier discussion about the development of the "reproductive justice" movement, and how its approach differs from the "pro-choice" reproductive rights framework, see London (2011).
6. The philosopher Mill ([1861] 1993) explained the relationship between justice and desert clearly, writing,

> It is universally considered just that each person should obtain that (whether good or evil) which he *deserves*; and unjust that he should obtain a good, or be made to undergo an evil, which he does not deserve. This is, perhaps, the clearest and most emphatic form in which the idea of justice is conceived by the general mind. ([1861] 1993, 46)

7. Disability studies scholars have identified the "medical model" and the "social model" of disability. Proponents of the medical model see disability as an individual medical condition. Accordingly, change should be primarily directed toward "fixing" the individual so that she is able to function in society. Disability is viewed a personal tragedy that the disabled person wants to overcome. By contrast, proponents of the social model argue that while *impairment* is a physiological condition, *disability* is socially induced through exclusionary policies and practices. They contend that once the disabling attitudinal, architectural, and socioeconomic barriers are removed, most people with impairments will be included in social and political life (see Shakespeare 2010).
8. Nietzsche describes ressentiment as the moralizing revenge of the powerless in *The Genealogy of Morals* ([1887] 1969):

> For every sufferer instinctively seeks a cause for his suffering, more exactly, an agent … some living thing upon which he can, on some pretext or other, vent his affects … This … constitutes actual physiological cause of ressentiment, vengefulness, and the like … (127)

In his view, ressentiment breeds a corrosive resentfulness among political actors who come to be defined by their suffering and the wrongs done them.

9. For a detailed account of the difference between negative and positive liberty see Berlin ([1958] 1969). For a feminist analysis of the negative/positive liberty distinction, see Hirschmann (2003).
10. Contemporary feminist theorists who have analyzed the concept of autonomy in detail include Mackenzie and Stoljar (2000) and Friedman (2003).
11. It should be noted that some feminist political theorists are reluctant to engage the state in the pursuit for freedom. For example, Brown (1995) views the state as an instrument of male domination. She is weary of feminist appeals to the state, arguing that state-centric strategies

paradoxically undermine women's liberty through the intensification of surveillance and regulation. As a result, emancipatory politics come to resemble the regimes they intend to subvert: "Whether one is dealing with the state, the Mafia, parents, pimps, police, or husbands the heavy price of institutionalized protection is always a measure of dependence and agreement to abide by the protector's rules" (1995, 169).

12. In this article, I discuss positive liberty theory broadly by emphasizing some of the shared features of this school of thought, although individual accounts of the meaning of positive freedom vary significantly. At the most general level, positive liberty theory originated in the classic Socratic-Stoic era, but its modern usage is often associated with Rousseau and an intellectual tradition that followed (see Wokler 1987). To date, a few feminist philosophers and legal theorists have borrowed from this intellectual tradition to advance the idea that reproductive liberty should be understood as form of positive freedom (see Copelon 1990; Pine and Law 1992; Mills 2011). In a certain sense, Roberts (1997) also endorses an affirmative conception of liberty. Thinking about the experiences of women of color, she is critical of a negative liberty approach since it masks social prejudices and the maldistribution of wealth and education (309). As an alternative, she supports "a notion of reproductive freedom that combines the values captured by both liberty and equality" (305). However, according to my reading, Roberts ultimately prefers to invoke the rhetoric of justice, as when she states, "Reproductive freedom is a matter of social justice" (6).

13. For more on disability discrimination within medical institutions, see Pendo (2008).

14. Piepmeier would undoubtedly find this dimension of positive freedom attractive because it is able to account for how our political communities "open and close particular possibilities" to potential parents with disabilities (2013, 176).

15. Currently, the Hyde Amendment, originally enacted in1977, is a legislative provision that bans the use of federal funds for abortion services in all but the most extreme circumstances – including cases of rape, incest, or life endangerment. This provision makes it difficult for poor women enrolled in Medicaid to obtain abortion services, and, due to systematic exclusion from the labor force, women with disabilities are more likely than their able-bodied counterparts to be enrolled in Medicaid (for more on disabled women and Medicaid coverage, see Musumeci 2014).

16. The film *The Other Sister* (1999) portrays an adult cognitively disabled woman who wants to live on her own and have a sexual and romantic relationship with a cognitively impaired man. When confronted with their disabled daughter's sexual desires, the parents express astonishment and disbelief. Their reactions reflect the culturally shared tendency to think of disabled people as asexual.

17. The film "I am Sam" (2001) depicts how state agency officials and others negatively assess a cognitively disabled parent's parental fitness before they have even conducted an individualized assessment of his actual parenting capabilities.

18. A noteworthy exception is the film *The Sessions* (2012), which is about a man in an iron lung who explores his sexuality with a sex surrogate.

19. See Wade's poem, "I Am Not One Of The" (2007). For more ideas about how to politically assert sexual agency see Wilkerson (2002).

20. As Nancy Hirschmann (2003) explains, "Autonomy is fundamentally about capabilities, specifically about the ability to assess one's options, reflect critically about them, and make choices that allow one to exert control over one's life" (2003, 36).

21. In the case of *Buck v. Bell* (1925), the Supreme Court upheld Virginia's state compulsory sterilization statute after a cognitively disabled woman named Carrie Buck was sterilized against her will due to her "incompetence." While many involuntary sterilization state statutes have been struck down since *Buck*, the case still has not been explicitly overruled almost a century later.

22. Legal theorists Kohn, Blumenthal, and Campbell (2013) describe supported decision-making as follows:

Proponents of supported decision-making tout it as a means to empower persons with disabilities by providing them with help in making their own decisions, rather than simply providing someone to make decisions for them ... As a general matter, supported decision-making occurs when an individual with cognitive disabilities is the ultimate decision-maker but is provided support from one or more persons who explain issues to the individual, and, where necessary, interpret the individual's words and behavior to determine his or her preferences. (1113–1120)

Acknowledgements

I would like to thank the anonymous reviewers, Gretchen Arnold, Amanda Grigg, Penny Weiss, and Jason Windett for comments on earlier drafts of this article.

Disclosure statement

No potential conflict of interest was reported by the author.

References

Adams, Rachel. 2015. "Privacy, Dependency, Discegenation: Toward a Sexual Culture for People with Intellectual Disabilities." *Disability Studies Quarterly* 35 (1).

Asch, Adrienne, and Michelle Fine. 1988. "Shared Dreams: A Left Perspective on Disability Rights and Reproductive Rights." In *Women with Disabilities: Essays in Psychology, Culture, and Politics*, edited by Michelle Fine, and Adrienne Asch, 297–305. Philadelphia, PA: Temple University Press.

Berlin, Isaiah. [1958] 1969. "Two Concepts of Liberty." In *Four Essays on Liberty*. Oxford: Oxford University Press.

Block, Pamela. 2002. "Sterilization and Sexual Control." In *Health of Women with Intellectual Disabilities*, edited by Patricia Noonan-Walsh, 76–89. Oxford: Blackwell Publishing Company.

Breeden, Christine, Rhoden Olkin, and Daniel Taube. 2008. "Child Custody Evaluations When One Parent Has a Physical Disability." *Rehabilitation Psychology* 53 (4): 445–455.

Brown, Wendy. 1995. *States of Injury: Power and Freedom in Late Modernity*. Princeton, NJ: Princeton University Press.

Calmes, Jackie. 2014. "Advocates Shun "Pro-Choice" to Expand Message." *The New York Times*. Accessed 23 June 2016. http://www.nytimes.com/2014/07/29/us/politics/advocates-shun-pro-choice-to-expand-message.html?_r=0.

Campion, Mukti Jain. 1995. *Who's Fit to Be a Parent?* London: Routledge.

Copelon, Rhonda. 1990. "Losing the Negative Right of Privacy: Building Sexual and Reproductive Freedom." *New York University Review of Law and Social Change* 18 (1): 15–50.

Cureton, Adam. 2016. "Some Advantages to Having a Parent with a Disability." *Journal of Medical Ethics* 42 (1): 31–34.

DeNavas, Carmen, Bernadette Proctor, and Jessica Smith. 2011. *Income, Poverty, and Health Insurance Coverage in the United States: 2010*. Washington, DC: U.S. Census Bureau.

DeVries, Brenda. 2009. "Health Should Not Be a Determinative Factor of Whether One Will Be a Suitable Parent." *Indiana Health Law Review* 6 (1): 137–169.

Dimova-Cookson, Maria. 2004. "Conceptual Clarity, Freedom, and Normative Ideas: Reply to Blau." *Political Theory* 32 (4): 554–562.

Finger, Ann. 1985. "Claiming All of Our Bodies: Reproductive Rights and Disability." In *With the Power of Each Breath: A Disabled Women's Anthology*, edited by Susan Browne, Debra Connors, and Nanci Stern, 292–307. Pittsburgh, PA: Cleis Press.

Friedman, Marilyn. 2003. *Autonomy, Gender, Politics*. Oxford: Oxford University Press.

Harris, John. 2007. *Enhancing Evolution: The Ethical Case for Making Better People*. Princeton: Princeton University Press.

Hirschmann, Nancy. 2003. *The Subject of Liberty: Toward a Feminist Theory of Freedom*. Princeton: Princeton University Press.

Hirschmann, Nancy. 2015. "Disability Rights, Social Rights, and Freedom." *Journal of International Political Theory* 12 (1): 1–16.

Jarman, Michelle. 2015. "Relations of Abortion: Crip Approaches to Reproductive Justice." *Feminist Formations* 27 (1): 46–66.

Kafer, Alison. 2013. *Feminist, Queer, Crip*. Bloomington, IN: Indiana University Press.

Kirshbaum, Megan, Daniel Taube, and Rosalind Lasian Baer. 2003. "Parents with Disabilities: Problems in Family Court Practice." *Journal of the Center for Families, Children and the Courts* 4: 27–48.

Kohn, Nina, Jeremy Blumenthal, and Amy Campbell. 2013. "Supported Decision Making: A Viable Alternative to Guardianship." *Penn State Law Review* 117 (4): 1111–1157.

Lewin, Ellen. 1993. *Lesbian Mothers: Accounts of Gender in American Culture*. Ithaca, NY: Cornell University Press.

Liu, Joy, and Eli Adashi. 2013. "Selective Justice: State Mandates for Assisted Reproductive Technology and Reproductive Justice." *American Journal of Clinical and Experimental Obstetrics and Gynecology* 1 (1): 53–61.

London, Sarah. 2011. "Reproductive Justice: Developing a Lawyering Model." *Berkeley Journal of African-American Law and Policy* 13 (1): 71–102.

Mackenzie, Catriona, and Natalie Stoljar. 2000. *Relational Autonomy: Feminist Perspectives on Autonomy, Agency, and the Social Self*. New York, NY: Oxford University Press.

MacKinnon, Catharine. 1987. *Feminism Unmodified: Discourses on Life and Law*. Cambridge, MA: Harvard University Press.

Mamo, Laura. 2007. *Queering Reproduction: Achieving Pregnancy and in the Age of Technoscience*. Durham, NC: Duke University Press.

McRuer, Robert, and Anna Mollow, eds. 2012. *Sex and Disability*. Durham, NC: Duke University Press.

Mill, John Stuart. [1861] 1993. *Utilitarianism, On Liberty, Considerations on Representative Government*, edited by Geraint Williams. London: Everyman.

Mills, Catherine. 2011. *Futures of Reproduction: Bioethics and Biopolitics*. New York, NY: Springer.

Musumeci, MaryBeth. 2014. "The Affordable Care Act's Impact on Medicaid Eligibility, Enrollment, and Benefits for People with Disabilities." *The Henry J. Keiser Foundation*. Accessed 8 February 2016. http://kff.org/health-reform/issue-brief/the-affordable-care-acts-impact-on-medicaid-eligibility-enrollment-and-benefits-for-people-with-disabilities/.

NCD. 2012. *Rocking the Cradle: Ensuring the Rights of Parents with Disabilities and their Children*. Washington, DC: National Council on Disability. Accessed 8 February 2016. https://www.ncd.gov … /2012/Sep272012.

Nielsen, Kim. 2012. *A Disability History of the United States*. Boston, MA: Beacon Press.

Nietzsche, Friedrich. [1887] 1969. *On the Genealogy of Morals*. Translated by W. Kaufmann and R.J. Hollingdale. New York, NY: Vintage.

O'toole, Corbett. 2002. "Sex, Disability and Motherhood: Access To Sexuality for Disabled Mothers." *Disability Studies Quarterly* 22 (4): 81–101.

Pendo, Elizabeth. 2008. "Disability, Equipment Barriers, and Women's Health: Using the ADA to Provide Meaningful Access." *Saint Louis University Journal of Health and Law Policy* 2 (1): 15–56.

Piepmeier, Alison. 2013. "The Inadequacy of " Choice': Disability and What's Wrong with Feminist Framings of Reproduction." *Feminist Studies* 39 (1): 159–186.

Pine, Rachael, and Sylvia Law. 1992. "Envisioning a Future for Reproductive Liberty: Strategies for Making the Rights Real." *Harvard Civil Rights-Civil Liberties Law Review* 27 (2): 407–463.

Pitkin, Hanna. 1988. "Are Freedom and Liberty Twins?" *Political Theory* 16 (4): 523–552.

Price, Camilla. 2010. "What is Reproductive Justice? How Women of Color Activists are Redefining the Pro-Choice Paradigm." *Meridians: Feminism, Race, Transnationalism* 10 (2): 42–65.

Price, Camilla. 2011. "It's Not Just About Abortion: Incorporating Intersectionality in Research About Women of Color and Reproduction." *Women's Health Issues* 21 (3): 55–57.

Roberts, Dorothy. 1997. *Killing the Black Body: Race, Reproduction, and the Meaning of Liberty*. New York, NY: Pantheon Books.

Roberts, Dorothy. 2009. "Race, Gender, and Genetic Technologies: The New Reproductive Dystopia?" *Signs* 34 (4): 783–804.

Robertson, John. 1996. *Children of Choice: Freedom and the New Reproductive Technologies*. Princeton, NJ: Princeton University Press.

Shakespeare, Tom. 2010. "The Social Model of Disability." In *The Disability Studies Reader*, 3rd ed., edited by Lennard Davis, 266–273. New York, NY: Routledge.

Skinner, Quentin. 1998. *Liberty before Liberalism*. Cambridge: Cambridge University Press.

Smith, Andrea. 2005. "Beyond Pro-Choice Versus Pro-Life: Women of Color and Reproductive Justice." *NWSA Journal* 17 (1): 119–140.

Solomon, Robert and Mark Murphy, ed. 2000. *What Is Justice? Classic and Contemporary Readings*. 2nd ed. New York, NY: Oxford University Press.

Wade, Cheryl Marie. 2007. "I Am Not One Of The." *The Gimp Parade*. Accessed 8 February 2016. http://thegimpparade.blogspot.com/2007/04/poetry-cheryl-marie-wade.html.

Wilkerson, Abby. 2002. "Disability, Sex Radicalism, and Political Agency." *NWSA Journal* 14 (3): 33–57.

Wokler, Robert. 1987. "Rousseau's Two Concepts of Liberty." In *Lives, Liberties, and the Public Good: New Essays in Political Theory*, edited by George Feaver, and Frederick Rosen, 61–100. London: Palgrave Macmillan Press.

White attitudes about descriptive representation in the US: the roles of identity, discrimination, and linked fate

Deborah J. Schildkraut

ABSTRACT
Many white Americans feel that whites are discriminated against, identify as white, and feel a sense of linked fate with whites. Scholars have studied these psychological connections to one's racial group among nonwhites, but little attention in political science has been given to how they operate among whites. However, changing social, demographic, and electoral patterns point to inevitable challenges to their traditional status and power. This study examines the extent to which these psychological connections to whites as a group exist and shape how whites feel about descriptive representation. Using a nationally representative survey, it finds that identifying as white, thinking whites are discriminated against, and seeing one's fate as tied to the fate of whites overall are common and make it more likely that whites will say it is important to have a political candidate who is white. These findings reveal a striking similarity in how whites and nonwhites form attitudes about descriptive representation. The implications of these findings given ongoing social and political trends are discussed.

The day after the 2012 election, a press release from the Pew Research Center claimed, "Changing Face of America Helps Assure Obama Victory" (Pew Research Center for People and the Press 2012). The *New York Times* stated, "Demographic Shift Brings New Worry for Republicans" (Shear 2012). It later reported, "For First Time on Record, Black Voting Rate Outpaced Whites in 2012" (Wheaton 2013). More dramatically, Bill O'Reilly told an election night audience, "The white establishment is now the minority" (Weinger 2012). In the days following the election, the inescapable narrative was that whites in America, especially conservative-leaning whites, were soon to be outnumbered, and they either need to brace themselves for an impending minority status or do a better job of finding common cause with racial minorities. In the following months, the US Supreme Court overturned a key provision of the Voting Rights Act (VRA), spurring nationwide discussions about whether racial bias continues to affect electoral institutions and whether Congress would attempt to craft a new version of the landmark civil rights legislation. When Congress undertakes its VRA revision in earnest, debates about race, group position, and representation will again be made salient.[1]

Given this demographic and political landscape, it is likely that a growing number of whites in the US are feeling an increased connection to their racial group and sense that the status of their group is threatened (Hutchings et al. 2012; Craig and Richeson 2014a, 2014b; Danbold and Huo 2014), and such perceptions likely have political consequences. Social scientists have already demonstrated that immigration-driven diversity, along with attitudes about immigrants and Latinos, leads some white Americans to identify more with the Republican Party, vote for Republican candidates, and adopt a more conservative political outlook (Craig and Richeson 2014b; Hajnal and Rivera 2014; Abrajano and Hajnal 2015). More generally, social identity theory suggests that our social and political context informs us about the aspects of our identity that will become salient (Tajfel 1982). Once salient, a group identity becomes a potent force shaping opinions. Perceptions of threat further lead members of socially salient groups to close ranks around the group and prefer policies and actions aimed at preserving the groups' interests (Branscombe et al. 1999; Schmitt and Branscombe 2002). This psychological perspective is similar to the sociological argument that perceived threats to group position generate group-interested attitudes and behaviors (Blumer 1958; Bobo and Hutchings 1996; Bobo 1999). According to these theories, the time is ripe for whites in the US to be thinking explicitly about whether proposed policies and political candidates will affect whites as a group and to be forming their preferences based on their assessments of group interests.

The goal of the present study is to investigate this possibility. Although it might sound obvious to some to posit that white Americans who perceive threats to their group's status would prefer to be represented by someone of the same race, few political scientists have examined empirically the political dynamics of white racial identity, and earlier studies concluded that it has low salience and influence (Wong and Cho 2005; Sears and Savalei 2006). The specific aim of the present study is, therefore, to advance research on white racial identification in the US by examining (1) the extent to which whites identify primarily as white, perceive discrimination against whites, and think that their fate is tied to the fate of whites as a whole (a sentiment known as linked fate) and (2) whether these factors shape how whites feel about descriptive representation, which is when a shared background exists between a constituent and her representative (Pitkin 1967). The focus is on descriptive representation because, as noted above, the current demographic and political climate increasingly raises the specter of whites on one side of electoral politics and nonwhites on the other. In recent years, scholars have begun to understand how *nonwhites* feel about the idea that they are better served in the political process by representatives who share their background (Tate 2004; Barreto 2010; Manzano and Sanchez 2010; McConnaughy et al. 2010; Schildkraut 2013b; Wallace 2014), but the views of whites remain largely unexplored (Casellas and Wallace 2015). Since whites will likely come to pay more attention to race and representation as their traditional status as the political majority is weakened and as race and partisanship continue to align, it is time to turn our attention to their views on descriptive representation.

In the sections that follow, I review the state of political science literature on white identity (and on racial identity more broadly) and on attitudes about descriptive representation. Then I rely on that research to lay out the hypotheses under investigation here. Next, I describe the data and measures used in the analysis, and I present the results. In the end, I find that identifying as white, thinking whites are discriminated against, and seeing one's fate as tied to the fate of whites overall make it more likely that white respondents will say it is important to be represented by someone who is white. These findings reveal a striking similarity in how whites and nonwhites form attitudes about descriptive representation. I end by discussing the implications of these findings given ongoing social and political trends.

Racial identification and perceptions of group standing

At the heart of this inquiry is the recognition that being a member of a social group is hardly a sufficient condition for having that group shape one's attitudes. A significant amount of research in political science over the years has relied on dummy variables to distinguish members of one racial group from members of another racial group, and when attitudinal differences between groups are found, the assumption is often made that such differences stem not from only the different positions that each group has in the sociopolitical hierarchy, but also an awareness about those differences (Lee 2008; Masuoka and Junn 2013). The types of survey questions needed to examine that assumption include questions about how important it is to be a member of that group, how one feels about the group's treatment in society, and whether one's own fate is tied to the fate of the group (Lee 2008; McClain et al. 2009). Measures of these factors include racial identification, perceptions of discrimination against the group, and linked fate. Such questions, however, are often lacking in public opinion surveys or are generally asked of nonwhites only. When available, these measures have been shown to be potent factors driving the political preferences of racial and ethnic minorities.

Racial identification: Assessing the extent to which people derive their sense of self from their membership in a racial or ethnic group (racial identification) is often the first step toward examining how racial group membership shapes political preferences. Including measures of racial identification in analyses underscores that identities are social, understood in terms of the social groups to which people belong and the connections they feel toward those groups (Tajfel 1982). Racial identification has been measured by asking people how important their group membership is to them, how close they feel to the group, whether they describe or think of themselves in terms of their group membership, and whether they prioritize their group membership over other groups to which they belong (Lien, Conway, and Wong 2004; Schildkraut 2005; Wong and Cho 2005; Sears and Savalei 2006; Schildkraut 2011; Fraga et al. 2012; Citrin and Sears 2014). Research on nonwhites has shown that identifying with one's racial group can influence political engagement, trust in government, attitudes toward race-related policies, voter turnout, and preferences for descriptive representatives (Miller et al. 1981; Tate 1991, 1994; Schildkraut 2005, 2011, 2013b; Wong and Cho 2005; Sears and Savalei 2006).

Perceptions of discrimination: Whether people feel that their group is mistreated in society has also come to be seen as an important element of group membership. Perceptions of discrimination against one's racial or ethnic group reveal a sense of group threat, indicate a sense of group vulnerability, and point to a recognition of societal disadvantage. Examinations of perceptions of discrimination among nonwhites have found that they lead to increased support for race-related policies such as affirmative action and bilingual education, lower levels of trust in government, greater political involvement, and greater ingroup solidarity (Masuoka 2006; Sanchez 2006a, 2006b; Sears and Savalei 2006; Schildk-raut 2011).

Linked fate: As originally conceived, a sense of linked fate, which is the idea that the fate of oneself depends on the fate of the group, served as a heuristic. Dawson (1994) posited that when people felt this type of connection to their group, it was rational for them to form their political preferences based on their view of what is best for the group, since what is good for the group is likely to be good for themselves as individuals. Dawson's argument, it should be noted, was centered on the analysis of black public opinion, derived from the unique experience of blacks in American political history and the persistent treatment of black individuals as members of their racial group. The original theory posits that the group serves as a rational heuristic for opinion formation based on the fact that slavery, disenfranchisement, and discrimination have long constrained the life chances of African Americans. An important conceptual and empirical question is whether the notion of linked fate holds any meaning for other groups in American society and if so, how its causes and influences on public opinion might vary across ethnic groups (McClain et al. 2009; Sanchez and Masuoka 2010; Masuoka and Junn 2013).

As the concept of linked fate has been applied to other groups, it has come to be interpreted not only as a heuristic, but also as a measure of group consciousness, racial solidarity, and even racial identification (Lee 2008; McClain et al. 2009; Masuoka and Junn 2013). Debate over what linked fate is remains ongoing (Gay, Hochschild, and White 2014). Despite the uncertainty over the precise psychological mechanism being tapped by measures of linked fate, its effect among nonwhites is wide ranging. Linked fate has been associated with greater support for economic redistribution and for race-related policies such as affirmative action and immigration reform (Dawson 1994; Sears and Savalei 2006; Masuoka and Junn 2013). It also leads to increased identification with the Democratic Party, greater political engagement, and greater likelihood of desire for descriptive representation (Lien, Conway, and Wong 2004; Sanchez 2006b; Barreto 2010; Manzano and Sanchez 2010; Hajnal and Lee 2011; Schildkraut 2013b).

One goal in the present analysis is to gauge white responses to questions about linked fate. Do whites answer affirmatively when asked whether what affects whites affects them individually, and does answering affirmatively promote support for white candidates? To date, few measures of white linked fate exist, yet as noted earlier, there are reasons to believe that current demographic trends and media narratives surrounding such trends might make linked fate both more common and more consequential for whites. At the same time, the political history of the white majority is so fundamentally different from the political history of the black minority, the group for which the theory of linked fate was developed, that what linked fate means for whites remains a very open question. The present research should be viewed as one component of the growing research agenda examining the meaning and impact of linked fate among different racial groups (Masuoka and Junn 2013; Gay, Hochschild, and White 2014).

In summary, when studying nonwhites, it has become more common to move beyond the use of dummy variables in order to inquire whether group membership affects political attitudes and behaviors. Group identification, perceptions of discrimination, and linked fate are three attitudinal factors that have helped illuminate the mechanisms that render group membership powerful. They tap into distinct aspects of group membership (sense of self, perceptions of threat, and interdependence), yet each one has been shown to elevate the salience and potency of group membership.

The fact remains, however, that studies that examine racial identity, perceptions of discrimination, and linked fate explicitly among whites are limited, with earlier studies concluding that the secure standing of whites as the numerical and political majority diminished both the level and impact of white identification (Wong and Cho 2005; Sears and Savalei 2006). Most research related to the impact of racial group membership on whites' political attitudes and behaviors comes instead from theories that originated in sociology and psychology. From sociology, Blumer's theory of group position frames racial prejudice as a response among dominant group members to perceptions of threat to their status and power (Blumer 1958). Such perceptions promote a sense of connection to the group and an aversion to policies seen as threatening to the group. For instance, perceived threats to group position among whites are associated with opposition to policies aimed at reducing racial inequality (Bobo 1999). In Blumer's formulation, "big events" that capture the public imagination and become "the focal points of the public discussion" are a critical source of information about group position (1958, 6). The demographic narrative following the 2012 election arguably serves as this type of big event. The years following the 2010 Census have also seen a parade of headlines and press releases that draw further attention to the looming critical demographic juncture in the US. Examples of such headlines include "Most Children Younger than Age 1 Are Minorities" (US Census Bureau 2012), "Asians Fastest-Growing Race or Ethnic Group in 2012" (US Census Bureau 2013), "U. S. Will Have a Majority-Minority Population by 2043, Census Predicts" (Wilson 2012), and "For First Time, Minority Students Expected to Be Majority in U.S. Public Schools" (Strauss 2014).

Many studies of group position theory focus on group competition and on attitudes toward race-related policies, such as affirmative action or immigration, rather than on the psychological processes that such perceptions ignite, namely group identification and a sense that the group is being treated poorly in society (e.g., Bobo and Hutchings 1996; Esses, Jackson, and Armstrong 1998; Stephan et al. 2002; Rosenstein 2008). Scholars across disciplines who have examined group position theory tend to use the racial and ethnic composition of one's context as a proxy for threat to the group's position rather than measure perceptions of threat directly (Smith 1981; Glaser 1994; Quillian 1995; Oliver and Mendelberg 2000; Glaser 2003; Lee et al. 2003; Oliver and Wong 2003; Campbell, Wong, and Citrin 2006; Donovan 2010).

Psychologists have likewise focused on the role that group identification and perceptions of group threat play in shaping attitudes among whites, employing the perspective offered by social identity theory described earlier, which maintains that social and political contexts shape which of our group memberships will become politically salient. Findings from this line of scholarship are similar to those that employ group position theory. Specifically, whites are more likely to think of themselves in terms of their racial identity when they are primed to consider threats to the group's status, and identification as white can promote group-interested preferences (e.g., Branscombe, Schmitt, and Schiffhauer 2007; Goren and Plaut 2012; Outten et al. 2012). Psychological investigations have also found that people prefer leaders who are prototypical group members and who favor the ingroup relative to the outgroup, whereas sympathy toward an outgroup can diminish support for group leaders (Haslam and Platow 2001; Platow and van Knippenberg 2001;

Platow et al. 2006). Such findings bolster the expectation that racial identities and perceptions of threat to the group will affect attitudes about whether one's representative should belong to one's racial ingroup.

Research in political science, however, has few studies that assess white racial identity and perceptions of group treatment directly. Some scholars have assessed direct measures of identity and perceptions of threat, and they determined that at the time of their research, these concepts were neither salient nor politically consequential. For example, Wong and Cho (2005) examined white identification from 1972 to 2000, using the group closeness measures in the American National Election Study (ANES). They found that an average of 51% of whites said they feel close to whites as a group during that time. Yet despite its prevalence, its influence on racial attitudes and racial policies was weak.

Similarly, Sears and Savalei wrote in their study of racial identification that, "Whites' whiteness is usually likely to be no more noteworthy to them than is breathing the air around them" (2006, 901). Using data from Los Angeles County in the late 1990s, they argued that the status of whites atop the political and social hierarchy was secure at the time, rendering racial threat minimal. The continuing color line in America, they maintained, was more a product of socialization about the racial hierarchy rather than a reaction to acute threats. They found that in the late 1990s, racial identification, perceptions of discrimination, and linked fate were more prevalent among nonwhites than among whites and that these factors were weak predictors of whites' attitudes on policies related to race and immigration.

Yet even in the 1990s, their data show that between 10% and 25% of whites exhibited concerns about the group, such as identifying strongly with other whites, saying that being white is very important to them, and perceiving both linked fate and discrimination against whites. Although these sentiments hardly represented the majority view among whites, they were at a notable level. Given the more recent social and political developments noted throughout this study, it is time to reconsider the levels of white identification, perceived discrimination, and linked fate, as well as their potential effects. As Wong and Cho noted,

> given previous research on social hierarchy, social identity, and racial threat, it is reasonable to hypothesize that demographic variation that affects whites' numerical majority status will lead to changes in the salience and centrality of white racial identification. (2005, 701)

Those threats to whites' majority status are upon us, and public discussion of them has become common. As such, some political scientists have begun to revisit direct measures of white racial identity, and have found that a sense of white identity can be heightened when whites are primed to consider threats to their group position (Hutchings et al. 2012; Jardina 2013). As psychologists have shown, this research finds that levels of white identity are responsive to discourse about politics and social change. Additionally, research suggests that both the level of white identification and the impact it has on policy preferences, such as immigration, have grown over time (Jardina 2013). It has also been documented that many American whites now consider anti-white bias to be a bigger problem than anti-black bias (Norton and Sommers 2011).

In these recent studies, the effect of white group membership on political outcomes has been demonstrated more firmly with respect to racial identification and perceptions of threat to the group than with respect to linked fate. Clearly, whites have not faced the generations of subjugation that has led many African Americans to rely on linked fate as a heuristic. Yet it is possible that the narrative of threats to whites' majority status could serve to promote a sense of interdependence (Jardina 2014). Masuoka and Junn maintain that linked fate should be understood as a measure of identification with the group, one that includes a recognition of "shared cultural constraints as a function of group membership" (2013, 105) and that whites high in linked fate will "recognize their interest in preserving the racial order" (111). They find 36% of whites feel a sense of linked fate, and that those whites are more likely than others to oppose affirmative action policies and are more likely to support both racial profiling and lowering the level of immigration. Gay, Hochschild, and White (2014), however, argue that linked fate is more of a measure of a desire to affiliate with others, and they find it is unrelated to whites' policy preferences or political behavior, though their analysis concentrated on policies and behaviors that were not racial in nature, such as partisan identification and voter registration.

Despite this growing body of scholarship on the political and electoral consequences of white identification and perceptions about the place of whites in American society, no study has yet examined the attitudes of whites regarding race and representation in the way that the attitudes of nonwhites have been examined. The mechanisms under investigation here are distinct, but all are related to how individuals understand their place in society vis-à-vis race, and all have been shown to promote support for descriptive representation among nonwhites, as I describe below. Whether they operate similarly for whites remains to be seen.

Attitudes about descriptive representation

To date, research on attitudes about descriptive representation, like research on racial identity, has focused on racial minorities. The reasons for that focus are obvious. Generations of political exclusion created legitimate claims among African Americans in the US regarding the need for group-specific redress. The passage of the VRA and its subsequent reauthorizations then created opportunities for racial minorities to elect representatives of their choice. The VRA was successful in raising the number of nonwhites elected to office, which promoted scholarly interest in investigating the extent to which the race of one's representative matters to nonwhite voters.

Existing studies generally have similar conclusions despite differing measures, samples, and time periods under investigation. Among racial minorities, feelings of linked fate are consistently influential (Tate 2003; Manzano and Sanchez 2010; Schildkraut 2013b; Wallace 2014). Similarly, perceptions of discrimination against one's racial group often promote support for descriptive representation, though not always (Manzano and Sanchez 2010; Schildkraut 2013b; Wallace 2014). Research also indicates that identifying strongly with the group in question increases support for descriptive representation. Such identification influences racial minorities as well as women (Rosenthal 1995; Sanbonmatsu 2002; Stokes-Brown 2006; Manzano and Sanchez 2010; Schildkraut 2013b). Among minorities connected to the immigrant experience, identifying with the panethnic group (i.e., Latino) and with the national origin group (i.e., Mexican) can both matter.[2] Notably, this set of findings is consistent across nonwhite groups in the US despite their different demographic and political histories.[3]

The question at hand is whether these factors operate similarly for whites. Some scholars have noted that the location of one's group in the racial hierarchy should condition the effect of racial identity and perceptions of threat on political outcomes. It has been argued that these factors will have opposite effects on race-related policy preferences and national attachments for those at the top of the political hierarchy compared to those at the bottom. Studies have found, for instance, that racial group attachments lead those at the top to support policies that protect the status quo and to have stronger attachments to the national group, whereas they lead those toward the bottom to support more egalitarian policies and to feel more alienated from the national group (Sidanius et al. 1997; Masuoka and Junn 2013). That racial location shapes the effects of group attachments is sensible and has received empirical support.[4] In the present inquiry, however, it is likely that racial identification and perceptions of threat and interdependence will work similarly for whites and nonwhites, enhancing support for co-racial representation across the board. Descriptive representation for nonwhites often means disrupting the status quo given the majority white membership in Congress and the fact that most racial minorities have a representative of a different race.[5] For whites, however, descriptive representation means preserving the racial status quo. If the analysis were examining how group threats affected white support for descriptive representation for outgroups, then the expectation would be different. Indeed, Glaser (2003) found that activating group threat experimentally led whites to be less supportive of majority–minority districts.

Clearly, group identification and perceptions of group position are essential factors to consider when examining attitudes about descriptive representation among racial minorities. Having a heightened sense of connection between one's own identity and the group, along with a sense of the group's tenuous position in the social hierarchy, strengthens support for co-ethnic representation, arguably as a means to ensure that the group's interests will be addressed. Is the same true for attitudes about descriptive representation among whites? Indirect investigations suggest that some whites do in fact care about having a white representative. Branton, Cassese, and Jones (2012) find that whites represented by whites in Congress give higher feeling thermometer scores to their representatives than whites with Latino or black representatives. Jones (2014) finds that whites believe that black and Latino legislators are more liberal and more Democratic than ideologically identical white legislators, even when the legislators adopt conservative positions. It is reasonable to suspect that the presence and persistence of such racial stereotypes regarding party and ideology would further bolster the perception among whites that the race of their representative matters. Finally, white racial identity has been shown to affect turnout and reported vote choice when a black candidate is on the ballot (Petrow 2010; Krupnikov and Piston 2015; Jardina 2014).

In sum, experimental research has established that white racial identity can be primed by political discourse and that the primed identity can affect political attitudes, while observational research has linked white racial identity and linked fate to policy preferences, reported electoral behavior, and candidate evaluations. My goal is to complement this growing body of research with an examination of whites' attitudes about descriptive representation. Research on racial minorities has examined the impact of racial identities on electoral politics from a variety of angles, including stated preferences for descriptive representation, and my aim is to contribute to a similar comprehensive approach with respect to whites.

Hypotheses

The current political climate and the existing scholarship reviewed in the previous sections lead to the following main hypotheses:

> H1: Whites who identify primarily as white are more likely than other whites to say that having a white representative is important.
>
> H2: Whites who feel that there is discrimination against whites in the US are more likely than other whites to say that having a white representative is important.
>
> H3: Whites with a sense of linked fate are more likely than other whites to say that having a white representative is important.

Additional secondary hypotheses are also considered. For instance, past research suggests that group-level discrimination is more influential over attitudes about descriptive representation than individual-level discrimination (Schildkraut 2013b; Wallace 2014). Nonetheless, it makes intuitive sense to expect that personal experiences with discrimination affect one's orientation toward the political system, and in some studies, this type of discrimination has political effects, particularly with respect to political trust (Michelson 2003; Lien, Conway, and Wong 2004; Schildkraut 2011). Thus, whether perceptions of individual-level discrimination affect attitudes about descriptive representation is also explored. Additionally, it is possible that whites are more likely to be concerned about the race of their representative when they are represented by someone who is not white. This possibility will also be examined.

Data and measures

Data come from the American Identity and Representation Survey (AIRS), which was commissioned by the author and conducted over the Internet in October of 2012 by Knowledge Networks (now GfK Custom Research).[6] The survey uses a probability sample and has 1702 respondents overall, 448 of whom are white, non-Hispanic. The median time for completion was 15 minutes. The completion rate (the percentage of completed interviews from among the total number of people GfK sampled for the survey) was 57%. Unless otherwise noted, statistical analyses employ weights provided by GfK to enable national representativeness.[7]

Dependent variables: The main dependent variable is measured with a question that asked respondents, "People can prefer a candidate for many different reasons. How important is it for you that a candidate is white?" Response options were very important, somewhat important, not very important, or not at all important.[8] Respondents were also asked whether they care about sharing their background with candidates in an unspecified way: one of the first questions in the survey (well before the race-specific question just described) asked, "How important is it for you that a candidate is like you in terms of his or her background?" I anticipated that whites who care about the race of their representative would be more likely than other whites to say that a generic shared background matters as well. I also wondered if whites who possess a heighted sense of white identity, racial threat, and linked fate would be concerned about expressing their desire for a white candidate. As such, I was curious to see whether white identity, linked fate, and perceptions of discrimination influence responses to this generic measure of descriptive representation; the analysis of this measure is admittedly exploratory.

The breakdown of responses on these two measures is presented in Table 1. They clearly show that whites are more likely to say that a shared background with a political candidate is important than they are to say a shared race is important. Nearly 56% say that having a shared background is very or somewhat important, while only 10% say a shared race is important. Nonetheless, there is variation on the race-specific measure, with nearly 27% saying "not very important" as opposed to "not at all important." Arguably, respondents who chose "not very important" instead of "not at all important" think that the race of their representative matters at least a little. To put it another way, nearly 37% of whites chose a response other than "not at all important." If concerns about descriptive representation become more common among whites, as is quite likely given the social and demographic trends outlined earlier, then it is important for us to begin to understand the sources of variation among whites when asked whether having a white representative matters.

Independent variables: The independent variable used to examine hypothesis 1 is one's psychological attachment to whites as a racial group relative to one's attachment to a national origin group or to being American. Specifically, respondents were asked (in random order) to indicate if they ever describe themselves as American, as white, and as their national origin (i.e., Irish, German, etc.). They were then asked which one best describes how they think of themselves most of the time. The answer to that question is used here to measure one's primary group attachment. Nearly 78% of white respondents identified primarily as American, 20.9% identified primarily as white, leaving a mere 1% that identified primarily with the national origin group. In all remaining analyses, white identifiers are contrasted with all other white respondents. As a point of comparison, the 2012 ANES asked respondents how important being white is to their identity (it did not ask them to choose white over American), and 34% said very or extremely important, while another 25% said moderately important.[9]

For hypothesis 2, respondents were asked how much discrimination there is in the US today against whites. Response options were a lot (coded as 1), some, a little, or none (coded as 0). Ten percent said there is a lot of discrimination against whites and 40% said there is some. In the 2012 ANES, 31% of non-Hispanic whites said that there is at least a moderate amount of discrimination against whites in the US.

To gauge personal experiences with discrimination, respondents were asked, "Have you ever been treated unfairly at work, school, or when you're out in public because of your racial background?" They could answer yes (coded as 1) or no (coded as 0). Seventeen percent of respondents said yes. The correlation between the group-level and individual-level discrimination measures is 0.19.

Table 1. Importance of descriptive representation.

	White	Shared background
Not at all important	63.02	14.21
Not very important	26.90	30.09
Somewhat important	7.43	44.74
Very important	2.65	10.95
Total	100	100

Note: Non-Hispanic whites only. Weighted results.
Source: Schildkraut (2012).

For hypothesis 3, respondents' sense of linked fate was measured with the following question: "Do you think what happens generally to white people in this country will have something to do with what happens in your own life?" They could answer yes (coded as 1) or no (coded as 0). A majority, 52.4%, of whites said yes.[10] In the 2012 ANES, 39% of whites said yes.

Levels of linked fate and discrimination among whites were somewhat higher in the AIRS than in the ANES, while levels of identification as white were higher in the ANES.[11] What is noteworthy, however, is the degree to which whites in both surveys report feeling a sense of racial identification, societal discrimination, and linked fate. Put simply, there appears to be a substantial amount of group identification and concern about group standing among whites, and their impact merits investigation.[12]

The models also include dummy variables indicating if the respondent has a white representative and if the representative is of the same political party as the respondent (=1 if yes, 0 otherwise). Whites with nonwhite representatives might be more attuned to the role of race in politics and might feel that their needs would be met better by a white candidate compared to whites with white representatives (e.g., Butler and Broockman 2011; Grose 2011). Similarly, whites with a representative from a different political party are likely to be dissatisfied with their current representation and should be more likely to feel that having a candidate who shares his or her background (i.e., who shares his or her political affiliation) is more important than whites who belong to the same party as their representative. Prior research has established that white Republicans care more about descriptive representation than white Democrats (Casellas and Wallace 2015), and so the analyses also control for partisan identification, using a standard seven-category measure (with "strong Republican" coded highest).[13] The analyses also include control measures for gender, age, years of education, whether the respondent is in the South, and income. Age, education, income, and partisanship were all rescaled to run from 0 to 1.

Findings

Results of bivariate cross-tabulations among each dependent variable and each key independent variable appear in Table 2. The top panel shows the results for whether people think it is important to have a white representative. It suggests that each measure of racial identification and group standing shapes how whites feel about the race of their representative. For instance, less than 1% of whites who do not identify primarily as white say that having a white representative is very important, compared to 10% of whites who identify primarily as white. Likewise, only 1% of whites who say that there is no discrimination against whites say that having a white representative is very important, compared to 12% of whites who say that there is a lot of discrimination against whites. The effect for linked fate appears to be weaker, but is in the expected direction.

The bottom panel of Table 2 shows the results for whether people think it is important that their representative share their background. The only measure of identification or group standing that seems to affect the responses is perceptions of discrimination: 5.42% of whites who do not perceive discrimination think that having a shared background is very important, compared to 21% of whites who perceive a lot of discrimination.

Table 2. Cross-tabulation of main independent variables and descriptive representation.

	Identity		Discrimination				Linked fate	
	White primary identity	Other primary identity	None	A little	Some	A lot	No	Yes
White representative								
Not at all important	50.99	67.15	88.86	65.87	54.50	54.11	66.69	59.05
Not very important	25.57	26.16	9.70	25.09	34.64	23.49	26.27	27.35
Somewhat important	13.25	5.84	0.45	7.07	9.34	10.34	5.52	9.20
Very important	10.19	0.85	1.02	1.96	1.52	12.06	1.52	3.60
Total	100	100	100	100	100	100	100	100
Shared backround								
Not at all important	13.60	14.18	22.98	13.77	10.16	19.17	13.68	15.12
Not very important	26.80	31.33	35.09	31.37	29.52	26.19	32.24	29.29
Somewhat important	45.62	43.48	36.5	45.79	48.42	33.58	43.89	43.55
Very important	13.99	11.01	5.42	9.08	11.91	21.05	10.19	12.03
Total	100	100	100	100	100	100	100	100

Note: Non-Hispanic whites only. Weighted results.
Source: Schildkraut (2012).

Table 3. Support for descriptive representation among non-Hispanic whites (ordered probit).

Independent variable	Shared race	Shared background
White identity	0.541**	0.024
	(0.189)	(0.166)
White discrimination	0.960**	0.530**
	(0.293)	(0.243)
Experienced discrimination	0.051	0.100
	(0.200)	(0.187)
Linked fate	0.254*	0.018
	(0.152)	(0.131)
Male	−0.116	−0.194
	(0.152)	(0.134)
Age	0.297	−0.767**
	(0.358)	(0.343)
Education	−1.484**	−1.125**
	(0.570)	(0.570)
Party	0.501**	0.154
(Republican coded higher)	(0.244)	(0.220)
South	−0.247	−0.115
	(0.165)	(0.144)
Income	0.222	0.614*
	(0.345)	(0.336)
White representative	−0.182	−0.259
	(0.359)	(0.321)
Same party as representative	0.062	−0.271*
	(0.165)	(0.150)
Cutpoint 1	0.296	−2.046
Cutpoint 2	1.349	−1.055
Cutpoint 3	2.101	0.343
Chi-square	45.49	24.97
N	396	394

Notes: Weighted results, robust standard errors in parentheses.
Source: Schildkraut (2012).
*$p < .1$.
**$p < .05$.

To conduct a more thorough examination of these responses, I analyzed the data using ordered probit models. Table 3 presents the results. The first column plainly demonstrates that the three main variables under investigation here are significant influences over whether whites say it is important that a political candidate is white. All the three hypotheses are confirmed. The coefficients for white identity and perceptions of discrimination are significant at the 95% confidence level, while the coefficient for linked fate is significant at 90% confidence. The only other significant variables in the model are education (which diminishes the importance placed on descriptive representation) and partisanship (with Republicans more likely to say it is important than Democrats). Personal experiences with discrimination are insignificant, as is having a representative of one's race or party.

In order to examine the magnitude of the effect of the three variables of interest, I calculated the predicted probability of offering each response to the race-specific dependent variable as each measure of group concern goes from its lowest to its highest value (Figures 1–3). I also calculated the predicted probability of saying that having a white candidate is important when all three measures are at their lowest and highest levels (Figure 4). The lowest level of group concern was characterized by not identifying primarily as white, not having a sense of linked fate, and thinking that there is no discrimination against whites in the US. The highest level of group concern was characterized by identifying primarily as white, having a sense of linked fate, and thinking that there is a lot of discrimination against whites.[14]

Figure 1 shows that identifying primarily as white pushes people out of the "not at all important" category, reducing the likelihood of offering this response by a full 20 percentage points. Figure 2 shows that perceptions of discrimination have an even more dramatic effect. Eighty-five percent of whites who say there is no discrimination against whites are predicted to say that having a white representative is not all important, vs. only 54% of whites who say there is a lot of discrimination against whites, a drop of 31 points. The percent saying that having a white candidate is not very or somewhat important rises considerably.

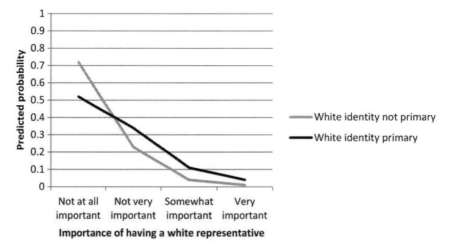

Figure 1. Predicted importance of having a white candidate among white respondents who identify primarily as white and who do not identify primarily as white.
Source: Schildkraut (2012).

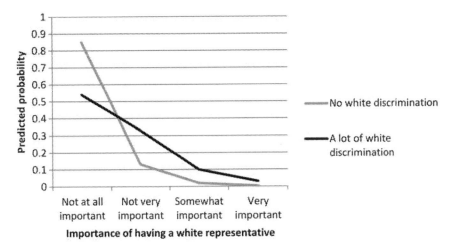

Figure 2. Predicted importance of having a white candidate among white respondents who perceive no discrimination against whites and who perceive a lot of discrimination against whites. Source: Schildkraut (2012).

Although few respondents say that a white representative is very important, the analysis indicates that whites who identify as white and feel that whites face discrimination care more about the race of their representative than other whites. With so many white respondents identifying as white (20.9%) and saying that there is some (40%) or a lot (10%) of discrimination against their group, the results point to the conclusion that a nontrivial portion of white Americans are interested in having a white candidate on the ballot.

Figure 3 shows the effect of linked fate, which has the weakest impact of the three measures of group concern under investigation here, leading to a predicted 8-point drop in saying that having a white candidate is not at all important.

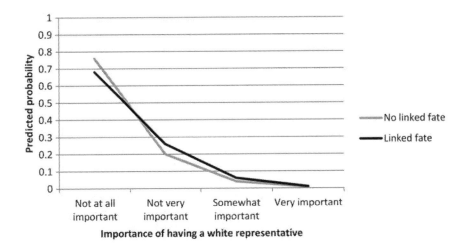

Figure 3. Predicted importance of having a white candidate among white respondents with and without a sense of linked fate. Source: Schildkraut (2012).

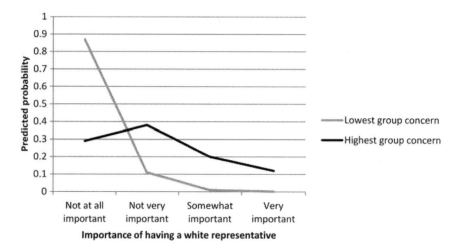

Figure 4. Predicted importance of having a white candidate among respondents with the highest and lowest levels of group concern.
Source: Schildkraut (2012).

Figure 4 shows the predicted outcomes when all three measures are set to either their lowest or their highest values. It shows that among whites with the lowest score on all three measures, the overwhelming majority, 84%, are expected to say that having a white candidate is not important at all. By contrast, only 25% of whites with the highest scores on all three measures are expected to say the same. Moreover, whites with high scores on all three measures are more likely to say that having a white candidate is very or somewhat important than to say that it is not important at all (37% vs. 25%). Put simply, whites who identify primarily as white, perceive discrimination, and feel a sense of linked fate have a substantively different pattern of responses about descriptive representation than whites who feel otherwise. Although the current proportion of people who scores high on all three measures may be low, it is reasonable to expect that proportion to increase over time (Hutchings et al. 2012; Danbold and Huo 2014). Examining the predicted effect of a high score on all three measures is instructive for it offers a glimpse at the potential future effects of media narratives regarding population change and for providing a base-line against which future studies can be compared as the proportion of whites in the US population continues to decline.

Turning back to Table 2, the results in column 2 show that asking people if they care about having a representative who shares their background does not yield the same results as asking if they care about having a white representative. Thinking that whites are discri-minated against in the US increases the likelihood of saying that it is important to have a candidate who shares one's background, but linked fate and white identity are insignifi-cant. Other factors, however, do matter here, namely, income, age, education, and having the same party affiliation as one's member of Congress. Having a higher income makes it more likely that whites will care about having a shared background with their representative, while the other three make it less likely. That people who are in the same party as their representative are less likely than others to say that a shared back-ground is important suggests, perhaps not surprisingly, that many people interpreted the question about shared background in terms of having a shared political orientation with one's representative. In fact, research involving focus group discussions among whites found that when asked if having a representative who is like them is important, concerns about party and ideology predominate (Schildkraut 2013a). Here, whites who have a representative of the same party already share the same background as their representative in this respect, and so the importance for them is diminished.

Discussion

The findings presented here are very much in line with results from existing research on the factors that shape nonwhite attitudes about descriptive representation. The power of racial group identification, perceptions of discrimination, and linked fate to increase support for having a representative of one's own race is ubiquitous. Moreover, these findings add to the small, but growing body of scholarship indicating that white racial identity and concerns about the status of whites in American society are becoming both more salient and more potent than they were previously.

This study demonstrates the presence and power of white racial identity, perceptions of discrimination against whites, and white linked fate. Many whites identify as white, think whites are discriminated against, and see their fate as tied to the fate of whites overall. These three factors shape support for having a white representative, and they do so more than they shape support for having a representative who shares one's background in some unspecified way. As the nation's population continues its trajectory toward becoming majority-minority, the role of racial identification, perceptions of discrimination, and linked fate in shaping political outlooks among whites merits continued investigation. One important avenue for future research is to continue tracking voter behavior in actual elections in which white voters face candidates of different races. While such elections are now common, election surveys that include the necessary measures related to racial identity and concerns about group standing are not. Another direction for future research is to conduct additional experiments in which political discourse regarding race and representation varies. Both types of inquiry will provide insights regarding the extent to which the attitudes examined here translate into voter behavior and whether, in the aggregate, such attitudes become more prevalent over time.

Moving beyond large-N opinion surveys will also be valuable in future research. In-depth studies would be particularly fruitful with respect to linked fate. Interviews and focus groups examining how whites feel about race, groups, and politics as the country becomes a majority–minority nation can provide valuable insights about perceived constraints due to whiteness that cannot be supplied solely by surveys or experiments. Both qualitative and quantitative approaches will also be needed to shed light on the factors that make some whites more likely than others to identify as white, perceive discrimination against whites, and feel a sense of linked fate with whites.

Finally, research on how descriptive representation affects the attitudes and behaviors of whites should also continue. Are whites who have a white representative more politically engaged than whites who lack descriptive representation? Do they have more optimistic evaluations of elected officials and political institutions? Does the racial makeup of one's local context condition how descriptive representation affects white constituents? To be sure, some extant research examines some of these questions (Gay 2001, 2002;

Barreto, Segura, and Woods 2004; Bowen and Clark 2014), but such investigations should continue as the composition of the population continues to evolve.

The research presented here found that attitudes about descriptive representation are responsive to perceptions about how the group is located in the political and social hierarchy. People who perceive an environment threatening to their racial group are more likely to feel that representatives who do not share their race are less likely to understand them and less likely to represent them well. A psychological connection to one's racial group also produces this sentiment. The desire for descriptive representation thus appears to be a targeted response to perceived social realities associated with the particular group mentioned in the survey question. What is especially noteworthy is the extent to which the factors under investigation here generate support for descriptive representation for whites and nonwhites alike (Stokes-Brown 2006; Manzano and Sanchez 2010; Schildkraut 2013b; Wallace 2014).

Conclusion

As this study is being written, the nation is pondering the implications of the US Supreme Court overturning a key section of the VRA in *Shelby County v. Holder*. The US Congress is now tasked with the question of whether and how to craft a new version of the VRA that would pass constitutional muster. Whether members of Congress support or oppose a revised VRA is likely to become a more prominent issue as reform efforts advance. Debates about reform will call attention to the treatment of groups in American society and will foster considerations of one's own location in the political and social hierarchy. Such debates have the potential to increase the salience that racial considerations play not only in how people form their views about particular candidates, but also their views about the very nature of political representation itself. Whether, in principle, people think it is important to be represented by someone like them is a question many Americans will consider at an explicit level when debates about the future of the VRA take place, whites included. Attention to group status and the treatment of groups in American society could increase the value that people of all racial backgrounds place on being represented by someone like them.

Although it is likely that many Americans will only pay minimal attention to legislative debates about the VRA, the positions representatives take on proposed VRA revisions are likely to become fodder for campaign discourse. It is also inevitable that debates about whether "demography is destiny" will dominate election commentary for the foreseeable future, as will discussion about the increased presence of ethnic minorities in all spheres of life, such as the public schools. Public discussions of the intersection of race and political power are here to stay. It is important that we continue to track their impact on Americans of all backgrounds.

Acknowledgements

The author wishes to thank Patricia Solleveld and Joshua Quan for research assistance.

Disclosure statement

No potential conflict of interest was reported by the author.

Funding

Funding was provided by the Russell Sage Foundation, the Jonathan M. Tisch College of Citizenship and Public Service at Tufts University, the Tufts Political Science Department, the Tufts Faculty Research Awards Committee, and the Office of the Dean of Academic Affairs at Tufts University.

Notes

1. As of this writing, the Voting Rights Amendment Act has been referred to the Judiciary Committees in the House of Representatives.
2. Aggregate-level analyses find that Latinos and Asians are more likely to vote for co-ethnic candidates than for white candidates (Collet 2005; Barreto 2010), and when presented with hypothetical candidates, shared ethnicity influences vote choice (Barreto 2010; McConnaughy et al. 2010). For contrasting findings, see Abrajano, Nagler, and Alvarez (2005) and Michelson (2005). The rise in minority representatives has also generated substantial research on the effect that descriptive representation has on constituents, which has found that descriptive representation leads racial minorities to become more likely to participate in politics and have more favorable opinions of political institutions (Bobo and Gilliam 1990; Monmonier 2001; Gay 2002; Tate 2003; Banducci, Donovan, and Karp 2004; Barreto, Segura, and Woods 2004; Tate 2004; Rahn and Rudolph 2005; Griffin and Keane 2006; Rocha et al. 2010; Sanchez and Morin 2011).
3. Although the antecedents of support for descriptive representation are consistent across non-white groups, the antecedents themselves, such as linked fate, might be a more transient and conditional sentiment among Latinos and Asian Americans than among African Americans, for whom linked fate is arguably more stable (Sanchez and Masuoka 2010; Schildkraut 2013b).
4. Though see Citrin and Sears (2014) for contrasting findings.
5. For example, in the 113th Congress, only 22.7% of Latinos had a Latino representative. Thanks to Sophia Jordán Wallace for providing this information.
6. The timing of the survey just prior to a federal election was coincidental. It is possible that respondents' thoughts about representation were more accessible during this time than they otherwise would be. Whether this is the case, and whether it affects the results, cannot be tested with this data set.
7. When this survey was conducted, Knowledge Networks (KN) used both random digit dialing and address-based sampling to recruit participants into their KnowledgePanel. In both cases, first contact with potential participants is through the mail, with telephone follow-up. KN draws a random sample from its panel and sends email invitations to complete the surveys, with reminders sent by email and telephone. Households that lack a computer or Internet service are provided both by KN.
8. This question was adopted from the 2006 Latino National Survey (Fraga et al. 2006).
9. Weighted results, face-to-face respondents only; data accessed from http://electionstudies.org/.
10. Note that the question about linked fate was asked before the question about perceptions of discrimination.
11. The ANES lacks questions about descriptive representation, making it unsuitable for the central analysis under investigation here.
12. An alternative possibility is that racial prejudice among whites increases the importance placed on descriptive representation. The AIRS, however, lacks measures of prejudice.
13. Ideology was included in alternative specifications but was dropped due to a high correlation with party ($r = 0.65$).
14. Predicted probabilities were calculated using CLARIFY, while holding all other variables at their weighted mean or, for dummy variables, their mode (King, Tomz, and Wittenberg 2000). In the sample as a whole, 1.5% of respondents scored the lowest on all the three measures, while 3.6% scored the highest on all the 3 measures. The majority of respondents were somewhere in between.

References

Abrajano, Marisa, and Zoltan Hajnal. 2015. *White Backlash: Immigration, Race, and American Politics.* Princeton, NJ: Princeton University Press.

Abrajano, Marisa, Jonathan Nagler, and R. Michael Alvarez. 2005. "A Natural Experiment of Race-Based Issue Voting: The 2001 City of Los Angeles Elections." *Political Research Quarterly* 58 (2): 203–218.

Banducci, Susan A., Todd Donovan, and Jeffrey A. Karp. 2004. "Minority Representation, Empowerment, and Participation." *The Journal of Politics* 66 (2): 534–556.

Barreto, Matt. 2010. *Ethnic Cues: The Role of Shared Ethnicity in Latino Political Participation.* Ann Arbor: University of Michigan Press.

Barreto, Matt, Gary Segura, and Nathan Woods. 2004. "The Effects of Overlapping Majority-Minority Districts on Latino Turnout." *American Political Science Review* 98 (1): 65–75.

Blumer, Herbert. 1958. "Race Prejudice as a Sense of Group Position." *Pacific Sociological Review* 1 (1): 3–7.

Bobo, Lawrence. 1999. "Prejudice as Group Position: Microfoundations of a Sociological Approach to Racism and Race Relations." *Journal of Social Issues* 55 (3): 445–472.

Bobo, Lawrence, and Franklin D. Gilliam Jr. 1990. "Race, Sociopolitical Participation, and Black Empowerment." *The American Political Science Review* 84 (2): 377–393.

Bobo, Lawrence, and Vincent Hutchings. 1996. "Perceptions of Racial Group Competition: Extending Blumer's Theory of Group Position to a Multiracial Social Context." *American Sociological Review* 61 (6): 951–972.

Bowen, Daniel C., and Christopher J. Clark. 2014. "Revisiting Descriptive Representation in Congress: Assessing the Effect of Race on the Constituent-Legislator Relationship." *Political Research Quarterly* 67 (3): 695–707.

Branscombe, Nyla R., Naomi Ellemers, Russell Spears, and Bertjan Doosje. 1999. "The Context and Content of Social Identity Threat." In *Social Identity*, edited by Naomi Ellemers, Russell Spears, and Bertjan Doosje, 35–58. Oxford: Blackwell.

Branscombe, Nyla R., Michael T. Schmitt, and Kristin Schiffhauer. 2007. "Racial Attitudes in Response to Thoughts of White Privilege." *European Journal of Social Psychology* 37 (2): 203–215.

Branton, Regina P., Erin C. Cassese, and Bradford S. Jones. 2012. "Race, Ethnicity, and US House Incumbent Evaluations." *Legislative Studies Quarterly* 37 (4): 465–489.

Butler, Daniel, and David Broockman. 2011. "Do Politicians Racially Discriminate Against Constituents? A Field Experiment on State Legislators." *American Journal of Political Science* 55 (3): 463–477.

Campbell, Andrea Louise, Cara Wong, and Jack Citrin. 2006. "'Racial Threat', Partisan Climate, and Direct Democracy: Contextual Effects in Three California Initiatives." *Political Behavior* 28 (2): 129–150.

Casellas, Jason P., and Sophia J. Wallace. 2015. "The Role of Race, Ethnicity, and Party on Attitudes Toward Descriptive Representation." *American Politics Research* 43 (1): 144–169.

Citrin, Jack, and David O. Sears. 2014. *American Identity and the Politics of Multiculturalism.* New York: Cambridge University Press.

Collet, Christian. 2005. "Bloc Voting, Polarization, and the Panethnic Hypothesis: The Case of Little Saigon." *Journal of Politics* 67 (3): 907–933.

Craig, Maureen, and Jennifer Richeson. 2014a. "More Diverse Yet Less Tolerant? How the Increasingly Diverse Racial Landscape Affects White Americans' Racial Attitudes." *Personality and Social Psychology Bulletin* 40 (6): 750–761.

Craig, Maureen, and Jennifer Richeson. 2014b. "On the Precipice of a 'Majority-Minority' America: Perceived Status Threat from the Racial Demographic Shift Affects White Americans' Political Ideology." *Psychological Science* 25 (6): 1189–1197.

Danbold, Felix, and Yuen J. Huo. 2014. "No Longer 'all-American'? Whites' Defenseive Reactions to their Numerical Decline." *Social, Psychological, and Personality Science.* doi:10.1177/1948550614546355.

Dawson, Michael C. 1994. *Behind the Mule: Race and Class in African-American Politics*. Princeton, NJ: Princeton University Press.

Donovan, Todd. 2010. "Obama and the White Vote." *Political Research Quarterly* 63 (4): 863–874.

Esses, Victoria M., Lynne M. Jackson, and Tamara L. Armstrong. 1998. "Intergroup Competition and Attitudes Toward Immigrants and Immigration: An Instrumental Model of Group Conflict." *Journal of Social Issues* 54 (4): 699–724.

Fraga, Luis R., John A. Garcia, Rodney Hero, Michael Jones-Correa, Valerie Martinez-Ebers, and Gary M. Segura. 2006. *Latino National Survey (LNS), 2006 ICPSR 20862*. Ann Arbor, MI: Inter-university Consortium for Political and Social Research. http://doi.org/10.3886/ICPSR20862.v6.

Fraga, Luis, John Garcia, Rodney E. Hero, Michael Jones-Correa, Valerie Martinez-Ebers, and Gary M. Segura. 2012. *Latinos in the New Millenium: An Almanac of Opinion, Behavior, and Policy Preferences*. New York: Cambridge University Press.

Gay, Claudine. 2001. "The Effect of Black Congressional Representation on Political Participation." *American Political Science Review* 95 (3): 589–602.

Gay, Claudine. 2002. "Spirals of Trust? The Effect of Descriptive Representation on the Relationship between Citizens and their Government." *American Journal of Political Science* 46 (4): 717–732.

Gay, Claudine, Jennifer L. Hochschild, and Ariel White. 2014. "Americans' Belief in Linked Fate: A Wide Reach but Limited Impact." Revision of paper presented at the 2010 Annual Meeting of the American Political Science Association. http://ssrn.com/abstract=1644497.

Glaser, James. 1994. "Back to the Black Belt: Racial Environment and White Racial Attitudes in the South." *Journal of Politics* 56 (1): 21–41.

Glaser, James. 2003. "Social Context and Inter-Group Political Attitudes: Experiments in Group Conflict Theory." *British Journal of Political Science* 33 (4): 607–620.

Goren, Matt, and Victoria Plaut. 2012. "Identity Form Matters: White Racial Identity and Attitudes Toward Diversity." *Self and Identity* 11 (2): 237–254.

Griffin, John D., and Michael Keane. 2006. "Descriptive Representation and the Composition of African American Turnout." *American Journal of Political Science* 50 (4): 998–1012.

Grose, Christian. 2011. *Congress in Black and White: Race and Representation in Washington and at Home*. New York: Cambridge University Press.

Hajnal, Zoltan, and Taeku Lee. 2011. *Why Americans Don't Join the Party: Race, Immigration, and the Failure of (Political Parties) to Engage the Electorate*. Princeton, NJ: Princeton University Press.

Hajnal, Zoltan, and Michael Rivera. 2014. "Immigration, Latinos, and White Partisan Politics: The New Democratic Defection." *American Journal of Political Science* 58 (4): 773–789.

Haslam, S. Alexander, and Michael J. Platow. 2001. "The Link between Leadership and Followership: How Affirming Social Identity Translates Vision into Action." *Personality and Social Psychology Bulletin* 27 (11): 1469–1479.

Hutchings, Vincent, Ashley Jardina, Robert Mickey, and Haynes Walton. 2012. "The Politics of Race: How Threat Cues and Group Position can Activate White Identity." Paper presented at Annual Meeting of the Midwest Political Science Association, Chicago, IL.

Jardina, Ashley. 2013. "Protecting Group Interests: The Role of White Racial Identity in Political Preferences." Paper presented at Annual Meeting of the American Political Science Association, Chicago, IL.

Jardina, Ashley. 2014. "Demise of Dominance: Group Threat and the New Relevance of White Identity for American Politics." Ph.D., University of Michigan.

Jones, Philip Edward. 2014. "Revisiting Stereotypes of Non-White Politicians' Ideological and Partisan Orientations." *American Politics Research* 42 (2): 283–310.

King, Gary, Michael Tomz, and Jason Wittenberg. 2000. "Making the most of Statistical Analyses: Improving Interpretation and Presentation." *American Journal of Political Science* 44 (2): 347–361.

Krupnikov, Yanna, and Spencer Piston. 2015. "Racial Prejudice, Partisanship, and White Turnout in Elections with Black Canddiates." *Political Behavior* 37 (2): 397–418.

Lee, Taeku. 2008. "Race, Immigration, and the Identity-to-Politics Link." *Annual Review of Political Science* 11: 457–478.

Lee, Jennifer, Frank Bean, Jeanne Batalova, and Sabeen Sandhu. 2003. "Immigration and the Black-White Color Line in the United States." *Review of Black Political Economy* 31 (2): 43–76.

Lien, Pei-te, M. Margaret Conway, and Janelle Wong. 2004. *The Politics of Asian Americans: Diversity and Community*. New York: Routledge.

Manzano, Sylvia, and Gabriel Sanchez. 2010. "Take One for the Team? The Limits of Shared Ethnicity and Candidate Preferences." *Political Research Quarterly* 63 (3): 568–580.

Masuoka, Natalie. 2006. "Together they Become One: Examining the Predictors of Panethnic Group Consciousness among Asian Americans and Latinos." *Social Science Quarterly* 87 (5): 993–1011.

Masuoka, Natalie, and Jane Junn. 2013. *The Politics of Belonging: Race, Public Opinion, and Immigration*. Chicago: Chicago University Press.

McClain, Paula, Jessica Johnson Carew, Eugene Walton, and Candis Watts. 2009. "Group Membership, Group Identity, and Group Consciousness: Measures of Racial Identity in American Politics." *Annual Review of Political Science* 12: 471–485.

McConnaughy, Corrine M., Ismail K. White, David L. Leal, and Jason P. Casellas. 2010. "A Latino on the Ballot: Explaining Coethnic Voting among Latinos and the Response of White Americans." *Journal of Politics* 72 (4): 1199–1211.

Michelson, Melissa R. 2003. "The Corrosive Effect of Acculturation: How Mexican Americans Lose Political Trust." *Social Science Quarterly* 84 (4): 918–933.

Michelson, Melissa R. 2005. "Does Ethnicity Trump Party? Competing Vote Cues and Latino Voting Behavior." *Journal of Political Marketing* 4 (4): 1–25.

Miller, Arthur, Patricia Gurin, Gerald Gurin, and Oksana Malanchuk. 1981. "Group Consciousness and Political Participation." *American Journal of Political Science* 25 (3): 494–511.

Monmonier, Mark. 2001. *Bushmanders and Bullwinkles: How Politicians Manipulate Electronic Maps and Census Data to Win Elections*. Chicago: Chicago University Press.

Norton, Michael I., and Samuel R. Sommers. 2011. "Whites See Racism as a Zero-Sum Game that they are Now Losing." *Perspectives on Psychological Science* 6 (3): 215–218.

Oliver, J. Eric, and Tali Mendelberg. 2000. "Reconsidering the Environmental Determinants of White Racial Attitudes." *American Journal of Political Science* 44 (3): 574–589.

Oliver, J. Eric, and Janelle Wong. 2003. "Intergroup Prejudice in Multiethnic Settings." *American Journal of Political Science* 47 (4): 567–582.

Outten, H. Robert, Michael T. Schmitt, Daniel A. Miller, and Amber L. Garcia. 2012. "Feeling Threatened about the Future: Whites' Emotional Reactions to Anticipated Ethnic Demographic Changes." *Personality and Social Psychology Bulletin* 38 (1): 14–25.

Petrow, Gregory. 2010. "The Minimal Cue Hypothesis: How Black Candidates Cue Race to Increase White Voting Participation." *Political Psychology* 31 (6): 915–950.

Pew Research Center for People and the Press. 2012. "Changing Face of America Helps Assure Obama Victory." Accessed November 25. http://www.people-press.org/2012/11/07/changing-face-of-america-helps-assure-obama-victory/.

Pitkin, Hanna. 1967. *The Concept of Representation*. Berkeley: University of California Press.

Platow, Michael J., and Daan van Knippenberg. 2001. "A Social Identtiy Analysis of Leadership Endorsement: The Effects of Leader Ingroup Prototypicality and Distributive Intergroup Fairness." *Personality and Social Psychology Bulletin* 27 (11): 1508–1519.

Platow, Michael J., Daan van Knippenberg, S. Alexander Haslam, Barbara van Knippenberg, and Russell Spears. 2006. "A Special Gift we Bestow upon You for being Representative of Us: Considering Leader Charisma from a Self-Categorization Perspective." *British Journal of Social Psychology* 45 (2): 303–320.

Quillian, Lincoln. 1995. "Prejudice as a Response to Perceived Group Threat: Population Composition and Anti-Immigrant and Racial Prejudice in Europe." *American Sociological Review* 60 (4): 586–611.

Rahn, Wendy M., and Thomas J. Rudolph. 2005. "A Tale of Political Trust in American Cities." *Public Opinion Quarterly* 69 (4): 530–560.

Rocha, Rene R., Caroline J. Tolbert, Daniel C. Bowen, and Christopher J. Clark. 2010. "Race and Turnout: Does Descriptive Representation in State Legislatures Increase Minority Voting?" *Political Research Quarterly* 63 (4): 890–907.

Rosenstein, Judith E. 2008. "Individual Threat, Group Threat, and Racial Policy: Exploring the Relationship between Threat and Racial Attitudes." *Social Science Research* 37 (4): 1130–1146.

Rosenthal, Cindy Simon. 1995. "The Role of Gender in Descriptive Representation." *Political Research Quarterly* 48 (3): 599–611.

Sanbonmatsu, Kira. 2002. "Gender Stereotypes and Vote Choice." *American Journal of Political Science* 46 (1): 20–34.

Sanchez, Gabriel. 2006a. "The Role of Group Consciousness in Latino Public Opinion." *Political Research Quarterly* 59 (3): 435–446.

Sanchez, Gabriel. 2006b. "The Role of Group Consciousness in Political Participation among Latinos in the United States." *American Politics Research* 34 (4): 427–450.

Sanchez, Gabriel, and Natalie Masuoka. 2010. "Brown-Utility Heuristic? The Presence and Contributing Factors of Latino Linked Fate." *Hispanic Journal of Behavioral Sciences* 32 (4): 519–531.

Sanchez, Gabriel, and Jason Morin. 2011. "The Effect of Descriptive Representation on Latinos' Views of Government and of Themselves." *Social Science Quarterly* 92 (2): 483–508.

Schildkraut, Deborah J. 2005. "The Rise and Fall of Political Engagement among Latinos: The Role of Identity and Perceptions of Discrimination." *Political Behavior* 27 (3): 285–312.

Schildkraut, Deborah J. 2011. *Americanism in the Twenty-First Century: Public Opinion in the Age of Immigration*. New York: Cambridge University Press.

Schildkraut, Deborah. J. 2012. *American Identity and Representation Survey.* http://ase.tufts.edu/polsci/faculty/schildkraut/.

Schildkraut, Deborah J. 2013a. "The Complicated Constituency: A Study of Immigrant Opinions about Political Representation." *Politics, Groups, and Identities* 1 (1): 26–47.

Schildkraut, Deborah J. 2013b. "Which Birds of a Feather Flock Together? Assessing Attitudes about Descriptive Representation among Latinos and Asian Americans." *American Politics Research* 41 (4): 699–729.

Schmitt, Michael T., and Nyla R. Branscombe. 2002. "The Meaning and Consequences of Perceived Discrimination in Disadvantaged and Privileged Social Groups." In *European Review of Social Psychology*, edited by Wolfgang Stroebe and Miles Hewstone, Vol. 12, 167–199. Essex: Psychology Press.

Sears, David O., and Victoria Savalei. 2006. "The Political Color Line in America: Many 'Peoples of Color' Or Black Exceptionalism?" *Political Psychology* 27 (6): 895–924.

Shear, Michael D. 2012. "Demographic Shift Brings New Worry for Republicans." *New York Times* 11/7/12.

Sidanius, Jim, Seymour Feshback, Shana Levin, and Felicia Pratto. 1997. "The Interface between Ethnic and National Attachment: Ethnic Pluralism Or Ethnic Dominance?" *Public Opinion Quarterly* 61 (1): 102–133.

Smith, A. Wade. 1981. "Racial Tolerance as a Function of Group Position." *American Sociological Review* 46 (5): 558–573.

Stephan, Walter G., Kurt A. Boniecki, Oscar Ybarra, Ann Bettencourt, Kelly S. Ervin, Linda A. Jackson, Penny S. McNatt, and C. Lausanne Renfro. 2002. "The Role of Threats in the Racial Attitudes of Blacks and Whites." *Personality and Social Psychology Bulletin* 28 (9): 1242–1254.

Stokes-Brown, Atiya Kai. 2006. "Racial Identitiy and Latino Vote Choice." *American Politics Research* 34 (5): 627–652.

Strauss, Valerie. 2014. "For First Time, Minority Students Expected to be Majority in U.S. Public Schools this Fall." *Washington Post*, August 21.

Tajfel, Henri, ed. 1982. *Social Identity and Intergroup Relations*. New York: Cambridge University Press.

Tate, Katherine. 1991. "Black Political Participation in the 1984 and 1988 Presidential Elections." *The American Political Science Review* 85 (4): 1159–1176.

Tate, Katherine. 1994. *From Protest to Politics: The New Black Voters in American Elections.* Cambridge, MA: Harvard University Press.

Tate, Katherine. 2003. "Black Opinion on the Legitimacy of Racial Redistricting and Minority-Majority Districts." *The American Political Science Review* 97 (1): 45–56.

Tate, Katherine. 2004. *Black Faces in the Mirror: African Americans and their Representatives in the U.S. Congress.* Princeton, NJ: Princeton University Press.

US Census Bureau. 2012 "Most Children Younger than Age 1 are Minorities, Census Bureau Reports." in U.S. Census Bureau [database online]. Accessed 01/03, 2013. http://www.census.gov/newsroom/releases/archives/population/cb12-90.html.

US Census Bureau. 2013 "Asians Fastest-growing Race or Ethnic Group in 2012." in U.S. Census Bureau [database online]. Washington, D.C. Accessed March 17, 2014. https://www.census.gov/newsroom/releases/archives/population/cb13-112.html.

Wallace, Sophia J. 2014. "Examining Latino Support for Descriptive Representation: The Role of Identity and Discrimination." *Social Science Quarterly* 95 (2): 311–327.

Weinger, Mackenzie. 2012. "Bill O'Reilly: 'The White Establishment is Now the Minority'." *Politico* 11/6/12.

Wheaton, Sarah. 2013. "For First Time on Record, Black Black Voting Rate Outpaced Rate for Whites in 2012." *New York Times* 5/8/13.

Wilson, Chris. "U.S. will have A majority-minority Population by 2043, Census Predicts." in Yahoo! News [database online]. Accessed March 17, 2014. http://news.yahoo.com/blogs/lookout/u-majority-minority-population-2043-census-predicts-164735561.html.

Wong, Cara, and Grace E. Cho. 2005. "Two-Headed Coins Or Kandinskys: White Racial Identification." *Political Psychology* 26 (5): 699–720.

Targeting young men of color for search and arrest during traffic stops: evidence from North Carolina, 2002–2013

Frank R. Baumgartner, Derek A. Epp, Kelsey Shoub and Bayard Love

ABSTRACT
North Carolina mandated the first collection of demographic data on all traffic stops during a surge of attention to the phenomenon of "driving while black" in the late 1990s. Based on analysis of over 18 million traffic stops, we show dramatic disparities in the rates at which black drivers, particularly young males, are searched and arrested as compared to similarly situated whites, women, or older drivers. Further, the degree of racial disparity is growing over time. Finally, the rate at which searches lead to the discovery of contraband is consistently lower for blacks than for whites, providing strong evidence that the empirical disparities we uncover are in fact evidence of racial bias. The findings are robust to a variety of statistical specifications and consistent with findings in other jurisdictions.

The US has been in a period of intense discussion of police shootings and relations with minority communities for the past three years. Beginning with the acquittal of George Zimmerman for the killing of Trayvon Martin (July 2013), through the killings by police officers of Eric Garner in Staten Island, NY (17 July 2014), Michael Brown in Ferguson, MO (9 August 2014), and Freddie Gray in Baltimore, MD (12 April 2015), these four unarmed black men have become symbols of a national movement made apparent with the #BlackLivesMatter and the "Hands up, don't shoot" slogans that have now become commonplace. Unequal treatment of black and white citizens is of course nothing new, as can be attested to by such works as those of Alexander, whose *New Jim Crow* (2010) dramatically and forcefully traced the history of racial disparities in the criminal justice system, brought, she argues, to a new level through the mass incarceration movement in the 1980s and beyond. As Stevenson (2014) notes, the US Department of Justice (DOJ) reported almost 7 million American adults were under some form of judicial control at the end of 2013 (see also Glaze and Kaeble 2014). This marked a dramatic shift from historical trends, as state and federal prisoners were no more in 1973 than they had been in 1960 (see BJS 1982). The dramatic shift toward mass incarceration began in 1974 and accelerated during the 1980s and the 1990s when the war on drugs generated not only large increases in incarceration rates overall, but also an increased focus on the minority community.

ⓑ Supplemental data for this article can be accessed here. http://dx.doi.org/10.1080/21565503.2016.1160413

Gary Webb's journalistic exposes of the "driving while black" phenomenon made clear in 1999 the extent to which black and brown drivers were subjected to systematic profiling as part of the war on drugs, also stressing the degree to which a previous police focus on safe driving was diverted into one focused on a needle-in-the-haystack search for drug couriers and largely reliant on very inefficient "behavioral" and racial profiles (see Webb 2007 [1999]).

The US Drug Enforcement Agency (DEA) promoted the use of profiles largely on the basis of the work of Florida state trooper Bob Vogel, later elected Sheriff of Volusia County, Florida. In a laudatory profile in the *Orlando Sentinel*, Fishman (1991) explains Vogel's laser-like focus on drug couriers, in spite of the fact that they typically were only in transit through his rural stretch of I-95 near Daytona Beach. Fishman writes:

> The pipeline wasn't causing much of a law enforcement problem for Vogel. (An early element of the courier profile, in fact, was that cars obeying the speed limit were suspect – their desire to avoid being stopped made them stand out.)

In fact, according to Webb (2007), Vogel's early work on drug interdiction was thrown out by various judges who considered his "hunch" that drugs may be in the car an unconstitutional violation of the need to have a probable cause before conducting a search. Vogel responded by studying the Florida vehicle code, finding that there were hundreds of reasons why he could legally pull a car over.

> He found them by the hundreds in the thick volumes of the Florida vehicle code: rarely enforced laws against driving with burned-out license plate lights, out-of-kilter headlights, obscured tags, and windshield cracks. State codes bulge with such niggling prohibitions, some dating from the days of the horseless carriage.

> "The vehicle code gives me fifteen hundred reasons to pull you over", one CHP [California Highway Patrol] officer told me. (Webb 2007)

In a major victory for this police strategy in the war on drugs, the Supreme Court decided in *Whren v. United States* (1996) that *any* traffic violation was a legitimate reason to stop a driver, even if the purported violation (e.g. changing lanes without signaling) was clearly a pretext for the officer's desire to stop and search the vehicle for other reasons, such as a general suspicion. There was no requirement that speeding laws, for example, be equitably enforced; if all the drivers are speeding, it is constitutionally permissible, said the Justices, to pick out just the minority drivers and enforce the speeding laws selectively. Of course, once a car is stopped, officers are often able to conduct a "consent" search when drivers do not object to the officer's request to search the vehicle. The *Whren* decision opened the floodgates to pretextual stops. Thus, tens of thousands of black and brown drivers have routinely been stopped and searched in an effort to reduce drug use. As Provine (2007) has pointed out, drug use is no different across race, though drug arrests differ dramatically.

Peffley and Hurwitz (2010) document the dramatic disparities in how white and black Americans experience, perceive, and relate to the police. Given the trends described above, it is no surprise that members of minority communities feel much less trustful of the police as compared to white Americans. Epp, Maynard-Moody, and Haider-Markel (2014) have provided the most comprehensive analysis of citizen interactions with the police in the particular context of traffic stop. They demonstrate that when blacks are stopped for legitimate reasons such as speeding, they show no difference in attitudes about the lawful-ness and appropriateness of the traffic stop nor in the behavior of the officer, as compared to whites. However, they note that drivers have a sense of when the stops are pretextual and that being subjected to these pretextual stops is humiliating, threatening, and unjus-tified. It dramatically reduces the driver's sense of belonging in the community and belief that they are equal citizens awarded the same level of respect and protection by the police as whites. Thus, the racialized character of traffic stops, as in other elements of the criminal justice system, may have dramatic consequences not just for traffic safety, crime, drugs, and incarceration, but for the nature of American democracy itself. It goes to the heart of the question of whether all Americans feel that they are part of a single nation rather than living in separate communities divided by color and subject to differing rights and burdens.

Recent studies by Burch (2013), Lerman and Weaver (2014), and Moore (2015) have further documented the adverse effects of such disparate police practices (see also the studies included in Rice and White (2010)). Burch shows the collective impact on entire neighborhoods stemming from high levels of police interaction and incarceration. While feelings of trust toward the police are highly related to neighborhood crime rates (which *increase* trust in the police, who are seen as helping solve the problem), the nature of those interactions matters as well. As Epp and colleagues argued, where individ-uals feel they cannot count on being treated fairly by the police, social connections, effi-cacy, voting, and participation in politics all decline, as does a full sense of citizenship. Lerman and Weaver document a wide variety of social ills stemming from adverse inter-actions with police, including reduced willingness to use relevant government programs, fear of reprisals that keeps individuals from asking for services to which they are entitled, and further involvement with the criminal justice system. In fact, they find that a mere interaction with a police officer (not resulting in arrest) is associated with a reduction in the probability of voting of almost 10% (223). Moore (2015, 5–7) documents relatively similar levels of interactions with the police, in particular in traffic stops, but significant differences in the reasons for the traffic stops and their outcomes, with black drivers much more likely to see adverse outcomes such as search and arrest. Interactions with the criminal justice system can have dramatic and adverse outcomes to individuals and to entire communities, as these scholars show.

For many, the first and most straightforward interaction with a criminal justice official comes in the context of a routine traffic stop. In this article we explore the degree to which motorists in North Carolina experience different outcomes when stopped by the police and add to our collective understandings about the degree of racial difference apparent in this most common form of police–citizen interaction. For most whites, a speeding ticket is unpleasant, certainly unwelcome, perhaps understandable, and most likely attrib-uted to a perhaps inadvertent lead foot. For many members of minority communities, traffic stops and their aftermaths represent something distinctly more alienating.

The US DOJ report on Ferguson

In March of 2015, the US Department of Justice released the results of its investigation of the Ferguson Police Department (FPD) (US DOJ 2015). The investigation took two lines of inquiry. The first was a qualitative assessment of department practices, based on interviews with Ferguson residents, police officers, and city officials; reviews of court documents, arrest records, and municipal budgets; and ride-alongs with on-duty officers. The second component was a quantitative analysis of patterns of police enforcement that compared the rate at which blacks were cited, arrested, and searched relative to whites.

Results from these inquiries were complementary and showed flagrant and systematic civil rights violations by the FPD. Among the most egregious violations was that city officials put great pressure on the police department to raise revenues by issuing traffic citations, and that these efforts were directed disproportionately toward the minority community. In effect, the city was subverting its traffic laws to balance municipal budgets, and doing so through the pockets of its black residents. Investigators also found that black motorists were more than twice as likely to be searched as whites following a traffic stop, but were 26% less likely to be found in the possession of contraband. The report concludes that

> the lower rate at which officers find contraband when searching African Americans indicates either that officers' suspicion of criminal wrongdoing is less likely to be accurate when interacting with African Americans or that officers are more likely to search African Americans without any suspicion of criminal wrongdoing. Either explanation suggest bias, whether explicit or implicit. (US DOJ 2015, 65)

The Department of Justice's logic in juxtaposing search rates with contraband hit rates as an indicator of racial discrimination finds support in the criminal justice literature. If studies discover that minority drivers are more likely to be searched, but less likely to be found with contraband, this disparity is taken as evidence of racial bias in police practice (Lamberth 1996; Harris 1999; Meehan and Ponder 2006; Persico and Todd 2008; Bates 2010). Conversely, when evidence shows that contraband hit rates are equal or higher among minorities, then the differences in search rates are considered to be part of good policing, not bias (Knowles, Persico, and Todd 2001). Others have used more complicated multivariate models that control for estimated rates of participation in crime across racial groups (Gelman, Fagan, and Kiss 2007). (Of course, higher contraband hit rates for relatively minor substances, such as user-amounts of marijuana, may not be an appropriate police focus, but this is a discussion beyond the scope of this analysis. We do not distinguish among the various types or amounts of contraband found here, which is a limitation we share with many previous analyses.)

Theory and expectations

We replicate the empirical component of the Ferguson investigation for North Carolina. North Carolina maintains the longest and most detailed record of traffic stops in the nation, allowing a wholescale replication of the quantitative segment of the report. We also push forward and measure the effects of other demographic factors that data limitations prevented the Department of Justice from considering in the Ferguson case. In particular, we consider how police enforcement varies not only by race, but also by age and gender. We determine that for North Carolina, racially disparate policing is predominantly a male-oriented phenomenon; female motorist experience only marginally different outcomes across racial lines.

We focus on particular empirical questions and draw out theoretical expectations from the literature on race and criminal justice as well as findings discussed above concerning the diversion of traffic control into part of the war on drugs. Our expectations are simply that the war on drugs has led to a sharp, but unjustified, focus on young men of color. Further, given that attention has only recently focused on the politically sensitive nature of these activities, and that no previous studies have given reason to expect any changes over time in the degree of racial disparities we might observe, we hypothesize no changes over time in these levels of disparity. Further, if the process is related to unjustified targeting, then any changes over time, if observed, should be uncorrelated with changes in contraband hit rates. Finally, we expect nothing in North Carolina to be exceptional. The Ferguson report showed an extreme case, perhaps, but incidents of racial profiling by the nation's police departments do not lend themselves to the conclusion that there is a single "hot spot" – rather there seems to be a broad and widespread institutional system at play. With that in mind, we lay out these hypotheses for testing:

> H1: Young men of color will be subjected to harsher outcomes following a traffic stop com-
> pared to any other demographic group.
> H2: These patterns are institutional rather than the results of individual "bad apple" police
> officers.
> H3: A focus on young men of color goes beyond what can be explained by higher rates of
> contraband found in those groups.
> H4: Trends over time will show no significant change in the degree of focus on young men of
> color over the study period of 2002–2013.
> H5: Any trends over time in the degree of disparity will not be justified by corresponding
> changes in contraband hit rates.
> H6: To the extent that it can be tested, the results from North Carolina analysis will be con-
> sistent with simple tests in other jurisdictions.

Data and preliminary analysis

North Carolina was the first state in the nation to mandate the collection of police-stop data, after public attention surged to this issue in the late 1990s. At least 15 states considered legislation during 1999 mandating the collection of police-stop information, and North Carolina was the first in the nation to pass such a law (GAO 2000, 15). Since 1 January 2002, the NC DOJ has collected information on every traffic stop from law-enforcement agencies throughout the state.[1] Our Supplemental Materials include a copy of the "SBI-122 Form", the two-page paper form which the officers fill out after any traffic stop. Data are relayed to the state DOJ and made available to the public in an online searchable database: http://trafficstops.ncdoj.gov/. Though the underlying legislation required the state to collect the data, police departments to report it, and the Attorney General to analyze it and issue reports on a biennial basis (see Mance 2012, fn. 3), the state has never issued any official analysis of the trends and patterns associated with the data collected. Because of the highly detailed nature of the NC database, we can add to the literature not only by exploring trends in stops, searches, and arrests as others have done (e.g. Moore 2015, using national data), but also with a multivariate analysis with controls not possible in other databases. We also note significant differences from one agency to the next (and from officer to officer), so we control for these in our statistical analyses as has not previously been possible in other studies.

North Carolina now makes an enormous amount of data available to the public: over 18 million traffic stops are documented in the NC DOJ database across the entire state, from 2000 to present. Before conducting any analysis, we drop observations from years where the data are incomplete. These include 2000 and 2001 when only the State Highway Patrol was reporting data, and 2014, which was the year of the last data update we received from the NC DOJ. We also drop observations relating to passengers and checkpoint stops. NC law requires these records to be collected only in the case when a search occurs, not for every stop. Therefore, we do not know how many drivers were stopped at a checkpoint, or how many passengers were in vehicles that were stopped. Table 1 presents an overview of the data.

The top part of Table 1 shows first how we move from 18.2 million observations to 15.99 million by eliminating years with incomplete data, checkpoint stops, and passengers. Then, based on the remaining cases, the bottom half of the table reports the number of times various outcomes have occurred following a traffic stop, with the right column showing the associated rates. Most traffic stops in NC result in a citation; this takes place in 66% of all cases. Searches occur in approximately 3% of the cases; arrests in 2.1%; and contraband in 0.8% of all stops, just 129,000 stops out of 16 million. The overall contraband hit rate (simply the number of contraband finds divided by the number of searches) is 25%. So a quarter of the searches conducted by NC officers are successful in the sense that they lead to contraband.[2]

Officers record the reason for each traffic stop and the State Bureau of Investigation (SBI) form allows for 10 different possibilities. For example, drivers can be stopped for speeding, safe movement violations, or not having their seat belt buckled. Table 2 shows how the 16 million stops are distributed across 9 of these stop purposes, excluding checkpoint stops. By far the most common reason NC motorists are pulled over is for speeding, followed by vehicle regulatory issues (having expired registration tags, for example). Other outcomes are less common. The table also shows the racial breakdown associated with each type of stop, making clear that the majority of motorists stopped for each type of violation are white. As whites greatly outnumber blacks in NC, this is not surprising. (The US Bureau of the Census reports that in 2013, 71.7% of North Carolinians identified as white, and 22.0% as black.) Overall 31% of stopped motorists are black and 63% are white, with the remainder belonging to other races. Reading down the two rightmost columns of the table tells us what types of stops break in a black or white direction relative to these baseline percentages. Vehicular issues skew strongly in the black direction. Blacks make up 31% of total stops, but 38% of stops relating to regulatory violations, 38% of those relating to

Table 1. Overview of the data.

Data subsets	Observations	Rates (%)
Total stops	18,194,110	–
2000	641,397	–
2001	598,733	–
2014	515,852	–
Passengers	298,459	–
Checkpoint stops	183,691	–
Stops for analysis	15,992,317	–
Citations	10,616,581	66.3
Searches	511,813	3.2
Arrests	349,136	2.1
Contraband	128,918	0.8

Table 2. Racial composition of traffic stops by purpose.

Purpose	Number	% Total	% White	% Black
Total stops	15,992,305	–	62.85	30.64
Driving impaired	158,264	0.99	66.22	22.32
Seat belt	1,492,624	9.33	66.88	26.56
Speed limit	6,665,939	41.68	66.64	26.65
Safe movement	886,090	5.54	62.93	29.82
Stop light/sign	758,136	4.74	62.63	31.18
Investigation	1,130,736	7.07	59.13	31.43
Other vehicle	851,550	5.32	57.49	33.53
Vehicle equipment	1,422,461	8.89	56.50	38.12
Vehicle regulatory	2,626,505	16.42	57.55	38.41

equipment issues, and 34% of "other vehicle" stops. The table also shows that some stops skew toward white drivers. These include speeding, seat belt violations, and driving impaired; white drivers are more likely to be stopped for one of these violations relative to their baseline rate of 63%. The data in Table 2 are for descriptive purposes only. As we do not know what percent of the driving public is black or white, or what percent of drivers engaging in various infractions are white or black, we do not interpret these results in any way at all, except to note dramatic differences in the proportions of blacks pulled over for various reasons (from 22% for driving while impaired to 38% for regulatory issues).

The Ferguson report focused on the rate at which blacks were searched, cited, and arrested relative to whites. We do the same in Table 3. For each of the nine stop purposes, the table shows the racial breakdown for experiencing these different outcomes. We also calculate a "percent difference", which describes the likelihood that a black driver experiences an outcome relative to a white driver. For example, if 10% of black motorists are searched following a stop for speeding and 5% of whites are searched, then the percent difference between them is 100%, indicating that blacks are 100% more likely to experience a search following a stop for speeding.[3] Percent differences will feature prominently in subsequent analysis as they highlight how black and white experiences with police differ. Table 3 thus starts our analysis of who experiences a relatively harsh outcome following their traffic stop. In contrast to Table 2, where we are limited because we do not know who was engaged in the behavior that led to the traffic stop, in Table 3 we know both the numerator and the denominator in the equation. Given all the people pulled over for a given reason, what was the outcome? And how does that differ by race?

Black drivers are much more likely to be searched or arrested than whites following each type of stop, with the exception of driving impaired. Blacks are 200% more likely to be searched and 190% more likely to be arrested after being pulled over for a seat belt violation; 110% are more likely to be searched or arrested following a stop for vehicle regulatory violations; and 60% are more likely to be searched or arrested after being stopped for equipment issues. In contrast, citations appear almost race-neutral. For six of the stop purposes, white motorists are slightly more likely to receive a citation and the only double-digit disparity is for driving impaired where black drivers are 11% more likely to be ticketed. Driving impaired appears to be an outlier; whites are more likely to be arrested and blacks more likely to be cited.

The only demographic distinction the Ferguson report makes is for race; but because the data for NC is more detailed and extensive than what is available for MO, we can

Table 3. Percent of drivers searched, cited, and arrested by race and purpose of stop.

Purpose	Searched			Cited			Arrested		
	Percent white	Percent black	Percent difference	Percent white	Percent black	Percent difference	Percent white	Percent black	Percent difference
Total	2.61	4.57	75	66.88	63.43	-5	1.90	2.71	43
Driving impaired	37.24	30.51	-18	24.56	27.25	11	56.26	46.82	-17
Safe movement	5.54	7.41	34	38.29	37.50	-2	3.25	3.62	11
Investigation	5.79	9.57	65	48.05	47.15	-2	4.03	6.39	59
Vehicle equipment	4.39	6.88	57	31.50	31.06	-1	1.75	2.78	59
Speed limit	0.95	1.67	76	78.35	79.16	1	0.69	1.12	62
Stop light/sign	2.31	4.55	97	57.03	56.89	0	1.42	2.33	64
Other vehicle	3.68	6.52	82	56.70	58.42	3	2.43	4.14	70
Vehicle regulatory	2.39	4.95	107	64.92	61.70	-5	1.23	2.56	108
Seat belt	1.09	3.30	203	90.00	84.21	-6	0.53	1.54	191

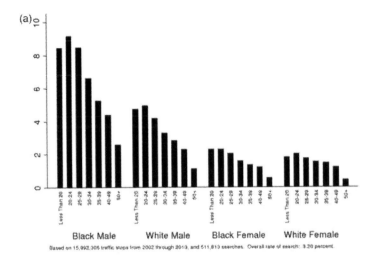

(a)

Black Male   White Male   Black Female   White Female

Based on 15,992,305 traffic stops from 2002 through 2013, and 511,813 searches. Overall rate of search: 3.20 percent.

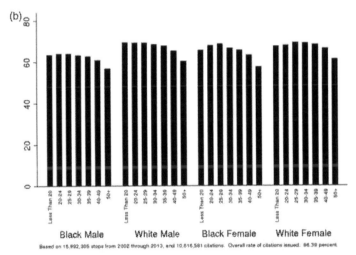

(b)

Black Male   White Male   Black Female   White Female

Based on 15,992,305 stops from 2002 through 2013, and 10,616,581 citations. Overall rate of citations issued: 66.39 percent.

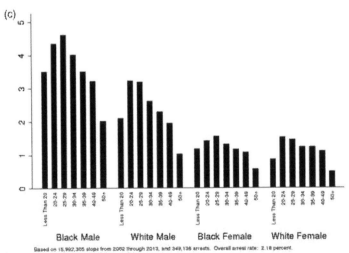

(c)

Black Male   White Male   Black Female   White Female

Based on 15,992,305 stops from 2002 through 2013, and 349,136 arrests. Overall arrest rate: 2.18 percent.

Figure 1. Rates by race, gender, and age group.

also separate motorists by age and gender, and still retain enough observations to ensure robust calculations. Figure 1 presents this analysis in a series of bar charts that show the rate at which different groups are searched, cited, or arrested following a stop. Looking first at searches, there are dramatic age disparities; older motorists are less likely to be searched and this holds true across racial and gender groups. There are also stark gender disparities. Male motorists of both races are more likely to be searched than their female counterparts. Comparing extremes, 9% of the black men between the ages of 20 and 24 years who are stopped are searched, while less than 1% of white women over the age of 50 years are searched. Young black men are 1800% more likely to be searched after a traffic stop than older white women.

Of particular interest is that the racial disparities so clearly visible between black and white males are only very modest for female drivers. In fact, black and white females are searched at a roughly equivalent rate across each age group and the same is true when looking at Panel C for arrests. This signals an important point of departure for our analysis from the Ferguson report. In NC, it appears that racially disparate policing predominately affects male drivers. Subsequent analysis will therefore focus only on males. Complementary analysis looking at female drivers is available in the appendix.

Finally, looking at Panel B it is clear that NC police approach citations differently than either searches or arrests. Table 2 indicates that ticketing was neutral with respect to race and Panel B suggests that it is also age- and gender-neutral. Black men of any age are actually marginally less likely to be ticketed than their white or female counterparts. In this respect, policing in NC and Ferguson is very different. Furthermore, the conventional wisdom that women are less likely to be ticketed after being pulled over appears to be false. Having established that pronounced disparities exist for searches and arrests (but not for citations), and having narrowed our focus to male drivers, we turn now to documenting trends over time and assessments of racial disparities.

Twelve years of NC policing

Table 2 shows that black drivers (men and women) are 75% more likely to be searched than whites, 5% less likely to be ticketed, and 43% more likely to be arrested. Figure 2 shows how these differences have varied over time, for male motorists. In 2002, black men were 70% more likely to be searched than whites and this disparity has grown steadily over the period of study. Beginning in 2007, black men were twice as likely to be searched and by 2013 this difference had grown to over 140%. Black men are also more likely to be arrested; however, this disparity has remained stable at about a 60% increased likelihood. We also see that black men are marginally less likely to receive citations and there is almost no variance; NC police are highly consistent over time in their relative treatment of whites and black men when it comes to ticketing.

Figure 3 shows the percent differences for citations, arrests, and searches across the various stop purposes. (Table 2 presents the same information for men and women combined.) Isolating men does little to change the overall pattern, except that the disparities are greater when we focus only on men. Compared to white men, black men are more likely to be searched and arrested for every type of stop, with the exception of driving while impaired. Disparities in ticketing are comparatively minor and fluctuate around zero.

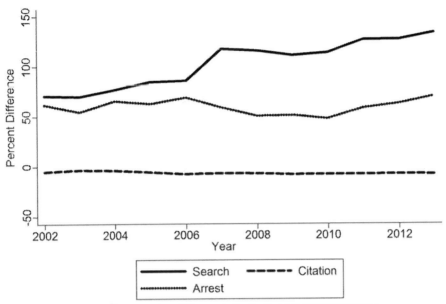

The figure shows the percentage difference in the likelihood of different outcomes for Blacks as compared to Whites.

Figure 2. Percent difference in the likelihood of search, citation, or arrest for black men.

There are two possible explanations for the disparities documented in Figures 2 and 3. One is racially differential policing and the other is racially differential possession of contraband.[4] Both explanations could account for higher search and arrest rates of black men, but they point to very different problems so we want to distinguish between them. To do so, we first take a closer look at the types of searches to which NC motorists are subjected. The SBI form lists five different search types and Table 4 shows the rate at which each type of search occurs. The three most common types of search are those based on driver consent, searches that occur incident to an arrest, and searches based on probable cause. Searches conducted when executing a warrant or as protective frisks are very rare. The top cell of the rightmost column shows the overall percent difference; black men are 97% more likely to be searched than white men. Reading down this column reveals how different types of search deviate from this baseline rate. Probable cause searches skew strongly toward blacks, indicating that officers are much more likely to be suspicious of criminal wrongdoing when interacting with black motorists. Black men are also twice as likely to be searched with consent. This indicates either that black men

Table 4. Rates of search by race for men.

Search type	Number	% Total	% White	% Black	Percent difference
Total stops	10,320623				
Total searches	427,677	4.14	3.23	6.38	97
Incident to arrest	148,326	1.44	1.23	1.90	55
Search warrant	1,127	0.01	0.01	0.01	61
Protective frisk	14,316	0.14	0.11	0.21	94
Consent	194,236	1.88	1.47	2.94	100
Probable cause	69,672	0.68	0.42	1.33	216

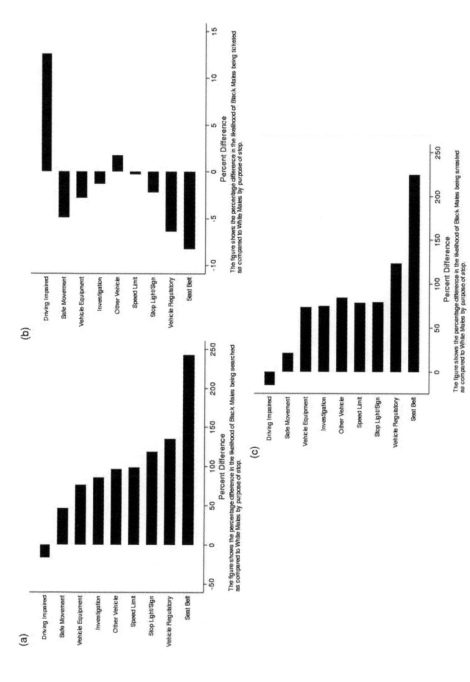

Figure 3. Percent difference in the likelihood of outcomes for blacks, by purpose of stop.

are more willing to give their consent to be searched or that officers are more likely to request consent after stopping a black driver. The other types of search take place under prescribed circumstances and in these instances may be a mandatory component of police protocol, such as making a search in conjunction with an arrest. They therefore have less to tell us about the decision-making of NC police, as officers have less discretion about when to carry out these searches.

Are the suspicions that lead officers to search black drivers at such disproportionately high rates justified? Table 5 provides the answer by showing the rates at which officers find contraband on drivers subsequent to conducting each type of search. Looking first at the row labeled "Total Contraband", we see that overall officers are 2% more likely to find contraband on black drivers after conducting a search. However, reading down the column shows that this increased likelihood is driven entirely by the searches where officers exercise the least discretion. For example, police are 9% more likely to find contraband on black motorists whom they have arrested and they are 11% more likely to find contraband on blacks after exercising a search warrant. These searches are mandated, not discretionary. When officers must make a judgment call about whether or not to search a motorist, they tend to be less successful at searching blacks; in other words, they use a lower probability threshold with blacks or have a "hunch" that is less likely to be accurate with regard to black male drivers than with others. Moreover, we know from Table 4 that consent and probable cause searches are much more likely to be employed on black motorists; so, taken together, these results paint a bleak picture of NC officer's abilities to discern when a black motorist should be searched. Indeed, it is just such a disparity that the US Department of Justice points to as evidence of racial bias in the Ferguson report.

Figure 4 shows trends in the differential use of probable cause searches and the success of these searches at recovering contraband from 2002 to 2013 between white and black males. A dramatic change is evident. Police today are much more suspicious of black motorists than they were in 2002. In 2002, officers were almost 125% more likely to search black men than white men using a probable cause search. By 2013, officers were almost 250% more likely to use probable cause as a justification for searching blacks – essentially doubling the disparity in the use of probable cause searches. Tracking the contraband hit rate associated with this type of search reveals that officers' suspicions of wrongdoing have always been less accurate when engaging with black motorists; officers consistently find contraband on black males at modestly lower rates than white males. So the increased reliance on probable cause to search blacks is not associated with more accurate assessments of the likelihood of blacks engaging in criminal behavior. And the increased racial disparities in probable cause searches over time appear to be unjustified in terms of any increased likelihood of finding contraband.

Table 5. Likelihood of finding contraband given a search for men, by race and type of search.

Search type	Number	% Total	% White	% Black	Percent difference
Total searches	427,677	4.14	3.23	6.38	97
Total contraband	108,198	25.30	25.64	26.07	2
Consent	194,236	20.91	23.30	19.13	−18
Probable cause	69,672	52.81	56.39	50.68	−10
Incident to arrest	148,326	18.92	18.68	20.39	9
Search warrant	1127	39.31	38.19	42.28	11
Protective frisk	14,316	15.95	15.79	17.76	12

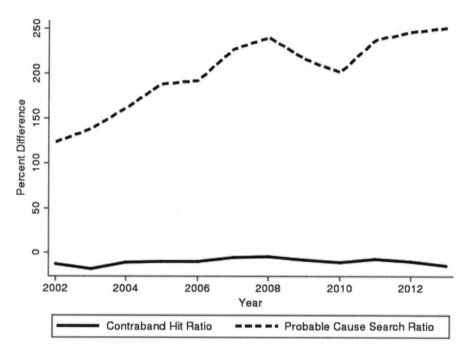

Figure 4. Percent difference in the likelihood of probable cause searches and finding contraband for black men.

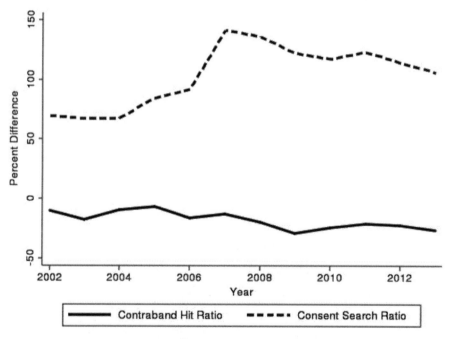

Figure 5. Percent difference in the likelihood of consent searches and finding contraband for black men.

Similar trends are apparent when looking at consent searches. Figure 5 shows that in 2002 officers were 75% more likely to conduct a consent search on a black man as compared to a white man, but by 2013 this disparity had grown even higher. During this time officers became less likely to find contraband on blacks; from 10% less likely in 2002 to 25% in 2013. The data make clear that with regard to consent and probable cause searches, an increased targeting of black males was completely unjustified by any corresponding increase in contraband hit rates. These were either flat or declining.

So far, we have looked at simple percentage differences in searches and contraband hits by race. In the next section we turn to multiple logistic regressions in order to control for possibly confounding factors.

Multivariate regression analyses

A number of factors could explain some of the apparent racial differences that we uncovered in the analyses above. The data collected as part of the North Carolina law allow us to control for the purpose of the stop, the time of day and day of week, and a number of other factors. In Table 6, we take advantage of these opportunities to present three statistical models. In each case, the dependent variable is whether the driver was (a) searched, (b) cited, or (c) arrested, and the independent variables include demographics, the purpose of the stop, the day and hour of the stop, whether the individual officer conducting the

Table 6. Predicting the occurrence of a search, citation, or arrest for men.

Variable	Search	Citation	Arrest
Demographics			
Black	1.75*(0.01)	1.08*(0.00)	1.51*(0.01)
Hispanic, not black	1.16*(0.01)	1.83*(0.01)	1.72*(0.01)
Age	0.97*(0.00)	0.99*(0.00)	0.99*(0.00)
Stop purpose			
Speed limit	–	–	–
Stop light	1.45*(0.01)	0.52**(0.00)	1.25*(0.02)
Impaired	23.65*(0.24)	0.08*(0.00)	59.21*(0.68)
Movement	2.96*(0.02)	0.21*(0.00)	2.04*(0.02)
Equipment	2.38*(0.02)	0.17*(0.00)	1.27*(0.01)
Regulatory	1.90*(0.01)	0.55*(0.00)	1.57*(0.01)
Seat belt	2.10*(0.02)	0.89*(0.00)	1.26*(0.02)
Investigation	5.38*(0.04)	0.27*(0.00)	3.98*(0.04)
Other	2.61*(0.02)	0.47*(0.00)	2.38*(0.03)
Officer type			
Black disparity[a]	1.20*(0.01)	0.98*(0.00)	1.12*(0.00)
White disparity[a]	0.84*(0.01)	0.97*(0.01)	1.32*(0.02)
Contraband			
Contraband Found	–	0.88*(0.01)	23.49*(0.19)
Time			
Hour of Day	Included	Included	Included
Day of Week	Included	Included	Included
Constant	0.09*(0.00)	2.63*(0.02)	0.03*(0.00)
N	4,752,908	4,752,908	4,752,908
Psuedo R^2	0.10	0.10	0.23

Notes: Entries are odds-ratios, with standard errors in parentheses. The number of observations is smaller than the total number of male stops because the "hour of stop" variable is missing in some cases. Race is coded in mutually exclusive categories here, with "White, non-Hispanic" being the reference category. "Other" race drivers are omitted in this table.
*$p < .05$.
[a]High disparity officers search white (black) drivers at more than twice the rate of a black (white) driver. Additionally, the office must have stopped at least 50 black drivers, 50 white drivers, and have a search rate greater than the statewide average of 3.20%.

stop was a "high disparity" officer, and, for the citation and arrest models, whether contraband was found. The models exclude a small number of motorists coded as "other" in the race category, so coefficients for the black and Hispanic variables can be interpreted as the differential likelihood of these groups experiencing a search, citation, or arrest relative to whites. Furthermore, we focus only on male drivers. Our appendix presents similar results for females, and a model in which we include a fixed-effects term for the agency conducting the stop, since different agencies have different overall rates of search, on average. (These robustness checks produce very similar results to those presented here, though the results for females show much lower levels of racial disparity.)

Table 6 provides clear evidence that the comparisons of percentages presented in earlier sections are robust to a more sophisticated set of controls. Coefficients indicate the percent difference in likelihood from a baseline of 1.00 that a search, arrest, or citation occurs. In the first model, black men are shown to have a 75% increased likelihood of search compared to white men, controlling for all other factors in the model, and based on over 4.7 million observations. The officer-disparity variables allow us to control for a "bad apple" hypothesis. While it is true that a driver stopped by an individual officer who tends to search many more blacks than whites will be more likely to be searched, inclusion of this variable in the model allows us to see if the race-of-driver variable remains significant even when that is controlled for. So the 75% increased likelihood can be interpreted as the increased chance, after controlling for all the other factors, including the "bad apple" hypothesis. Clearly, there are some officers with great disparities in their behaviors. However, the patterns we document here cannot be explained away with reference only to these individuals; these are widespread patterns of differential treatment.

The single greatest predictor of being searched, it is important to note, is being stopped for impaired driving. Overall 32.77% of male drivers stopped for impaired driving are searched, as compared to 3.2% of drivers overall, and the large coefficient for this variable accurately reflects this huge increase in likelihood. In fact, all the search purpose variables are relatively large (and of course are all significant, which we expect since there are almost five million observations); this means that the baseline category, speeding, is significantly less likely to lead to a search than any other type of traffic stop. Safe movement, equipment, and seat belt violations have high coefficients in the search model, and of course stops relating to investigations have very high rates of both search and arrest.

Looking at the citation model, as speeding tends to lead to a ticket, all the other stop purposes have low coefficients (a coefficient of 0.90 would indicate a 10% lower likelihood of that outcome, compared to the baseline, which in our model is speeding). Driving while impaired has an extremely low coefficient for citation, and a very high one for arrest, indicating that such drivers are more likely to be searched and/or arrested, not simply given a ticket. These common-sense outcomes are evidence that the models are indeed capturing the results of most traffic stops, giving confidence that the other coefficients can similarly be interpreted with confidence.

In the second (citation) and third (arrest) models, we include a variable for whether contraband was found. Again, consistent with common sense, these coefficients indicate that the presence of contraband is a strong predictor that the driver will be arrested, not ticketed. In the citation and arrest models, we can see that blacks are marginally more likely to be cited (with an 8% increased likelihood) and much more likely to be arrested (51% increased likelihood), all other factors equal. Hispanic males show a 16%

increased likelihood of search; 83% increased likelihood of citation, and 72% increased chance of arrest. In all cases, the odds of these outcomes decline with age.

In general, the results from Table 6 present a stark picture of the odds of negative outcomes for black and Hispanic male drivers in North Carolina. Controlling for why and when they were stopped, which officer pulled them over, and whether or not they had contraband in the car, young men of color are much more likely to see adverse outcomes. Of course, the analysis is limited in that we do not know the extent to which motorists were breaking the law when they were pulled over. It may be that minorities systematically break the law in more egregious ways than whites, as the Lange, Johnson, and Voas (2005) study found. In part, we account for this possibility by controlling for contraband, but this is incomplete as there are many ways to break law beyond carrying contraband. Still, these multivariate results corroborate and extend the findings from our earlier presentations of simple percentage differences in the rates of search or arrest. Minorities are much more likely to be searched and arrested than similarly situated whites, controlling for every variable that the state of North Carolina mandates to be collected when traffic stops are carried out.

Conclusion

The war on drugs comes with readily apparent costs, both fiscal and in lost human opportunity. Much has been written about the price of incarcerating minor drug users and the effects on community development of "missing black men". Burch's (2013) careful work has shown the enormous collective costs to entire communities of mass incarceration. Epp, Maynard-Moody, and Haider-Markel (2014) have clearly documented how pretextual traffic stops alienate, humiliate, and demean minority drivers, depriving them of a full sense of citizenship and promoting distrust with government. An insidious but growing consequence of the war on drugs, we believe, has been the gradual alienation of minority communities whose residents feel that the police unreasonably target them; a trend that recent events in Ferguson, New York, and Baltimore have forced the nation to confront. Having conducted an extensive statewide analysis of traffic stops using state-of-the-art data, we can conclude that blacks in North Carolina appear to have good reasons to be mistrustful of the police, and that these trends appear to be growing over time. This is particularly true for North Carolina's black men, who are searched at much higher rates than their white counterparts, but are less likely to be found with contraband in discretionary police searches. If we follow the precedent used by the US Department of Justice in the Ferguson report, then this discrepancy points strongly toward racial bias in the policing of NC motorways.

Our most surprising and worrisome finding is that evidence for racial discrimination appears to be growing stronger over time. Black motorists today are much more likely to be searched relative to whites than they were 10 years ago and these higher search rates find no justification in contraband hit rates. This is a trend that deserves immediate attention by NC and national policy-makers. In a recent study of the Texas Department of Highway Safety (their Highway Patrol), Baumgartner et al. (2015) show that black drivers in Texas were subject to search 51% more often than white drivers in 2003, but that this disparity has also grown over time, reaching 97% in 2011, and 86% in 2014, the most recent year available. If the US DOJ report on Ferguson was troubling, these two statewide reports document something perhaps even more troubling: these racial disparities are increasing over time.

Our findings confirm all of our hypotheses but one, and all of the findings are troubling, if not all unexpected. Young men of color are indeed targeted for harsher outcomes (searches and arrest); these patterns cannot be explained by our high disparity officer variable, debunking a "bad apple" hypothesis; this targeting cannot be explained by contraband hit rates; trends over time disconfirm our naïve hypothesis that there would be no trends, as disparities are sharply increasing; these disparities are uncorrelated with contraband hit rates and therefore cannot be explained by them; and the findings in North Carolina are similar to the extent that they can be replicated in Texas, with the limited data available there.

Notes

1. The law exempts only police departments in towns with fewer than 10,000 population. The State Highway Patrol has been subject to the law since 1 January 2000, but it was phased in for other agencies in 2002.
2. Other outcomes that can result from a traffic stop include verbal or written warnings and "no enforcement action". In concert with the Ferguson report, we focus on only citations, arrests, and searches because they are the most invasive and punitive of the possible outcomes.
3. The mathematics behind this calculation are straightforward: $((10/5)*100)-100$.
4. For example, a study by Lange, Johnson, and Voas (2005) of drivers on the New Jersey Turnpike found that speeders were more likely to be black and that patterns of police traffic stops accurately reflected the racial make-up of speeders, rather than the racial composition of the surrounding communities.

Disclosure statement

No potential conflict of interest was reported by the authors.

References

Alexander, Michelle. 2010. *The New Jim Crow: Mass Incarceration in the Age of Colorblindness.* New York: The New Press.

Bates, Timothy. 2010. "Driving While Black in Suburban Detroit." *Du Bois Review: Social Science Research on Race* 7: 133–150.

Baumgartner, Frank R., Bryan D. Jones, Julio Zaconet, Colin Wilson, and Arvind Krishnamurthy. 2015. "Racial Disparities in Texas Department of Public Safety Traffic Stops, 2002–2014." Testimony presented to the Texas House of Representatives Committee on County Affairs, November 18. http://www.unc.edu/~fbaum/TrafficStops/Baumgartner-TexasDPS-Nov2015.pdf.

Burch, Traci. 2013. *Trading Democracy for Justice.* Chicago, IL: University of Chicago Press.

Bureau of Justice Statistics. 1982. *Prisoners, 1925–81.* Washington, DC: US DOJ. http://www.bjs.gov/content/pub/pdf/p2581.pdf.

Epp, Charles R., Steven Maynard-Moody, and Donald Haider-Markel. 2014. *Pulled Over: How Police Stops Define Race and Citizenship.* Chicago, IL: University of Chicago Press.

Fishman, Charles. 1991. "Sheriff Bob Vogel: He's The Mayor of I-95, and a Terror to Drug Smugglers." *Orlando Sentinel,* August 11. Accessed June 6, 2015. http://articles.orlandosentinel.com/1991-08-11/news/9108091173_1_bob-vogel-drug-trade-drug-traffic.

GAO (Government Accounting Office). 2000. *Racial Profiling: Limited Data on Motorist Stops.* Washington, DC: US General Accounting Office.

Gelman, Andrew, Jeffrey Fagan, and Alex Kiss. 2007. "An Analysis of the New York City Police Department's "Stop-and-Frisk" Police in the Context of Claims of Racial Bias." *Journal of the American Statistical Association* 102: 813–823.

Glaze, Lauren E., and Danielle Kaeble. 2014. *Correctional Populations in the United States, 2013.* Washington, DC: US DOJ. http://www.bjs.gov/content/pub/pdf/cpus13.pdf.

Harris, David A. 1999. *Driving While Black: Racial Profiling on Our Nation's Highways.* New York: American Civil Liberties Union.

Knowles, John, Nicola Persico, and Petra Todd. 2001. "Racial Bias in Motor Vehicle Searches: Theory and Evidence." *Journal of Political Economy* 109: 203–229.

Lamberth, John. 1996. *A Report to the ACLU.* New York: American Civil Liberates Union.

Lange, James E., Mark B. Johnson, and Robert B. Voas. 2005. "Testing the Racial Profiling Hypothesis for Seemingly Disparate Traffic Stops on the New Jersey Turnpike." *Justice Quarterly* 22: 193–223.

Lerman, Amy E., and Vesla M. Weaver. 2014. *Arresting Citizenship.* Chicago, IL: University of Chicago Press.

Mance, Ian A. 2012. *Racial Profiling in North Carolina: Racial Disparities in Traffic Stops 2000 to 2011.* Raleigh, NC: North Carolina Advocates for Justice.

Meehan, Albert J. and Michael C. Ponder. 2006. "Race and Place: The Ecology of Racial Profiling African American Motorists." *Justice Quarterly* 19: 399–430.

Moore, Nina M. 2015. *The Political Roots of Racial Tracking in American Criminal Justice.* New York: Cambridge University Press.

Peffley, Mark, and Jon Hurwitz. 2010. *Justice in America: The Separate Realities of Blacks and Whites.* New York: Cambridge University Press.

Persico, Nicola and Petra Todd. 2008. "The Hit Rates Test for Racial Bias in Motor-Vehicle Searches." *Justice Quarterly* 25 (1): 37–53.

Provine, Doris Marie. 2007. *Unequal Under Law: Race in the War on Drugs.* Chicago, IL: University of Chicago Press.

Rice, Stephen K., and Michael D. White, eds. 2010. *Race, Ethnicity and Policing: New and Essential Readings.* New York: New York University Press.

Stevenson, Bryan. 2014. *Just Mercy: A Story of Redemption.* New York, NY: Spiegel & Grau.

United States Department of Justice, Civil Rights Division. 2015. *Investigation of the Ferguson Police Department.* March 4. Washington: US DOJ.

Webb, Gary. 2007. "Driving While Black: Tracking Unspoken Law-Enforcement Racism." *Esquire,* January 29. Accessed May 21, 2015. www.esquire.com/news-politics/a1223/driving-while-black-0499. [Originally published as: DWB, Esquire 131, 4 (April 1999): 118–127].

Appendix 1. Alternative model specifications

Table 6 presented a model for the entire state. Each agency has a different baseline rate of search, however, so it may be appropriate to include fixed effects for the agency. We do so in Table A1, limiting our analysis in this case to the 25 largest police agencies in the state. Note that the N here declines from 4.75 million in Table 6 to just over 3 million, as we exclude many smaller agencies. Results in Table A1 suggest that the findings in Table 6 are highly robust.

Table A1. Predicting the occurrence of a search, citation, or arrest for men for the top 25 agencies.

Variable	Search	Citation	Arrest
Demographics			
Race	2.08*(0.01)	0.94 *(0.00)	1.61*(0.01)
Hispanic	1.23*(0.01)	1.70*(0.01)	1.78*(0.02)
Age	0.97*(0.00)	0.97*(0.00)	0.99*(0.00)
Stop purpose			
Speed limit	–	–	–
Stop light	1.62*(0.02)	0.45*(0.00)	1.23*(0.02)
Impaired	29.44*(0.42)	0.05*(0.00)	75.48*(1.18)
Movement	2.85*(0.03)	0.20*(0.00)	2.11*(0.03)
Equipment	2.52*(0.02)	0.15*(0.00)	1.28*(0.02)
Regulatory	1.98*(0.02)	0.43*(0.00)	1.49*(0.02)
Seat belt	2.55*(0.03)	0.68*(0.00)	1.35*(0.03)
Investigation	5.52*(0.05)	0.22*(0.00)	4.07*(0.05)
Other	2.96*(0.03)	0.39*(0.00)	2.59*(0.04)
Officer type			
Black disparity[a]	1.30*(0.01)	0.92*(0.00)	1.10*(0.00)
White disparity[a]	0.90*(0.02)	1.07*(0.01)	1.42*(0.03)
Contraband			
Contraband found	–	0.76*(0.01)	26.90*(0.30)
Time			
Hour of day	Included	Included	Included
Day of week	Included	Included	Included
Agency fixed effects	Included	Included	Included
N	3,052,024	3,052,024	3,052,024
Log likelihood	−627,322.11	−1,839,413.2	−366,595.01

Notes: Entries are odds-ratios, with standard errors in parentheses. Constant suppressed. The number of observations is smaller than the total number of male stops because the "hour of stop" variable is missing in some cases.
*p < .05.
[a]High disparity officers search white (black) drivers at more than twice the rate of a black (white) driver. Additionally, the office must have stopped at least 50 black and white drivers, and have a search rate greater than 3.20%.

Appendix 2. Analysis of female drivers

Our main text focuses on males. Here we provide parallel information for female drivers, generally showing much more muted racial disparities. Figure A1 presents basic information on the differential likelihood of various outcomes of a stop for black women as compared to white women. As can be seen, women have essentially the same likelihood of being cited; this remains constant over the time period of the study. Over time, black women are increasingly more likely to be searched after being stopped than white women; in 2002 there was no difference, but by 2013 there is a 25% increased likelihood of being searched. The difference in the likelihood of being arrested fluctuates over this time.

Moving on from the basic trends in time of differences in stop outcomes, Figure A2 presents the percent difference in the likelihood of outcomes for black women as

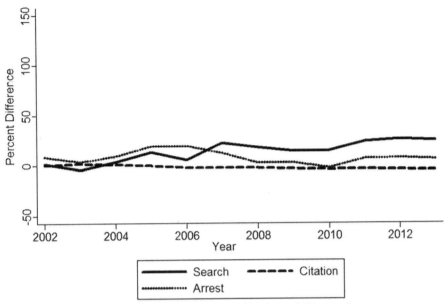

The figure shows the percentage difference in the likelihood of different outcomes for Blacks as compared to Whites.

Figure A1. Percent difference in the likelihood of traffic stop outcomes for black women.

compared to white women by purpose of stop. Unlike for men, there is more variation in the percent differences by purpose and outcome. White women are more likely to be searched after being stopped for driving while impaired, safe movement violations, and vehicle equipment. Black women have an essentially equal rate of search when stopped for an investigation. Black women are more likely to be searched following any other type of stop. All women are roughly as likely as being cited following any of type of stop; the differences are all within 5%. Finally, black women are consistently more likely to be arrested following a stop except for driving while intoxicated and safe movement stops.

These differences in the likelihood of being searched following a stop once again lead us to examine whether this difference is being driven by the differential use of specific types of searches. Table A2 begins to answer this question. While there are modest differences for consent searches, searches executed per a search warrant, and incident-to-arrest searches, the real differences are in the use of probable cause searches. In these cases, black women are much more likely to be subject to search.

Table A3 extends this line of enquiry by presenting the contraband hit rates following a search-by-search type. In every case, the police are less to find contraband on black women. This is emphasized in Figures A3 and A4 where the percent difference in the likelihood of a consent and probable cause searches are presented alongside the percent difference in the likelihood of finding contraband following a search for black women as compared to white women. While these trends are more dramatic than those for men, they are smaller and fluctuate more over time.

Table A4 presents the same model from Table 6 for women. Findings indicate much more muted racial disparities: Black women are 10% less likely to be searched, 21%

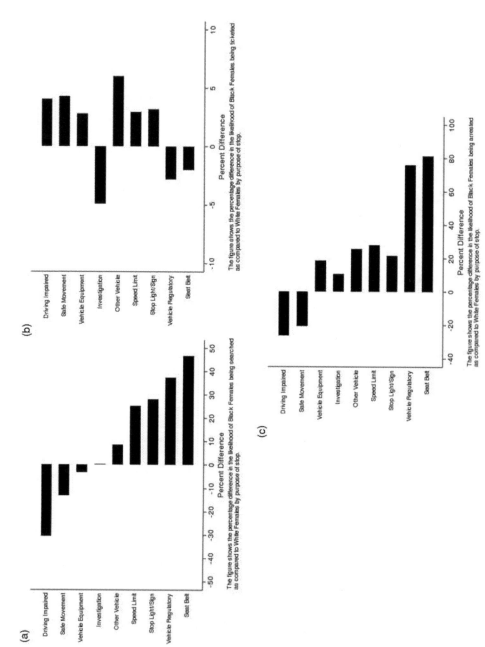

Figure A2. Percent difference in the likelihood of outcomes for black women by purpose of stop.

Table A2. Rates of search by race for women.

Search type	Number	% Total	% White	% Black	Percent difference
Total stops	5,671,694	–	62.42	33.06	–
Total searches	84,136	1.48	1.45	1.63	12
Consent	36,974	0.68	0.68	0.65	−5
Search warrant	218	0	0	0	0
Incident to arrest	31,457	0.55	0.55	0.59	7
Protective frisk	1917	0.03	0.03	0.04	33
Probable cause	13,570	0.19	0.19	0.35	84

Table A3. Likelihood of Finding Contraband Given a Search for Women, by Race and Type of Search.

Search type	Number	% Total	% White	% Black	Percent difference
Total searches	84,136	1.48	1.45	1.63	12
Total contraband	20,720	24.63	25.75	23.03	−11
Protective frisk	1917	12.26	12.49	11.99	−32
Incident to arrest	31,457	15.43	16.88	13.21	−22
Probable cause	13,570	50.36	54.22	46.29	−21
Search warrant	218	31.65	35.17	23.94	−15
Consent	36,974	23.61	25.48	20.23	−11

more likely to get a ticket, and six percent more likely to be arrested, compared to similarly situated white women. Table A5 presents the fixed-effects agency model showing only slightly different results for the race variable: 12%, 6%, and 14% increased likelihoods. In no case, however, are the black/white differences among women close to as great as those we document among men.

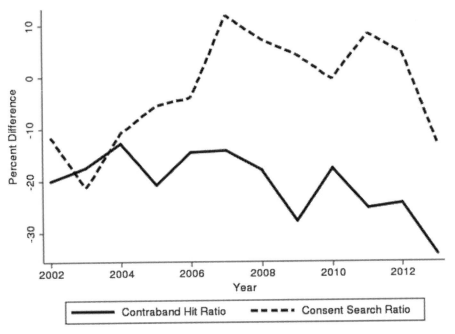

Figure A3. Percent difference in the likelihood of probable cause searches and finding contraband for black women.

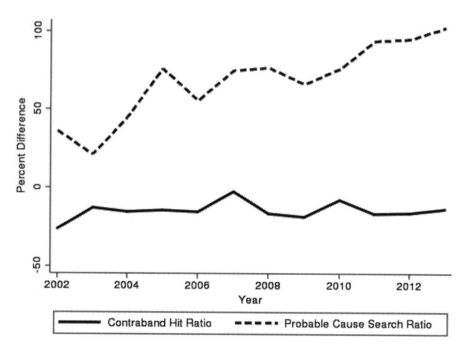

Figure A4. Percent difference in the likelihood of consent searches and finding contraband for black women.

Table A4. Predicting the occurrence of a search, citation, or arrest for women.

Variable	Search	Citation	Arrest
Demographics			
Race	0.90*(0.01)	1.21 *(0.00)	1.06*(0.01)
Hispanic	0.48*(0.01)	1.80*(0.01)	0.69*(0.02)
Age	0.97*(0.00)	0.99*(0.00)	0.99*(0.00)
Stop purpose			
Speed limit	–	–	–
Stop light	1.63*(0.03)	0.45*(0.00)	1.36*(0.03)
Impaired	37.05*(0.75)	0.08*(0.00)	93.64*(2.01)
Movement	3.77*(0.06)	0.19*(0.00)	2.90*(0.06)
Equipment	3.06*(0.05)	0.13*(0.00)	1.65*(0.04)
Regulatory	2.44*(0.03)	0.50*(0.00)	1.99*(0.03)
Seat belt	2.79*(0.07)	0.89*(0.01)	1.68*(0.06)
Investigation	9.70*(0.15)	0.26*(0.00)	7.14*(0.14)
Other	3.86*(0.07)	0.43*(0.00)	3.51*(0.08)
Officer type			
Black disparity[a]	1.12*(0.01)	0.96*(0.00)	1.16*(0.02)
White disparity[a]	0.96*(0.03)	0.95*(0.01)	1.24*(0.04)
Contraband			
Contraband Found	–	1.24*(0.02)	35.93*(0.68)
Time			
Hour of Day	Included	Included	Included
Day of Week	Included	Included	Included
Constant	0.04	2.26	0.01
N	2,906,964	2,906,964	2,906,964
R^2	0.12	0.11	0.24

Notes: Entries are odds-ratios, with standard errors in parentheses. The number of observations is smaller than the total number of male stops because the "hour of stop" variable is missing in some cases.
*$p < .05$.
[a]High disparity officers search white (black) drivers at more than twice the rate of a black (white) driver. Additionally, the office must have stopped at least 50 black and white drivers, and have a search rate greater than 3.20%.

Table A5. Predicting the occurrence of a search, citation, or arrest for women for the top 25 agencies.

Variable	Search	Citation	Arrest
Demographics			
Race	1.12 *(0.01)	1.06 *(0.00)	1.14*(0.01)
Hispanic	0.52*(0.02)	1.60*(0.01)	0.69*(0.02)
Age	0.97*(0.00)	0.99*(0.00)	0.98*(0.00)
Stop purpose			
Speed limit	–	–	–
Stop light	1.76*(0.05)	0.39*(0.00)	1.36*(0.04)
Impaired	45.54*(1.27)	0.06*(0.00)	112.24*(3.26)
Movement	3.49*(0.08)	0.17*(0.00)	2.93*(0.09)
Equipment	2.96*(0.06)	0.11*(0.00)	1.61*(0.05)
Regulatory	2.40*(0.04)	0.38*(0.00)	1.90*(0.04)
Seat belt	2.94*(0.10)	0.74*(0.01)	1.72*(0.08)
Investigation	9.27*(0.20)	0.20*(0.00)	7.35*(0.19)
Other	3.90*(0.10)	0.36*(0.00)	3.75*(0.11)
Officer type			
Black disparity[a]	1.23*(0.02)	0.91*(0.00)	1.15*(0.02)
White disparity[a]	1.13*(0.04)	1.06*(0.01)	1.36*(0.06)
Contraband			
Contraband Found	–	1.03*(0.03)	45.13*(1.20)
Time			
Hour of Day	Included	Included	Included
Day of Week	Included	Included	Included
Agency fixed effects	Included	Included	Included
N	1,905,026	1,905,026	1,905,026
Log likelihood	−154,994.72	−1,122,016.30	−106,235.63

Notes: Entries are odds-ratios, with standard errors in parentheses. Constant suppressed.
The number of observations is smaller than the total number of male stops because the "hour of stop" variable is missing in some cases.
$*p < .05$.
[a]High disparity officers search white (black) drivers at more than twice the rate of a black (white) driver. Additionally, the office must have stopped at least 50 black and white drivers, and have a search rate greater than 3.20%.

Refusing to know a woman's place: the causes and consequences of rejecting stereotypes of women politicians in the Americas[†]

Amy Erica Smith, Katherine Warming and Valerie M. Hennings

ABSTRACT

What are the sources and effects of gendered leadership stereotypes for women's representation? We explore the role of stereotypes in shaping public attitudes toward women's representation using AmericasBarometer survey data from 25 countries. We report three key results. First, the modal respondent in almost every country rejects gendered leadership stereotypes, affirming that women and men leaders are equally qualified on corruption and the economy. This holds even after we attempt to account for social desirability bias. Second, there are significant individual- and country-level *determinants* of stereotyping. In countries with higher women's representation and labor force participation but without gender quotas, citizens are more likely to choose pro-female and neutral responses over pro-male stereotypes. At the individual level, those rejecting stereotypes are less authoritarian, more supportive of labor market equality, and more leftist than those reporting pro-female stereotypes. Third, the *consequences* for representation vary by partisanship and country context. Pro-female leadership stereotypes boost support for women presidential candidates and for legislative gender quotas, but they matter *less* among copartisans of women candidates, and they matter *more* when women candidates are viable but gendered outsiders. Those rejecting leadership stereotypes altogether are less supportive of quotas.

What are the nature and consequences of gendered leadership stereotypes in developing democracies? We address this question in the case of the Americas, where the number of women elected to presidential office has risen dramatically in the past decade, yet women remain substantially underrepresented at all levels. Growing bodies of work examine the institutional causes and policy consequences of women's representation in Latin America; at the mass level, scholars examine public opinion toward women leaders in the abstract,

[†]A previous version of this paper was presented at the 2013 Annual Meeting of the Midwest Political Science Association. LeeAnn Banaszak, Tessa Ditonto, Jana Morgan, Dave Peterson, and Robert Urbatsch provided very helpful feedback. The underlying replication code for this paper can be accessed at: http://amyericasmith.org/wp-content/uploads/2016/06/Smith-Warming-Hennings-Replication-Code.zip. The data can be accessed from the AmericasBarometer, www.americasbarometer.org

and how candidate gender affects vote choice. Yet, the connection from mass attitudes such as stereotypes to women's representation in the region has yet to be addressed.

Scholars of the US show that gendered leadership stereotypes remain prevalent but are declining, and in recent elections only indirectly affect vote choice; some suggest they do not matter at all (Bauer 2015a, 2015b; Brooks 2013; Ditonto, Hamilton, and Redlawsk 2014; Dolan 2014; Dolan and Lynch 2015). We analyze 2012 public opinion data to understand citizens' stereotypes of the political capabilities of men and women politicians. We make two advances over prior work. First, we examine the extent to which developing democracies exhibit similar gendered leadership stereotypes as in the US. There are reasons to expect differences. For instance, the Americas contain a great range in levels of development, and development is associated feminist attitudes more generally (e.g., Banaszak and Plutzer 1993; Inglehart and Norris 2003; Morgan and Buice 2013; Paxton and Hughes 2007). Second, we distinguish theoretically and empirically between rejecting stereotypes and holding *both* pro-female and pro-male stereotypes.

We then use the same public opinion data to examine the determinants and consequences of stereotypes supporting women leaders and of refusal to stereotype. Stereotypes on economic leadership vary by a country's level of women's legislative representation and workforce participation, and by whether countries have gender quota laws. At the individual level, leftists and non-authoritarians are more likely to say both sexes are equal than to give pro-female responses.

Turning to consequences, we assess how stereotypes are associated with two public opinion outcome variables: self-reported voting for women presidential candidates and support for legislative gender quotas, a policy tool increasingly adopted across the Western Hemisphere. Results indicate pro-female stereotypes are associated with support for gender quotas and with saying one voted for women candidates. However, those saying men and women are equally competent are less supportive of gender quotas than the ambivalent.

Beyond varying levels of development, the Americas also present a wide range of party systems and levels of women's representation. This variation allows us to contextualize conclusions regarding stereotypes and women's representation heretofore based solely on the US. We find that stereotypes are *not* associated with voting for women among copartisans of women candidates. Moreover, gendered leadership stereotypes appear to matter only in elections with viable women candidates whose principal competitors are all male.

Gender stereotypes of leaders in the Americas: causes and consequences

The return to democracy in Latin America and the Caribbean beginning in the 1970s coincided with a gradual rise in women's representation (Jalalzai 2016; Schwindt-Bayer 2010). In legislatures, proportional representation and gender quotas have contributed to this rise (dos Santos and Wylie, Forthcoming; Hinojosa 2012; Hinojosa and Franceschet 2012; Jones 2009; Krook 2009; McAllister and Studlar 2002; Schwindt-Bayer 2010). In presidencies, many women elected have been spouses of former presidents or had charismatic male patrons (Jalalzai 2016; Jalalzai and dos Santos 2015; Ríos-Tobar 2008). We know less about the impact of public opinion on representation; scholars present conflicting evidence on gendered leadership preferences in the Americas (Aguilar, Cunow, and Desposato 2015; Batista Pereira 2015; Morgan 2015; Morgan and Buice 2013; Shair-Rosenfield and Hinojosa 2014). We have yet to understand the role of stereotypes.

The nature and determinants of gendered leadership stereotypes

We define stereotypes as culturally learned and shared "knowledge … associated with a group of people" (Moskowitz and Li 2011, 103). We are concerned with such "knowledge" of men's and women's political leadership abilities, which may differ from knowledge of other gendered roles (Eagly and Karau 2002; Schneider and Bos 2014). A rich literature in the US developed over several decades documenting gendered leadership stereotypes; US citizens tend to associate women candidates with "feminine" traits and policy areas, and to link them to the Democratic Party (Alexander and Andersen 1993; Diamond 1977; Dolan 2004; Holman, Merolla, and Zechmeister 2011; Huddy and Terkildsen 1993; Kahn 1996; Koch 2000; Lawless 2004; McDermott 1998; Sanbonmatsu 2003; Sapiro 1983; Winter 2010). Yet stereotypes are undeniably changing in the US. Dolan and Lynch observe that "the American public is more supportive of a role for women in political life today than it has ever been," and that only relatively small minorities today endorse statements such as that men are better suited emotionally for politics (2015, 112). Moreover, citizens express traditional stereotypes of women leaders to a much lesser extent than of women generally (Schneider and Bos 2014). These new results suggest that while gendered leadership stereotypes still exist, their expression and effects may be subtler than just a few decades ago.

Have gendered leadership stereotypes gradually changed in other democracies, as in the US? Women's public roles have changed dramatically in the past four decades across the North and South America. As citizens have become accustomed to women in the workplace and public office and as generational replacement has brought new cohorts of adults socialized in non-traditional roles, attitudes may have adjusted across many countries in the Americas. Diekman et al. (2005) compare dynamic gender stereotypes in the US, Chile, and Brazil; they find that in all three countries citizens believe women are becoming increasingly masculine in personality, cognitive, and physical traits, and are converging toward the mean traits of men. Hence, we have reason to expect that citizens may also increasingly say they believe there is little difference between women and men politicians.

Our first goal is thus descriptive: to understand the extent to which citizens in developing country contexts report gendered leadership stereotypes. We distinguish between citizens who reject positive and negative statements about either sex, and those who hold counter-traditional stereotypes: for instance, that women leaders are better than men on the economy.

Our second goal is to understand the *determinants* of stereotypes. At the country level, we examine the effects of levels of human development, women's representation, women's labor force participation, and of legislative gender quotas. First, the "developmental theory" of the gender gap posits that as human development rises, increasing postmaterialism boosts support for women's leadership (Inglehart and Norris 2003). Second, women's entry into office may affect women's representation long term by raising support for women leaders (e.g., Bhavnani 2009; Kerevel and Atkeson 2015). However, gender quotas can heighten stereotypes by implying that women candidates need special preferences (Bos 2015; Franceschet and Piscopo 2008). Fourth, rising female labor force participation can change perceptions of women's leadership capabilities. We hypothesize:

H1. As human development, women's legislative representation, and women's labor force participation rise, both positive stereotypes of women leaders and rejection of stereotypes will rise, compared to pro-male stereotypes. Controlling for legislative representation, in countries with gender quotas, both pro-female leadership stereotypes and neutrality will drop, compared to pro-male stereotypes.

At the individual level, who expresses either neutral views of women leaders or pro-female stereotypes? First we examine gender. Those in positions of relative power are more likely to stereotype the less powerful; women may tend to report both neutral and pro-female stereotypes due to gender affinity (Bauer 2015a; Dépret and Fiske 1993; Fiske 1993; Fulton 2014). Education may reduce both positive and negative stereotypes, as stereotyping can be considered a heuristic employed more frequently by those with limited cognitive and attentional resources (Bauer 2015a; Sherman, Macrae, and Bodenhausen 2000). Also, education can socialize citizens into changing gendered leadership norms (Hietanen and Pick 2015 Inglehart and Norris 2003; Morgan and Buice 2013). In addition, age might matter, as younger people are also more likely to have been socialized in a world with non-traditional gender roles (Fullerton and Stern 2010). Next, marriage may foster traditional attitudes, leading to greater stereotyping, and in particular more pro-male stereotyping (Hayes 1993). Fifth, we control for household wealth and skin color.

Turning to attitudes, we hypothesize that authoritarians – those endorsing hierarchical family structures – will endorse gendered leadership stereotypes, especially pro-male ones (Hetherington and Weiler 2009; Schaller et al. 1995). Leftists and committed democrats might tend to choose egalitarian responses due to associations among equality, leftism, and democracy (Feldman 1988; Haidt 2012). However, leftists' historical support for women's representation might be driven instead by *pro-female* stereotypes (Banaszak and Plutzer 1993; Kenworthy and Malami 1999). Those rejecting traditional gender roles in the workforce may also reject pro-male leadership stereotypes (Alexander and Andersen 1993, 541; Paxton and Kunovich 2003). Finally, those dissatisfied with the political system may support women political leaders, perceiving them as outsiders (Brown, Diekman, and Schneider 2011; Morgan and Buice 2013).

H2. Women, those with more education, youth, the unmarried, leftists, non-authoritarians, and those who support democracy will all be more likely to endorse neutrality, compared to positive and negative stereotypes of women leaders.
H3. Women, those with more education, youth, the unmarried, leftists, those with general feminist attitudes, and those dissatisfied with the political system will be more likely to endorse pro-female than pro-male stereotypes.

The consequences of gendered leadership stereotypes

Our third goal is to understand the *consequences* of leadership stereotypes for attitudes toward gender quotas and for presidential voting. Quotas have been adopted across the Americas, most recently in Bolivia (2010), Colombia (2011), El Salvador (2013), Nicaragua (2015), and Chile (to be implemented in 2017). But does *rejecting stereotypes* or *endorsing pro-female stereotypes* more effectively boost such support? We hypothesize that those stating there are no differences between men and women leaders – whether they actually believe there is no difference, or refuse to acknowledge differences they privately believe exist – will be less likely to support measures addressing structural inequalities, including legislative quotas. As the US struggle for racial equality has shown, abstract belief in equality can lead citizens to oppose measures perceived as favoritism, even when intended to redress historical disadvantages (Sears, Henry, and Kosterman 2000; see also Bos 2015 on gender quotas and egalitarianism). Hence, we expect that those rejecting both positive and negative stereotypes will be less supportive of gender quotas, but will be likely to vote for individual women candidates.

What about those with *pro-female* leadership stereotypes? Some scholars argue that gendered stereotypes no longer affect vote choice in the US, in part overwhelmed by partisanship (Brooks 2013; Dolan 2014; Dolan and Lynch 2015). Others instead hold that the effect is indirect, as politicians' gender shapes communication and information-gathering strategies (Bauer 2015a, 2015b; Ditonto, Hamilton, and Redlawsk 2014; Fridkin and Kenney 2014). Women politicians in the US may now be evaluated primarily based on their *political* roles and leadership stereotypes on "masculine" issues, rather than based on feminine stereotypes (Bauer 2015a; Brooks 2013; Dolan 2010; Fulton 2012, 2014; Schneider 2014; Schneider and Bos 2014).

To what extent are findings about the impact of gender stereotypes in the US applicable across North and South America? The range of institutional and competitive landscapes in the Americas provides an opportunity to examine how the effects of stereotypes on the vote vary across contexts. Gender stereotypes might matter more for vote choices in the region's third wave "delegative democracies," characterized by voter deference to charismatic, personalist leaders (O'Donnell 1994). Voters in such countries are likely to reward stereotypically masculine characteristics.

The effects of gendered leadership stereotypes could also vary from country to country. First, levels of partisanship vary greatly across the region, and gendered leadership stereotypes appear to matter more when partisanship matters less. In the AmericasBarometer data used here, the percentage of the population identifying with a political party varies from about 13% in Guatemala to 63% in the Dominican Republic; the US is tied with the Dominican Republic for highest levels of partisanship in the hemisphere. Second, given multipartism, the competitive scenarios facing women candidates across the Americas vary greatly. In some races, women candidates represent minor parties with few real chances of winning, and in others they are viable. In some races a single woman runs, and in others there are multiple women. We expect that gendered leadership stereotypes will be activated more strongly when women candidates are viable, but when there is a single viable female candidate. When multiple viable women are on the ballot, gender may become less salient in voters' evaluations of candidates. We hypothesize:

> H4. Those who reject stereotypes will be reluctant to support gender quotas, but will tend to support women candidates. Those with pro-female stereotypes will support both gender quotas and female candidates.
> H5. The effects of pro-female stereotypes will be stronger for non-partisans and in races in which there is a single viable woman.

Data and methods

Our study is based on the 2012 AmericasBarometer, in which over 41,000 citizens were interviewed in 26 countries (Seligson, Smith, and Zechmeister 2012). In 24 countries, the questionnaire was administered in face-to-face interviews in respondents' homes, while it was conducted using a web interface in the US and Canada (Canada is excluded due to missing data, and only descriptive data on stereotypes are available in the US). Outside these two countries, the survey was based on a common sample design, involving a multi-stage, stratified probability sample (with household-level quotas) of approximately 1500 individuals per country. Coefficients and standard errors have been adjusted to take into account the complex sample design (Kish 1965).

These countries present great diversity in women's incorporation into politics. The US was the first to grant women suffrage, in 1920. In the ensuing decades suffrage was granted in every country; finally in 1967 voting became compulsory for Ecuadoran women, after previously being compulsory only for men (Inter-Parliamentary Union 2015). At the elite level, 18 countries have legislated candidate quotas, and 10 have voluntary party quotas (Quota Project 2013). As of 2015, 6 had had woman as prime minister and 11 as president (women had filled both positions in Guyana and Haiti; see Hawkesworth 2012; Jalalzai 2008). In 2015, legislatures ranged from 3–4% female in Belize and Haiti to 42–53% in Ecuador and Bolivia.

In 2012, the AmericasBarometer included two questions regarding gendered leadership stereotypes: "Who do you think would be more corrupt as a politician, a man or a woman, or are both the same?" and "If a politician is responsible for running the national economy, who would do a better job, a man, or a woman or does it not matter?" (see Appendix Table A1 for frequencies). These questions were administered to half of respondents in each country.[1] When these items are used as dependent variables, they are coded so that the omitted categories are the pro-male responses. The measures have limitations, in that they do not capture the full range of gendered stereotypes that might affect attitudes toward women's leadership. First, they deal only with perceptions of *leaders*, and not perceptions of women's political capabilities in general. Second, they measure only beliefs about women's and men's relative competence in key areas of political performance; they do not address perceptions of other leader characteristics, such as ideology or personality traits. Third, they measure only attitudes with respect to stereotypically masculine traits, and exclude stereotypically feminine ones. Nonetheless, these data *do* address one important domain of stereotypes, and they provide an unrivaled opportunity to study stereotypes across a great range of countries.

We assess the association between stereotypes and two dependent variables. The first addresses support for gender quotas: "The state ought to require that political parties reserve some space on their lists of candidates for women, even if they have to exclude some men. How much do you agree or disagree?" Responses ran from "Strongly Disagree" (1) to "Strongly Agree" (7). The second measures voting for a woman presidential candidate, following Morgan (2015). In each country, respondents were asked whom they had supported in the most recent presidential or parliamentary general election (in countries with two round elections, respondents were asked about the first round). In countries with a woman presidential candidate, an indicator variable is coded 1 if the respondent voted for a woman and 0 if for a man. Non-voters and parliamentary systems are excluded, since in parliamentary races votes are cast for parties rather than the likely eventual head of government.[2] After excluding countries in which fewer than 20 respondents had voted for the female candidate(s) in the most recent election, the countries analyzed are Argentina, Brazil, Costa Rica, Guatemala, Haiti, Panama, Paraguay, and Peru.

Of 46 presidential candidates coded, 13 were women, 8 of whom won over 10% of the vote (see Appendix Table A2). One (Cristina Fernández de Kirchner of Argentina) was an incumbent, and three were from the incumbent party. Fernández was reelected in 2011; Dilma Rousseff from Brazil's incumbent PT and Laura Chinchilla from Costa Rica's incumbent PLN were both elected to first terms in 2010. None of the other women was elected.[3]

Multivariate analysis includes four country-level variables: human development, women's legislative representation, women's labor force participation rate, and gender quota laws.[4] In voting models, we also control for identification with the same or a different party from the woman candidate(s), based on a question that asks simply "Do you identify with a political party?" In many countries of the Americas, partisanship is low, and affiliations unstable; partisanship is often endogenous to vote choice, especially when both are reported months or years after the election. Hence, controlling for partisanship runs the risk of overcorrecting for a downstream effect of the vote. Only about 35% of our sample reports partisan affiliation, split approximately evenly between copartisans and out-partisans of the woman candidate(s).

We control for other individual characteristics. *Support for women's labor participation* is measured by asking, "Some say that when there is not enough work, men should have a greater right to jobs than women. To what extent do you agree or disagree?" Responses were originally from 1 to 7; they are reverse coded so that higher values represent more egalitarian responses and converted to a 0–1 scale. This item is a classic measure of gender ideology (Inglehart and Norris 2003; Paxton and Kunovich 2003). *Support for democracy* is the extent to which respondents agree that "democracy may have problems, but it's better than the alternatives"; again, responses were originally scaled 1–7 but recoded from 0 to 1. This classic from the AmericasBarometer has been validated in many studies, and is powerfully associated with political behavior in Latin America (Booth and Seligson 2009; Smith 2009).

Support for the political system is a 0–1 index derived from classic studies (Muller 1979). It averages responses to five questions about the respondent's country: the extent to which "courts … guarantee a fair trial"; "you respect [your country's] political institutions"; "citizens' basic rights are well protected"; "you feel proud of living under the political system"; and "you think that one should support" the system. *Leftism* is a 10 category variable, running from 0 (far right) to 1 (far left).[5] Measurement of *authoritarianism* follows Hetherington and Weiler (2009). Respondents were asked which was more important for a child: (a) independence versus respect for adults; (b) obedience versus autonomy; and (c) creativity versus discipline. Responses of (a) respect for adults, (b) obedience, and (c) discipline each received a value of 1; their opposites 0. Volunteered answers that "both are important" received .5. The scale is the mean of responses. Across the Americas, 40.3% of respondents score a 1.0, and only 9% below 0.5.

Educational attainment is a four category ordinal variable running from 0 to 1, adjusted to each country: no formal education; primary education (1 to 6–8 years of schooling, varying by country); secondary education; and university/post-secondary education. *Age* is coded in six groups (16–25, 26–35, 36–45, 46–55, 56–65, and 66+).[6] Indicator variables measure gender and marital status. *Household wealth* is coded in quintiles within each country by the AmericasBarometer (Córdova 2009); this variable has lower levels of missing data than income. Finally, to capture race cross-nationally, interviewers surreptitiously coded *skin color* using a printed card running from 1 (very light) to 11 (very dark).

We also include an indicator for interviewer gender. Individuals may suppress stereotypic and prejudiced responses (Devine 1989; Devine et al. 2002; Krupnikov, Piston, and Bauer 2016). Citizens who actually believe one sex is superior may avoid saying so due to social desirability bias (Presser and Traugott 1992). Such citizens might choose not to answer the questions; they might give neutral or egalitarian responses; or they might actually endorse stereotypes contrary to private inclinations. While controlling for the sex of the interviewer does not fully address the problem, it provides some leverage on this issue. When the interviewer is male, we expect fewer respondents to give neutral and pro-female responses, and more to report pro-male stereotypes, compared to when the interviewer is female.

Results and discussion

Before evaluating our hypotheses, we examine the incidence of stereotypes. Across the Americas, a near majority rejects leadership stereotypes on both dimensions; 49% say that leaders' sex does not matter for either corruption or the economy. The US is among the countries with highest stereotype rejection, but at least half of respondents in 13 of the 25 countries rejects stereotypes on both issues (Figure 1). Examining the content of stereotypes, 31% of respondents across the Americas say men are more corrupt and only 5% say women are more corrupt. Thirteen percent say they prefer men's leadership on the economy, and 28% prefer women's leadership (see Appendix for the distribution by country). Thus, most citizens exhibit some discomfort with

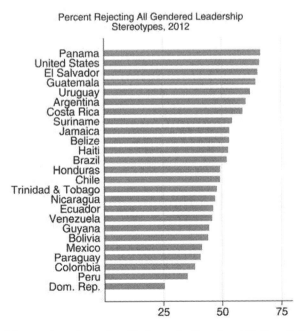

Figure 1. Percent of Respondents Reporting "Both are the Same" and "It Does Not Matter" on Leadership Questions.

stereotypes, but (except in Guyana, Trinidad and Tobago, Haiti, and Guatemala) those reporting stereotypes tend to favor women leaders in both performance areas.

Were respondents self-censoring? If social desirability leads citizens to overstate neutrality, the effect may be somewhat weaker with male interviewers. Bivariate analysis provides minor evidence of interviewer effects. Having a male interviewer decreases the percentages saying women are better at the economy from 29% to 26%, and it decreases neutral responses from 59% to 58%. It is not significantly associated with responses on corruption.

What leads to gendered leadership stereotypes? We had hypothesized that both positive pro-female stereotypes and rejection of stereotypes would be positively associated with a

Table 1. Hierarchical multinomial logit models: determinants of gendered leadership stereotypes in the Americas, 2012.

	Who is less corrupt?		Who is better at economy?	
	A woman	Both equal	A woman	Both equal
Individual-level determinants				
Leftism	0.008	0.132	0.106	**0.300****
	(0.158)	(0.153)	(0.107)	(0.098)
Support for women's labor participation	0.924***	**1.117****	0.759***	**1.032****
	(0.125)	(0.120)	(0.085)	(0.078)
Authoritarianism	0.348^	**−0.123**	−0.368**	**−0.563****
	(0.184)	(0.176)	(0.127)	(0.118)
Male interviewer	−0.099	−0.055	−0.483***	**−0.342****
	(0.093)	(0.090)	(0.061)	(0.056)
Support for democracy	0.620***	**0.323***	0.244*	−0.068
	(0.151)	(0.144)	(0.107)	(0.099)
Support for the political system	−0.291	−0.219	−0.220	−0.131
	(0.206)	(0.199)	(0.137)	(0.126)
Educational level	0.682***	0.700***	0.368**	0.443***
	(0.207)	(0.200)	(0.137)	(0.126)
Age	0.418**	0.437**	−0.037	−0.102
	(0.150)	(0.144)	(0.099)	(0.091)
Female	0.329***	**0.195***	0.850***	**0.475****
	(0.091)	(0.088)	(0.062)	(0.057)
Married/partner	0.085	0.126	0.054	0.063
	(0.088)	(0.085)	(0.060)	(0.055)
Quintile of household wealth	0.027	−0.005	−0.005	0.016
	(0.032)	(0.031)	(0.022)	(0.020)
Skin color	−0.051*	−0.061*	−0.039*	−0.040*
	(0.026)	(0.025)	(0.017)	(0.016)
Country-level determinants				
Human Development Index	2.952	1.848	1.292	0.771
	(2.256)	(1.774)	(1.153)	(1.139)
Women in legislature	0.999	−0.832	2.178***	1.566**
	(1.590)	(1.297)	(0.582)	(0.568)
Gender quota laws	0.032	−0.171	−0.212	−0.445*
	(0.374)	(0.305)	(0.203)	(0.200)
Women in labor force	1.900	1.160	2.328*	**0.270**
	(1.906)	(1.589)	(1.055)	(1.042)
Number of observations	14,092		13,932	
Number of countries	20		20	
Log likelihood	−10794.157		−12751.432	

Notes: The base outcome for each model is the pro-male response (i.e., men are less corrupt and better at the economy). Coefficients in the "both equal" equations marked in **bold** are statistically significantly different from the respective coefficients in the pro-female equations at $p < .05$. Coefficients are statistically significant at ^ $p < .10$; * $p < .05$; ** $p < .01$; *** $p < .001$. Countries included in the analysis: Argentina, Bolivia, Brazil, Chile, Colombia, Costa Rica, Dominican Republic, El Salvador, Guatemala, Guyana, Haiti, Honduras, Mexico, Nicaragua, Panama, Paraguay, Peru, Trinidad & Tobago, Uruguay, and Venezuela.

country's levels of human development, women's legislative representation, and women's labor force participation, and negatively associated with gender quotas. In Table 1 we present two hierarchical multinomial logit models (Gelman and Hill 2007). As the omitted category in both models is the pro-male response, coefficients represent determinants of choosing pro-female or neutral responses relative to pro-male ones. In the "both the same" columns, coefficients in **bold font** are significantly different from those for pro-female stereotypes at $p < .05$.[7] At the country level, corruption stereotypes are not significantly associated with any variable. However, women's legislative representation boosts both pro-female economic stereotypes and neutrality. Gender quotas *decrease* neutral responses relative to pro-male ones, while women's labor force participation *increases* pro-female relative to pro-male stereotypes.

At the individual level, we had hypothesized that women, those with more education, youth, the unmarried, and leftists would all tend to endorse both neutrality and pro-female stereotypes. We also expected that non-authoritarians and supporters of democracy would tend to choose the neutral option, while those with feminist attitudes and those dissatisfied with the political system would tend to endorse pro-female stereotypes. Results indicate that those saying men and women are the same are distinct from those giving pro-female and pro-male responses in non-centrist ways. Leftists and those most supportive of women's labor market participation tend to choose the neutral option on the economy, rather than favor women's leadership. Those rejecting stereotypes are also less authoritarian; authoritarianism actually increases pro-female responses on corruption. In partial contradiction of Hypothesis 2, however, support for democracy is associated with pro-female stereotypes, not the neutral option.

Congruent with our hypotheses, education increases pro-female and neutral responses. Women are much more likely than men to report positive stereotypes of women leaders, and somewhat more likely to *reject* stereotypes. Marriage and income are unassociated with stereotypes, while older citizens are somewhat less likely to see men as corrupt, and those with darker skin somewhat more likely to choose pro-male responses. Last, confirming the bivariate analysis, the interviewer's sex affects answers on economic leadership, but not corruption.

How do attitudes affect women's representation? Do *pro-female stereotypes* or *neutrality* more effectively promote women's inclusion? We had hypothesized that both those rejecting stereotypes and those with pro-female stereotypes would be more likely to vote for women candidates, but that those rejecting stereotypes would fail to support gender quotas. In Figure 2, we present bivariate relationships between leadership stereotypes and two outcome measures. We code a single categorical variable distinguishing those who give two pro-female, two pro-male, or two neutral responses, or an ambivalent combination (pro-female-neutral, pro-male-neutral, or pro-female-pro-male). Comparing consistent pro-female to consistent pro-male respondents, support for gender quotas is one point higher on the one-to-seven scale and support for women candidates nineteen percentage points higher in the simple, bivariate analysis. Those rejecting stereotypes are significantly less supportive of gender quotas than either of the other groups, but they support women *candidates* at similar rates as those who are pro-female.

In Table 2 we present multivariate hierarchical models assessing how stereotypes are associated with support for gender quotas. Both pro-female and neutral responses on corruption are associated with higher support for gender quotas. However, respondents

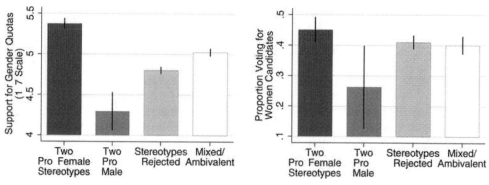

Figure 2. Consequences of Stereotyping in the Americas, 2012.

saying men and women leaders perform equally on the economy support gender quotas at the same level as those saying men are better. Turning to the other independent variables, women and committed democrats are substantially more supportive of gender quotas. Controlling for other variables, however, those supporting women's equal labor force participation actually have *lower* support for legislative gender quotas. None of the country-level variables – even the actual presence of gender quota laws – is significantly associated with support for gender quotas.[8]

In Table 3, we assess determinants of self-reported vote for a woman versus a man in the eight countries with women candidates in the most recent presidential election. The first column presents a non-interactive model. Across these countries, corruption stereotypes are unassociated with prior vote choice, while pro-female stereotypes on the

Table 2. Hierarchical model: determinants of support for legislative gender quotas.

	Coefficient	Standard error
A woman is less corrupt	0.443***	0.077
Both equal on corruption	0.327***	0.077
A woman better on economy	0.375***	0.053
Both equal on economy	0.024	0.050
Support for women's labor participation	−0.273***	0.047
Authoritarianism	0.111^	0.066
Male interviewer	−0.047	0.034
Support for democracy	0.856***	0.057
Leftism	0.025	0.058
Educational level	0.044	0.074
Age	−0.078	0.054
Woman	0.309***	0.033
Married/common law married	−0.001	0.032
Quintiles of wealth	−0.006	0.012
Skin color	−0.003	0.010
Human Development Index	−0.706	2.190
Women in legislature	1.006	1.553
Gender quota laws	0.207	0.364
Constant	4.088*	1.636
Number of observations	*13,437*	
Number of countries	*20*	
R-squared	*0.0506*	

Notes: Coefficients are statistically significant at ^ $p < .10$; * $p < .05$; ** $p < .01$; *** $p < .001$.

Table 3. Hierarchical logistic regression models: determinants of voting for women politicians.

	(1)	(2)
Women less corrupt	−0.239	−0.189
	(0.248)	(0.259)
Both equal on corruption	−0.222	−0.202
	(0.246)	(0.250)
Women better on economy	0.366*	0.383*
	(0.152)	(0.174)
Both equal on economy	0.150	0.191
	(0.143)	(0.161)
In-party supporter		2.461***
		(0.413)
Women better economy*in-party		−0.680
		(0.462)
Equal on economy*in-party		−0.192
		(0.448)
Out-party supporter		−1.256***
		(0.145)
Woman	0.355***	0.341***
	(0.087)	(0.093)
Education	−0.511*	−0.501*
	(0.202)	(0.217)
Age	−0.243	−0.340*
	(0.153)	(0.164)
Married/common law married	0.064	0.07
	(0.091)	(0.097)
Quintiles of wealth	0.003	−0.005
	(0.032)	(0.034)
Skin color	0.014	0.02
	(0.025)	(0.026)
Number of observations	*3567*	*3567*
Number of countries	*8*	*8*
Log likelihood	*−1753.30*	*−1553.78*

Notes: Models based only on Argentina, Brazil, Costa Rica, Guatemala, Haiti, Panama, Paraguay, and Peru. Coefficients are statistically significant at $^\wedge p < .10$; $* p < .05$; $** p < .01$; $*** p < .001$.

economy are associated with an increased probability of voting for a woman. Those who say the genders are equal on the economy are somewhat but not significantly more likely to say they voted for a woman than those with pro-male stereotypes. In addition, women are more likely than men to support women candidates, confirming findings from Europe and the Americas (Fulton 2014; Goodyear-Grant and Croskill 2011; Holli and Wass 2010; Morgan 2015; Paolino 1995; Seltzer, Newman, and Leighton 1997; Simon and Hoyt 2008).

Do results vary from one country to another? We had hypothesized that pro-female stereotypes would more strongly affect vote choice among non-partisans and in races with a single viable woman. In eight countries, developing hierarchical models is risky, but we run analysis within each country. We find gender stereotypes are associated with vote choice *only* in Costa Rica, and weakly in Argentina.[9] In the former, the effects are quite large (see Table 4). In the latter, *neutrality* significantly raises the probability of voting for a woman, but *pro-female stereotypes* do not. So why were stereotypes associated with voting only in Costa Rica and Argentina? Recall that these are two of the three countries in which women won the presidency. In Brazil, the third country, candidate Dilma Rousseff's third place competitor was also a woman. The presence of two strong, arguably viable women candidates within one race may have reduced the salience of gendered leadership stereotypes. In Argentina and Costa Rica, stereotypes might also have been activated by quotas that led to high women's legislative representation but

Table 4. Predicted probability of voting for a woman candidate, by gendered leadership stereotypes.

	Man better at economy	Woman better	Both the same
Guatemala 2011	0.03	0.04	0.05
Costa Rica 2010	0.46	0.81	0.72
Panama 2009	0.34	0.23	0.26
Peru 2011	0.27	0.31	0.31
Paraguay 2008	0.20	0.27	0.14
Brazil 2010	0.82	0.80	0.76
Argentina 2011	0.77	0.83	0.88
Haiti 2010/2011	0.12	0.16	0.13

Note: Results are from individual-country logistic regression models.

emphasized special treatment of women candidates (Franceschet and Piscopo 2008). Though Brazil has gender quotas, they have been extraordinarily ineffective in that country (dos Santos and Wylie, Forthcoming). In the remaining countries, by contrast, women candidates might not have been salient enough in many voters' choice sets to activate stereotypes.

Returning to the pooled model, we hypothesize that partisanship conditions the effect of stereotypes. In weak party systems, controlling for partisanship can understate the effect of stereotypes because partisanship is often endogenous to vote choice. Still, interactive analysis provides the opportunity to verify US-based findings that gender stereotypes matter less among partisans. The second column of Table 3 indicates gender stereotypes do not matter for copartisans of the woman candidate, while they *do* affect gendered voting among independents and out-party supporters.[10] Among independents, the probability of voting for a woman is .29 for those who believe male leaders are better on the economy, but .37 and .33 for those with pro-female and neutral views. Effects among out-partisans are larger than among non-partisans, though differences are not statistically significant. Among these countries, levels of partisanship vary from 18% (in Peru) to 58% (in Paraguay); in the broader sample, the US and the Dominican Republic are tied for the highest partisanship, at 63%. Thus, varying party systems could lead to variation in the impact of stereotypes.

Conclusion

To what extent do citizens of the Americas hold gendered leadership stereotypes, and what are the consequences for representation? We report three sets of findings. First, most citizens reject gendered leadership stereotypes, at least on some indicators. Of those who *do* accept stereotypes, the majority support women's leadership, though we cannot fully rule out social desirability bias. These data do not measure the full range of gendered leadership stereotypes, but they do represent a great range of countries. We find substantial cross-national variation in stereotyping; rejection of stereotypes is most pronounced in the US and Panama, and least in the Dominican Republic.

Second, stereotypes vary systematically by women's labor force participation, legislative representation, and gender quota laws. At the individual level, those saying "both are the same" are more leftist, more likely to oppose labor market preferences for men, and less authoritarian than those saying women leaders are superior. Meanwhile, women and committed democrats tend to choose pro-female over neutral responses.

Third, we examine the consequences of gendered leadership stereotypes. In pooled analysis, pro-female stereotypes boost support for gender quotas, but rejecting stereotypes is associated with lower support for quotas. Both pro-female *and* neutral responses are associated with voting for women candidates when ones are available. However, the association between stereotypes and voting for women varies cross-nationally. It may be highest when women candidates are viable and salient, yet are positioned as gendered outsiders. Relatively low partisanship can also exacerbate the impact of gendered leadership stereotypes.

What are the lessons for institutional designers? Previous studies identify a combination of legislative institutions highly effective in boosting women's representation: closed list proportional representation, gender quotas, and strong parties. Yet the present study highlights concerns. Gender quotas can exacerbate stereotypic thinking about women leaders, while support for gender quotas may be inhibited by norms of equality. Thus, a challenge faces proponents of gender quotas: to frame quotas to appeal to the majority of citizens who support – at least in principle – gender equality in political leadership.

And what about party strategies? In only 8 of the 16 presidential systems studied did women candidates receive more than tiny vote shares. Even in those eight countries, male candidates greatly outnumbered women, and less than half of citizens who preferred women leaders on both issues voted for women candidates. Promoting women's leadership, then, requires attention to elite recruitment. Major parties considering nominating women may find the experiences of major women presidential candidates in the Americas instructive. It is telling that gendered stereotypes have affected voting for women only in certain conditions, and that even in those cases, women won. Women candidates may find it especially helpful to seek advantages on issues traditionally viewed as men's strengths (e.g., Schneider 2014). Thus, a lesson from studies in the US also applies to presidential politics across the hemisphere: when women run, they can win.

Notes

1. The questions were omitted entirely in Canada, which consequently is excluded from all analysis.
2. The only parliamentary countries with women party heads were Trinidad and Tobago and Jamaica. The presidential elections with women candidates that are excluded are Mexico, Colombia, Ecuador, and Bolivia; the woman candidates are Patricia Mercado, from Mexico's Social Democratic and Peasant Alternative Party (0.4% of reported votes); Noemí Sanín, from Colombia's Conservative Party (1.6%); Martha Roldos Bucaram, from Ecuador's Ethics and Democracy Network (1.5%) and Melba Jacome, from Ecuador's Fertile Earth Movement (0.3%); and Ana María Flores, from Bolivia's Movement for Patriotic Social Unity (0.1%).
3. One might wonder about the interaction between gender and incumbency (e.g., Shair-Rosenfield 2012; Shair-Rosenfield and Hinojosa 2014). In the 17 presidential elections here (including US 2008), it is difficult to draw inferences on this issue. Among the eight incumbent candidates, the lone woman and six of the seven men were reelected. Among non-incumbents from the incumbent party, two of the five men and two of the four women were elected.
4. *Human development* is from the UNDP Human Development Index (2012). *Labor force participation* is from the World Bank (2012), and is rescaled as a proportion (i.e., to run from 0 to 1): http://data.worldbank.org/indicator/SL.TLF.CACT.FE.ZS. *Women in the legislature* is

from the Inter-Parliamentary Union (March 2012), and is also rescaled as a proportion: http://www.ipu.org/wmn-e/arc/classif310312.htm. Gender quotas are coded by the Quota Project, http://www.quotaproject.org.

5. Non-response on ideology is relatively high (19%). Personal and contextual variables affect non-response (Ames and Smith 2010; Harbers, de Vries, and Steenbergen 2013; Zechmeister and Corral 2013). To include non-respondents, we assign them a value of 5.5 (the midpoint). Results are similar if we exclude them or simply use dummy variables for the scale endpoints.

6. Sixteen and seventeen-year-olds were included only in countries where they are considered of majority age and have voting rights.

7. The US, Belize, Ecuador, Jamaica, and Suriname are excluded due to missing data. Countries included in each analysis are listed in table notes.

8. The country-level coefficients remain statistically insignificant when entered individually.

9. Standard errors may be inflated due to small samples, yet coefficients are also small in most countries.

10. This interactive effect is also evident in Costa Rica.

Acknowledgements

Thanks to the Latin American Public Opinion Project (LAPOP) and its major supporters (the United States Agency for International Development, the United Nations Development Program, the Inter-American Development Bank, and Vanderbilt University) for making the data available. The data utilized here are publicly available at http:www.lapopsurveys.org.

Disclosure statement

No potential conflict of interest was reported by the authors.

References

Aguilar, Rosario, Saul Cunow, and Scott Desposato. 2015. "Choice Sets, Gender, and Candidate Choice in Brazil." *Electoral Studies* 39: 230–242.

Alexander, Deborah, and Kristi Andersen. 1993. "Gender as a Factor in the Attribution of Leadership Traits." *Political Research Quarterly* 46 (3): 527–545.

Ames, Barry, and Amy Erica Smith. 2010. "Knowing Left from Right: Ideological Identification in Brazil, 2002–2006." *Journal of Politics in Latin America* 2 (3): 3–38.

Banaszak, Lee Ann, and Eric Plutzer. 1993. "Contextual Determinants of Feminist Attitudes: National and Subnational Influences in Western Europe." *American Political Science Review* 87 (1): 145–157.

Batista Pereira, Frederico. 2015. "Electoral Rules and Aversive Sexism: When Does Voter Bias Affect Female Candidates?" Unpublished manuscript.

Bauer, Nichole M. 2015a. "Who Stereotypes Female Candidates? Identifying Individual Differences in Feminine Stereotype Reliance." *Politics, Groups, and Identities* 3 (1): 94–110.

Bauer, Nichole M. 2015b. "Emotional, Sensitive, and Unfit for Office? Gender Stereotype Activation and Support Female Candidates." *Political Psychology* 36 (6): 691–708.

Bhavnani, Rikhil R. 2009. "Do Electoral Quotas Work after They Are Withdrawn? Evidence from a Natural Experiment in India." *American Political Science Review* 103 (1): 23–35.

Booth, John A., and Mitchell A. Seligson. 2009. *The Legitimacy Puzzle in Latin America: Political Support and Democracy in Eight Latin American Nations*. Cambridge: Cambridge University Press.

Bos, Angela L. 2015. "The Unintended Effects of Political Party Affirmative Action Policies on Female Candidates' Nomination Chances." *Politics, Groups, and Identities* 3 (1): 73–93.

Brooks, Deborah. 2013. *He Runs, She Runs: Why Gender Stereotypes Do Not Harm Women Candidates*. Princeton, NJ: Princeton University Press.

Brown, Elizabeth R., Amanda B. Diekman, and Monica C. Schneider. 2011. "A Change Will Do Us Good: Threats Diminish Typical Preferences for Male Leaders." *Personality and Social Psychology Bulletin* 37 (7): 930–941.

Córdova, Abby. 2009. *Methodological Note. Measuring Relative Wealth Using Household Asset Indicators. AmericasBarometer Insights*. Nashville, TN: Latin American Public Opinion Project, Vanderbilt University.

Dépret, Eric, and Susan T. Fiske. 1993. "Social Cognition and Power: Some Cognitive Consequences of Social Structure as a Source of Control Deprivation." In *Control Motivation and Social Cognition*, edited by Gifford Weary, Faith Gleicher, and Kerry L. Marsh, 176–202. New York: Springer.

Devine, Patricia G. 1989. "Stereotypes and Prejudice: Their Automatic and Controlled Components." *Journal of Personality and Social Psychology* 56 (1): 5–18.

Devine, Patricia G., E. Ashby, David M. Amodio, Eddie Harmon-Jones, and Stephanie L. Vance. 2002. "The Regulation of Explicit and Implicit Race Bias: The Role of Motivations to Respond without Prejudice." *Journal of Personality and Social Psychology* 82 (5): 835–848.

Diamond, Irene. 1977. *Sex Roles in the State House*. New Haven, CT: Yale University Press.

Diekman, Amanda B., Alice H. Eagly, Antonio Mladinic, and Maria Cristina Ferreira. 2005. "Dynamic Stereotypes about Women and Men in Latin America and the United States." *Journal of Cross-Cultural Psychology* 36 (2): 209–226.

Ditonto, Tessa, Allison Hamilton, and David Redlawsk. 2014. "Gender Stereotypes, Information Search, and Voting Behavior in Political Campaigns." *Political Behavior* 36 (2): 335–358.

Dolan, Kathleen. 2004. *Voting for Women: How the Public Evaluates Women Candidates*. Boulder, CO: Westview Press.

Dolan, Kathleen. 2010. "The Impact of Gender Stereotypes Evaluations on Support for Women Candidates." *Political Behavior* 32 (1): 69–88.

Dolan, Kathleen. 2014. *When Does Gender Matter?* New York: Oxford University Press.

Dolan, Kathleen, and Timothy Lynch. 2015. "Making the Connection? Attitudes about Women in Politics and Voting for Women Candidates." *Politics, Groups, and Identities* 3 (1): 111–132.

dos Santos, Pedro G., and Kristin Wylie. Forthcoming. "A Law on Paper Only: Electoral Rules, Parties, and the Persistent Underrepresentation of Women in Brazilian Legislatures." *Politics & Gender*.

Eagly, Alice H., and Steven J. Karau. 2002. "Role Congruity Theory of Prejudice Toward Female Leaders." *Psychological Review* 109 (3): 573–598.

Feldman, Stanley. 1988. "Structure and Consistency in Public Opinion: The Role of Core Beliefs and Values." *American Journal of Political Science* 32 (2): 416–440.

Fiske, Susan T. 1993. "Controlling Other People: The Impact of Power on Stereotyping." *The American Psychologist* 48 (6): 621–628.

Franceschet, Susan, and Jennifer M. Piscopo. 2008. "Gender Quotas and Women's Substantive Representation: Lessons from Argentina." *Politics & Gender* 4 (3): 393–425.

Fridkin, Kim L., and Patrick J. Kenney. 2014. *The Changing Face of Representation: The Gender of U.S. Senators and Constituent Communications*. Ann Arbor: University of Michigan Press.

Fullerton, Andrew S., and Michael J. Stern. 2010. "Explaining the Persistence and Eventual Decline of the Gender Gap in Voter Registration and Turnout in the American South, 1956–1980." *Social Science History* 34 (2): 129–169.

Fulton, Sarah. 2012. "Running Backwards and in High Heels: The Gendered Quality Gap and Incumbent Electoral Success." *Political Research Quarterly* 65 (2): 303–314.

Fulton, Sarah. 2014. "When Gender Matters: Macro-Dynamics and Micro-Mechanisms." *Political Behavior* 36 (3): 605–630.

Gelman, Andrew, and Jennifer Hill. 2007. *Data Analysis Using Regression and Multilevel/Hierarchical Models*. Cambridge: Cambridge University Press.

Goodyear-Grant, Elizabeth, and Julie Croskill. 2011. "Gender Affinity Effects in Vote Choice in Westminster Systems: Assessing 'Flexible' Voters in Canada." *Politics & Gender* 7 (2): 223–250.

Haidt, Jonathan. 2012. *The Righteous Mind: Why Good People Are Divided by Politics and Religion*. New York: Pantheon Books.

Harbers, Imke, Catherine E. de Vries, and Marco R. Steenbergen. 2013. "Attitude Variability Among Latin American Publics: How Party System Structuration Affects Left/Right Ideology." *Comparative Political Studies* 46 (8): 946–967.

Hawkesworth, Mary. 2012. *Political Worlds of Women: Activism, Advocacy, and Governance in the Twenty-First Century*. Boulder, CO: Westview Press.

Hayes, Bernadette C. 1993. "Partisanship and Political Attitudes: Is There a Marriage Gap?" *Australian Journal of Political Science* 28 (2): 242–257.

Hetherington, Marc J., and Jonathan Weiler. 2009. *Authoritarianism and Polarization in American Politics*. Cambridge: Cambridge University Press.

Hietanen, Anna-Emilia, and Susan Pick. 2015. "Gender Stereotypes, Sexuality, and Culture in Mexico." In *Psychology of Gender Through the Lens of Culture*, edited by Saba Safdar, and Natasza Kosakowska-Berezecka, 285–305. Cham: Springer International.

Hinojosa, Magda. 2012. *Selecting Women, Electing Women: Political Representation and Candidate Selection in Latin America*. Philadelphia: Temple University Press.

Hinojosa, Magda, and Susan Franceschet. 2012. "Separate but Not Equal: The Effects of Municipal Electoral Reform on Female Representation in Chile." *Political Research Quarterly* 65 (4): 758–770.

Holli, Anne Maria, and Hanna Wass. 2010. "Gender-Based Voting in the Parliamentary Elections of 2007 in Finland." *European Journal of Political Research* 49 (5): 598–630.

Holman, Mirya R., Jennifer L. Merolla, and Elizabeth J. Zechmeister. 2011. "Sex, Stereotypes, and Security: A Study of the Effects of Terrorist Threat on Assessments of Female Leadership." *Journal of Women, Politics & Policy* 32 (3): 173–192.

Huddy, Leonie, and Nayda Terkildsen. 1993. "Gender Stereotypes and the Perception of Male and Female Candidates." *American Journal of Political Science* 37 (1): 119–147.

Hughes, Melanie M., Mona Lena Krook, and Pamela Paxton. 2015. "Transnational Women's Activism and the Global Diffusion of Gender Quotas." *International Studies Quarterly*. doi:10.1111/isqu.12190.

Inglehart, Ronald, and Pippa Norris. 2003. *Rising Tide: Gender Equality and Cultural Change Around the World*. New York: Cambridge University Press.

Inter-Parliamentary Union. 2012. *Women in Politics: 2012*. http://www.ipu.org/wmn-e/pdf/publications/wmnmap12_en-.pdf.

Inter-Parliamentary Union. 2015. *Women's Suffrage*. June. http://www.ipu.org.

Jalalzai, Farida. 2008. "Women Rule: Shattering the Executive Glass Ceiling." *Politics & Gender* 4 (2): 1–27.

Jalalzai, Farida. 2016. *Women Presidents of Latin America: Beyond Family Ties?* New York: Routledge.

Jalalzai, Farida, and Pedro G. dos Santos. 2015. "The Dilma Effect? Women's Representation under Dilma Rousseff's Presidency." *Politics & Gender* 11 (1): 117–145.

Jones, Mark P. 2009. "Gender Quotas, Electoral Laws, and the Election of Women: Evidence from the Latin American Vanguard." *Comparative Political Studies* 42 (1): 56–81.

Kahn, Kim Fridkin. 1996. *The Political Consequences of Being a Woman: How Stereotypes Influence the Conduct and Consequences of Political Campaigns*. New York: Cambridge University Press.

Kenworthy, Lane, and Melissa Malami. 1999. "Gender Inequality in Political Representation: A Worldwide Comparative Analysis." *Social Forces* 78 (1): 235–268.

Kerevel, Yann P., and Lonna Rae Atkeson. 2015. "Reducing Stereotypes of Female Political Leaders in Mexico." *Political Research Quarterly* 68 (4): 732–744.

Kish, Leslie. 1965. *Survey Sampling*. New York: Wiley.

Koch, Jeffrey. 2000. "Do Citizens Apply Gender Stereotypes to Infer Candidates' Ideological Orientations?" *The Journal of Politics* 62: 414–429.

Krook, Mona Lena. 2009. *Quotas for Women in Politics: Gender and Candidate Selection Reform Worldwide*. New York: Oxford University Press.

Krupnikov, Yanna, Spencer Piston, and Nichole M. Bauer. 2016. "Saving Face: Identifying Voter Responses to Black Candidates and Female Candidates." *Political Psychology* 37 (2): 253–273.

Lawless, Jennifer. 2004. "Women, War, and Winning Elections: Gender Stereotypes in the Post-September 11th Era." *Political Research Quarterly* 57 (3): 479–490.

McAllister, Ian, and Donley T. Studlar. 2002. "Electoral Systems and Women's Representation: A Long-Term Perspective." *Representation* 39 (1): 3–14.

McDermott, Monika L. 1998. "Race and Gender Cues in Low-Information Elections." *Political Research Quarterly* 51 (4): 895–918.

Morgan, Jana. 2015. "Gender and the Latin American Voter." In *The Latin American Voter*, edited by Ryan E. Carlin, Matthew Singer, and Elizabeth Zechmeister, 143–167. Ann Arbor: University of Michigan Press.

Morgan, Jana, and Melissa Buice. 2013. "Latin American Attitudes Toward Women in Politics: The Influence of Elite Cues, Female Advancement, and Individual Characteristics." *American Political Science Review* 107 (4): 644–662.

Moskowitz, Gordon B., and Peizhong Li. 2011. "Egalitarian Goals Trigger Stereotype Inhibition: A Proactive Form of Stereotype Control." *Journal of Experimental Social Psychology* 47 (2011): 103–116.

Muller, Edward N. 1979. *Aggressive Political Participation*. Princeton: Princeton University Press.

O'Donnell, Guillermo. 1994. "Delegative Democracy?" *Journal of Democracy* 5: 55–69.

Paolino, Phillip. 1995. "Group-Salient Issues and Group Representation: Support for Women Candidates in the 1992 Senate Elections." *American Journal of Political Science* 39 (2): 294–313.

Paxton, Pamela, and Melanie M. Hughes. 2007. *Women, Politics, and Power: A Global Perspective*. Thousand Oaks, CA: Pine Forge Press/Sage.

Paxton, Pamela, and Sheri Kunovich. 2003. "Women's Political Representation: The Importance of Ideology." *Social Forces* 82 (1): 87–113.

Presser, Stanley, and Michael Traugott. 1992. "Little White Lies and Social Science Models: Correlated Response Errors in a Panel Study of Voting." *Public Opinion Quarterly* 56: 77–86.

Quota Project. 2013. "Global Database of Quotas for Women." International Institute for Democracy and Electoral Assistance (IDEA), Inter-Parliamentary Union, and Stockholm University. http://www.quotaproject.org.

Ríos-Tobar, Marcela. 2008. "Seizing a Window of Opportunity: The Election of President Bachelet in Chile." *Politics & Gender* 4 (3): 509–519.

Sanbonmatsu, Kira. 2003. "Political Knowledge and Gender Stereotypes." *American Politics Research* 31 (6): 575–594.

Sapiro, Virginia. 1983. *The Political Integration of Women: Roles, Socialization, and Politics*. Urbana: University of Illinois Press.

Schaller, Mark, Carrie Boyd, Jonathan Yohannes, and Meredith O'Brien. 1995. "The Prejudiced Personality Revisited: Personal Need for Structure and Formation of Erroneous Group Stereotypes." *Journal of Personality and Social Psychology* 68 (3): 544–555.

Schneider, Monica C. 2014. "The Effects of Gender-Bending on Candidate Evaluations." *Journal of Women, Politics & Policy* 35 (1): 55–77.

Schneider, Monica C., and Angela L. Bos. 2014. "Measuring Stereotypes of Female Politicians." *Political Psychology* 35 (2): 245–266.

Schwindt-Bayer, Leslie A. 2010. *Political Power and Women's Representation in Latin America*. New York: Oxford University Press.

Sears, David O., P. J. Henry, and Rick Kosterman. 2000. "Egalitarian Values and Contemporary Racial Politics." In *Racialized Politics: The Debate about Racism in America*, edited by David O. Sears, Jim Sidanius, and Lawrence Bobo, 75–117. Chicago, IL: University of Chicago Press.

Seligson, Mitchell A., Amy Erica Smith, and Elizabeth J. Zechmeister, ed. 2012. *The Political Culture of Democracy in the Americas, 2012: Toward Equality of Opportunity*. Nashville, TN: Latin American Public Opinion Project.

Seltzer, Richard, Jody Newman, and Melissa Voorhees Leighton. 1997. *Sex as a Political Variable: Women as Candidates and Voters in U.S. Elections*. Boulder: Lynne Rienner.

Shair-Rosenfield, Sarah. 2012. "The Alternative Incumbency Effect: Electing Women Legislators in Indonesia." *Electoral Studies* 31 (3): 576–587.

Shair-Rosenfield, Sarah, and Magda Hinojosa. 2014. "Does Female Incumbency Reduce Gender Bias in Elections? Evidence from Chile." *Political Research Quarterly* 67 (4): 837–850.

Sherman, Jeffrey W., C. Neil Macrae, and Galen V. Bodenhausen. 2000. "Attention and Stereotyping: Cognitive Constraints on the Construction of Meaningful Social Impressions." *European Review of Social Psychology* 11 (1): 145–175.

Simon, Stefanie, and Crystal L. Hoyt. 2008. "Exploring the Gender Gap in Support for a Woman for President." *Analyses of Social Issues and Public Policy* 8 (1): 157–181.

Smith, Amy Erica. 2009. "Legitimate Grievances: Preferences for Democracy, System Support, and Political Participation in Bolivia." *Latin American Research Review* 44 (3): 102–126.

Winter, Nicholas J. G. 2010. "Masculine Republicans and Feminine Democrats: Gender and Americans' Explicit and Implicit Images of the Political Parties." *Political Behavior* 32 (4): 587–618.

Zechmeister, Elizabeth, and Margarita Corral. 2013. "Individual and Contextual Constraints on Ideological Labels in Latin America." *Comparative Political Studies* 46 (6): 675–701.

Appendix

Table A1. Percentages choosing each response, AmericasBarometer 2012

	Which more corrupt?			Which better on economy?			% supporting gender quotas
	A man	A woman	Both the same	A man	A woman	It does not matter	
Argentina	23.3	2.7	74.0	13.4	21.0	65.6	68.4
Belize	25.9	7.7	66.4	12.2	28.2	59.6	63.3
Bolivia	37.8	3.7	58.4	14.9	36.8	48.3	61.7
Brazil	37.2	1.1	61.6	8.6	25.1	66.3	48.4
Chile	26.5	4.9	68.6	9.5	35.5	54.9	74.8
Colombia	40.6	6.4	52.9	6.7	47.4	45.9	74.0
Costa Rica	25.1	2.9	72.0	7.8	22.3	69.9	63.1
Dom. Republic	65.2	2.9	31.8	20.7	41.5	37.8	81.1
Ecuador	31.3	6.6	62.1	12.4	32.7	54.9	69.1
El Salvador	21.0	1.7	77.3	9.6	17.6	72.7	84.7
Guatemala	21.6	2.2	76.2	16.5	15.6	67.9	54.0
Guyana	29.3	17.3	53.4	27.9	19.5	52.5	66.9
Haiti	24.5	6.4	69.1	18.9	19.3	61.8	52.0
Honduras	26.8	9.6	63.6	11.7	38.2	50.1	54.9
Jamaica	32.2	2.7	65.0	13.3	21.2	65.5	50.6
Mexico	41.8	4.4	53.8	11.7	33.5	54.8	64.9
Nicaragua	36.6	6.3	57.1	13.0	29.0	58.0	72.5
Panama	20.2	9.1	70.8	9.0	19.9	71.2	56.0
Paraguay	38.5	2.1	59.4	11.5	39.4	49.1	79.6
Peru	43.9	3.0	53.1	14.3	42.9	42.8	53.8
Suriname	25.9	6.0	68.1	7.5	27.8	64.7	62.3
Trinidad & Tobago	29.4	8.9	61.7	21.1	19.5	59.4	39.1
US	25.5	1.4	73.2	5.3	10.1	84.6	N/A
Uruguay	24.2	1.1	74.7	7.6	23.1	69.3	77.8
Venezuela	39.2	5.2	55.6	18.6	35.0	46.4	58.3

Notes: Means are adjusted for complex survey sample design. The item on gender quotas was not asked in the U.S. Those who choose responses of 5, 6, or 7 on a 1–7 scale are coded as supporting gender quotas.

Table A2. Women presidential candidates analyzed.

Country	Year of election	Candidate	Party	% of respondents	Actual vote %	Incumbent candidate/ party?	Won?
Argentina	2011	Cristina Fernández de Kirchner	Frente para la Victoria/ Partido Justicialista	81.5	54.12	Incumbent candidate	Yes
Brazil	2010	Dilma Rousseff	PT, PMDB, PDT, PCdoB, PSB	68.4	46.91	Incumbent party	Yes
Brazil	2010	Marina Silva	Partido Verde	7.7	19.33	Neither	
Costa Rica	2010	Laura Chinchilla	PLN	68.0	46.90	Incumbent party	Yes
Guatemala	2011	Adela de Torrebiarte	Partido Accion de Desarrollo Nacional	0.4	0.42	Neither	
Guatemala	2011	Patricia de Arzu	Partido Unionista	1.1	2.19	Neither	
Guatemala	2011	Rigoberta Menchu	Winaq/Urng/ann – Frente Amplio	3.0	3.22	Neither	
Haiti	2010/ 2011	Josette Bijou	Independent	0.3	1.00	Neither	
Haiti	2010/ 2011	Mirlande Marigat	RDNP (Rassemblement des Démocrates Nationaux Progressistes)	14.3	31.37	Neither	
Panama	2009	Balbina Herrera	Partido Revolucionario Democrático	31.1	37.54	Incumbent party	
Paraguay	2008	Blanca Ovelar	Asociación Nacional Republicana (Partido Colorado)	21.3	30.70	Incumbent party	
Peru	2011	Keiko Fujimori	Fuerza 2011	29.1	23.57	Neither	

Using experiments to understand public attitudes towards transgender rights

Brian F. Harrison and Melissa R. Michelson

ABSTRACT

While lesbian, gay, and bisexual Americans have seen recent legal victories and declining explicit discrimination, transgender and gender non-conforming individuals (TGNC) remain astoundingly vulnerable. An area of recent public debate is the right of transgender individuals to use the bathroom that corresponds to their gender identity, regardless of the sex they were assigned at birth. Little is known, however, about how the public forms their views of transgender people and rights, particularly the issue of bathroom access. Our research agenda seeks to better understand public attitudes about transgender bathroom access. In this paper, we describe our use of experiments to investigate how issue framing and identity priming affects public opinion toward the key transgender right of bathroom access and provide results from a recent pilot study.

While lesbian, gay, and bisexual Americans have seen recent legal victories and declining explicit discrimination, there are fewer legal victories and less support for the rights of transgender and gender non-conforming (TGNC) individuals. The term transgender refers to people whose gender identity is different from the sex they were assigned at birth. Gender non-conforming people do not adhere to stereotypes or expectations from others about how they should behave or look based on the sex they were assigned at birth (Sylvia Rivera Law Project, n.d.).

TGNC people are astoundingly vulnerable to explicit discrimination, unemployment, detachment from family structures and social institutions, drug and alcohol abuse, homelessness, extreme poverty, suicide, and violence. A 2011 survey of self-identified TGNC individuals found that 63% had experienced at least one serious act of discrimination that would have a major impact on a person's quality of life (Grant et al. 2011). TGNC people also remain a largely invisible population: one recent poll found that almost 25% of Americans do not know what the term "transgender" means and another found that only 8% of Americans say they personally know someone who is transgender. Overall, little is known about how the public forms their views of transgender people and rights. We recently launched a research agenda focused on better understanding public attitudes toward the rights of transgender people and in particular, their right to use the bathroom that corresponds to their gender identity.

In 1995, a group of transgender activists issued the International Bill of Gender Rights which claimed that transgender bathroom rights stem from the right of all individuals to free expression of their self-defined gender identity (www.transgenderlegal.com/ibgr.htm). Resistance to bathroom access rights has sprung from disparate points on the political spectrum. Opponents on the right see access as indecent, incompatible with privacy rights, and as giving sexual predators access to children, while some feminist scholars argue that transgender bathroom access rights deny the reality of male domination and forget that women's toilets are "essential to women's equality" (Jeffreys 2014, 46). Cavanaugh (2010, 30) claimed this opposition is rooted in transphobia and homophobia:

> There seems to be a fetishistic quality to the obsessive interest in the gender of bathroom users. Separating bodies by urinary capacities – real and imagined – is a way to ensure sexual difference when our bodies do not always lend themselves to absolute and exacting divisions by gender.

Our research agenda, grounded in theory and methods from political science, communication, and social psychology, seeks to better understand public attitudes about transgender bathroom access and how framing the issue in different ways affects those attitudes. In short, we want to test how to increase support for the protection of transgender bodies by changing the attitudes of people in non-transgender bodies, people who may not be aware of or concerned about transgender people in the first place. Or, to put it another way, "How do bodies that do not matter become bodies that matter?" (Boyd 2006, 136).

Our research methodology combines traditional sources of public opinion and political communication – framing and priming – with the relatively newer method of testing causal relationships – randomized experiments. Specifically, we use randomized experiments to expose participants to common frames and to identity primes expected to shape attitudes toward transgender bathroom rights and then measure their support for those rights. Observed differences in support can then be attributed to the framing assignment or the primed identity, providing insight into what shapes those attitudes and how advocates might seek to change them. We hypothesize that elements of the public debate (i.e., issue framing) are strongly determinant of overall attitudes toward transgender people and that awareness of and concern for transgender rights and bodies can be affected by framing that makes their bodies matter, for example, if their bodies become sites of contention over American core values of freedom and equality or of public safety.

After a brief discussion of experiments generally, we discuss how they can be used to investigate questions about identity politics, specifically about attitudes toward transgender people and rights. Finally, we present the results of a pilot survey experiment and discuss its implications and the future of our research agenda.

Experiments as identity politics methodology

Randomized experiments have experienced an explosion of interest in the past 15 years, sparked by a get-out-the-vote experiment conducted in New Haven in 1998 (Gerber and Green 2000). Since then, thousands of randomized experiments have been conducted by scholars to test causal theories about not just voter turnout but a range of constructs, including the effects of persuasive communication, including mass media and interpersonal communication; identity and social group membership on public opinion; and framing on preference formation (see Druckman et al. 2011). When properly designed and executed, experiments can provide firm evidence about the causal effect of the experimental treatment in a way that cross-sectional survey data and other observational data simply cannot. While experiments are not suitable for answering every research question – they are, for example, better at testing theories than for exploring less well-understood topics, and not everything can be ethically randomized – they are a powerful methodology.

Randomized experiments are perhaps best understood as parallel to medical trials. In the medical field, controlled trials are often used to test new drugs or procedures. Individuals are recruited for a test and randomly divided into treatment and control groups. Those in the treatment group are administered the new drug or procedure while those in the control group receive a placebo such as sugar pills or sham surgeries. Subsequent differences in health outcomes between individuals in the two groups can be clearly attributed to the treatment.

Similarly, experiments in political science randomly assign individuals to receive a treatment expected to generate a change in attitude or behavior while others are randomly assigned to receive a placebo treatment or to no treatment whatsoever. Subsequent observed differences in attitudes or behavior can then be clearly attributed to the treatment message. For example, an experiment seeking to increase voter turnout might expose some individuals to a postcard or telephone blandishment to vote while those in the control group would receive either no message or one encouraging recycling (a message not expected to affect voter turnout). Thousands of randomized experiments of this sort have been conducted over the last decade, generating valuable insights in a variety of social science disciplines.

We have used a similar combination of methods to investigate attitudes toward marriage equality for same-sex couples, including the effect of framing on donations to a gay and lesbian rights organization (Harrison and Michelson 2012), the effect of religious identity priming on support for marriage equality (Harrison and Michelson 2015), and, most recently, the effect of priming a professional football fan identity on support for marriage equality (Harrison and Michelson 2016a). Working with advocacy organizations, we have used randomized experiments to explore how to use framing and priming to shift supporters of marriage equality to also engage in efforts to expand other rights to lesbian, gay, bisexual, and transgender people (Harrison and Michelson 2017). For our new research project, we use randomized experiments and the theories of priming and framing to better understand support for (or opposition to) transgender individuals and rights, including bathroom access.

Experiments in identity studies

Political scientists and scholars who engage with identity studies rarely study personality per se but rather look at self-concepts and identities and how they affect political attitudes and behavior. The "self" is a process; we construct a sense of who we are through interaction with others (Rohall, Milkie, and Lucas 2013). Identity refers to our internalized, stable sense of who we are, including role identities, social categories, and personal characteristics. Identity theory examines the ways society shapes how we view ourselves and how those views, or identities, subsequently affect our attitudes and behavior. Tajfel (1981, 255) described social identity as "that part of an individual's self-concept which derives from [her or] his membership in a social group (or groups) together with the value and emotional significance attached to that membership." In other words, our social identity is the part of our identity derived from the social groups to which we belong and to which we do not. The latter part of this formula is often the most important (Rohall, Milkie, and Lucas 2013). When a social identity is salient, individuals tend to think and act like group members (Brewer 1991) and to rely on the in-group as a guide for their own thoughts and behaviors (Terry and Hogg 1996). Social psychologists suggest that we derive self-esteem by positively differentiating our in-group from out-groups ("us" and "them") and therefore tend to categorize our social environment into groups, privileging our in-groups over our out-groups.

Social identity and attitudes are inextricably linked. Lazarsfeld, Berelson, and Gaudet (1948, 27) concluded, "a person thinks, politically, as he is socially. Social characteristics determine political preferences." As a result, the manner in which people see themselves will be an important predictor of how they view others, particularly those that may not conform to traditional concepts of identities like gender. Priming and framing are increasingly common theoretical bases to investigate identity, communication effects, and attitudinal change, with relevant extant work showing that both issues and identities can be primed and framed by both context and cues (Druckman and Holmes 2004; Chong and Druckman 2007).

First, priming theory suggests that emphasizing or highlighting an identity will increase the salience of that identity as well as increase a person's concern for identity-based interests (Iyengar and Kinder 1987; Druckman 2004; McLeish and Oxoby 2008). Further, primed attributes are more likely to serve as an overall basis of evaluation (Krosnick and Brannon 1993). Extant research on gender priming in particular has shown that gender self-concepts among both men (McCall and Dasgupta 2007) and women (Haines and Kray 2005; Rudman and Phelan 2010) can be experimentally manipulated using priming theory. For example, in one of our recently conducted experiments, we hypothesized that support for transgender bathroom access is related to individual-level gender identity and salience. We posited that priming (and threatening) a cisgender identity will be more likely to generate opposition to bathroom access among those with stronger gender identities, particularly among men (Harrison and Michelson 2016b).

Second, framing effects occur when differences in the presentation of an issue or event changes one's opinion about that issue or object; it is a process by which people orient their thinking toward an object. For example, Sniderman and Theriault (2004) showed that 85% of respondents support allowing a hate group rally when a free-speech frame is emphasized whereas support drops to 45% when the issue is framed in terms of the potential for violence. Similarly, Rasinski (1989) showed that support for government expenditures on welfare drops markedly when framed as "assistance to the poor" versus "welfare." Relatedly, Chong and Druckman (2007) presented frames in an expectancy model in which different considerations toward an object are weighted by different considerations about that object, leading to what is known as a *frame in thought*. Frames in thought are often influenced by frames in communication, defined as information that attempts to change the emphasis on different considerations toward an object. As a result, a framing effect is defined as the instance where a frame in communication influences a frame in thought, ultimately changing an evaluation toward the attitude object.

In the pilot experiment described below, we framed the issue of transgender bathroom access as either about safety or freedom. Individuals were randomly assigned to view images and storyboards about the issue, either framing it as an issue of transgender rights and important for the safety of transgender individuals (including children) or as an issue of protecting the privacy and safety of women and girls; in each case, half of the messages were supportive of transgender bathroom access rights while the other half opposed those rights. A placebo treatment condition exposed participants to an unrelated image and storyboard, about using fewer paper towels in the bathroom. Overall, our experiments investigate how (a) individuals' identities can be primed and (b) transgender rights and individuals can be framed to increase support for this marginalized and underserved group of people.

Pilot experiment: methodology

We designed an initial study to test how framing effects impact public opinion toward transgender people accessing bathrooms that correspond to their gender identity. In this online survey experiment, we expose participants to frames and then measure their levels of support. Participants are randomly assigned to one issue frame. We recruited participants through Amazon.com's Mechanical Turk (MTurk). This online tool matches employers with workers who are paid to complete tasks, often including online surveys and experiments. Berinsky, Huber, and Lenz (2012) found that while MTurk workers are younger and more ideologically liberal than the general public, the tool is a valid low-cost method of conducting experiments (also see Levay, Freese, and Druckman 2016).

We posted our survey experiment "job" to MTurk on February 24, 2016, offering payment of $0.50 for a completed survey, consistent with fair wages and best practices on the site. MTurk workers who agreed to complete the job were randomly assigned to one of five conditions (described below). All participants were then asked a set of questions about bathroom access (our dependent variables), and a few demographic questions. The experiment tested our hypothesis that framing could make transgender bodies matter in ways that increased or decreased support for transgender bathroom access rights.

The experimental conditions framed bathroom access as about either safety or freedom compared to a placebo condition that exposed participants to a statement about reducing their use of paper towels. For the safety and freedom frames, participants were further split into conditions that either framed the issue negatively (that bathroom access for transgender people would reduce safety/freedom) or positively (that bathroom access would increase safety/freedom). In sum, the purpose of the experiment was to examine how respondents answered questions about transgender bathroom choice differently depending on their random assignment to different statements framing the issue in different ways. In the safety frame in the supportive condition (Condition A), the text read:

> Keeping kids safe means allowing them to use the restroom without worrying about getting attacked or harassed. To do this, we need to allow transgender youth to use the restroom of their choice.

> Keep kids safe. Allow kids to use the restroom they prefer.

In the safety frame in the opposition condition (Condition B), the text read:

> Keeping kids safe means allowing them to use the restroom without worrying about getting attacked or harassed. To do this, we need to keep men who say they are transgender out of women's restrooms.

> Keep kids safe. Keep men out of the ladies room.

In the freedom frame in the supportive condition (Condition C), the text read:

> Transgender people should have the freedom to use the bathroom of their choice. No one should be forced to go into a bathroom they don't want to use.

> It's all about freedom. Allow everyone to choose the restroom they prefer.

In the freedom frame in the opposition condition (Condition D), the text read:

> Men and women should have the freedom to use a bathroom just for them, just for men or just for women.

> It's all about freedom. Allow everyone to choose the restroom that is just for them.

The placebo condition (Condition E) encouraged respondents to use fewer paper towels when using the bathroom; the text read:

> Using fewer paper towels when you use the restroom helps save trees and protect our planet.

> Protect our trees. Protect the world. Use fewer paper towels.

Pilot experiment: results

Overall, 443 MTurk workers completed the survey.[1] As shown in Table 1, Condition B produces the weakest level of support (50.6%), while support is strongest in the placebo condition (E) and also very strong in Condition A (67.5%). This suggests that without framing, individuals (at least, liberal-leaning MTurk workers) are open to the idea of transgender bathroom access but that anti-choice framing of the issue by opponents can easily erode that support. The results support our contention that framing can affect support for transgender bathroom rights. However, the supportive frames failed to increase support. We believe that if framing can erode support for transgender rights, it can also be used to increase that support. The key point is finding a frame that makes transgender bodies matter. Further experiments, with different frames and larger samples, are needed to further investigate how to do so.

Table 1. Support for transgender bathroom access, pilot framing experiment.

Condition	Percent supportive (N)	Percentage-point difference from placebo
(A) Safety, Pro	67.5 (52/77)	−1.8
(B) Safety, Anti	50.6 (42/83)	−18.7*
(C) Freedom, Pro	64.0 (48/75)	−5.3
(D) Freedom, Anti	59.2 (42/71)	−10.1
(E) Placebo	69.3 (57/82)	n/a

Note: Responses were collected on February 24, 2016. Overall, 443 responses were collected; 55 respondents reported having a TGNC family member or close friend and were not included in the analysis. * = $p \leq .05$, two-tailed.

Discussion and conclusion

Transgender individuals are beginning to enter public consciousness – for example, former Olympian Caitlin Jenner; imprisoned whistleblower Chelsea Manning; Laverne Cox and her character Sophia Burset on the Netflix series Orange Is the New Black. However, transgender people remain a largely unknown, invisible population, and public support for their rights, including bathroom access rights, is low includes opposition from both feminists and conservatives. Combining the powerful social science methodology of randomized experiments with theories of framing and priming, our ongoing research project on this issue promises to deliver insights on several fronts.

First, we are interested in how attitudes are formed about transgender people and rights; second, we want to extend what we learn to help advocates work to increase support for not only bathroom access rights but other transgender rights as well. Using randomized experiments allows us to identify causal relationships between gender identity and political communication. Relying on theories with deep roots in attitude change and identity allow us to add to an expansive literature on how to change minds on important social and political issues but applying the concepts to transgender individuals, a vulnerable group deserving of additional attention. As evidenced by the pilot experiment discussed here, attitudes toward transgender people are easily influenced by framing effects. In other work (Harrison and Michelson 2016b), we find these attitudes are also strongly affected by one's own gender identity and perceived threats to that identity.

We are conducting additional research to investigate the power of framing and identity priming to affect attitudes toward transgender individuals. For example, little extant research focuses on different attitudes toward male-to-female (MTF) transgender people, individuals assigned a male gender at birth but who now identify as female, compared to attitudes toward female-to-male (FTM) transgender people, individuals assigned a female gender at birth but who now identify as male. In our pilot experiment, Condition B alludes only to MTF individuals, mirroring the real-world examples of perceived threat against men invading women's spaces. One example comes from Houston, Texas. In 2014, the city council approved a city ordinance banning discrimination based on sexual orientation or gender identity: the Houston Equal Rights Ordinance (HERO). Opponents dubbed HERO the "bathroom bill" and denounced the bill as a danger to women and girls, featuring the rallying cry, "No men in women's bathrooms." Their strategy worked: HERO was repealed in a 2015 referendum with almost 70% of the popular vote.

While not a component of current real-world debates, we believe that framing could also test the effect of frames featuring FTM transgender individuals. A safety frame using the issue of bathrooms would be unlikely to be effective for the bathroom access issue given that men and boys are not generally considered endangered by the presence of FTM people in their restrooms. However, a safety frame might incorporate stereotypes about FTM members of the armed forces and an alleged threat to the nation's security of allowing them to serve, for example. Additional research should evaluate the differences in perception of threat between MTF and FTM individuals and the implications of those differences.

While body politics have traditionally been applied to the rights of women to control their own bodies, we extend it here to the rights of transgender individuals to control their own bodies and specifically their right to decide for themselves which public restrooms they want to use. It is not about their genitalia or how their physical body presents to the outside world; body politics as applied to the transgender community is about the power of individuals to have autonomy over their own bodies regardless of whether they fit easily into the existing gender binary.

Framing and identity priming allows us to better understand how the public (mis)understands transgender bodies. Future research can uncover new ways to reduce misunderstandings about those bodies and harness the power of framing and identity priming to increase equal access and rights for all. It is important to better understand the basis of public opinion toward transgender people and rights to shift conversations and minds to greater appreciation for those who do not conform to the dominant gender binary. Our methodology and theory seeks to do just that: to find the most effective ways to extend norms of body politics and rights to transgender people and to empower them to live their lives as openly and safely as possible.

Note

1. Fifty-five respondents who said that they had a TGNC family member or close friend were excluded from the analysis.

Disclosure statement

No potential conflict of interest was reported by the authors.

References

Berinsky, Adam J., Gregory A. Huber, and Gabriel S. Lenz. 2012. "Evaluating Online Labor Markets for Experimental Research: Amazon.com's Mechanical Turk." *Political Analysis* 20: 351–368.

Boyd, Nan Alamilla. 2006. "Bodies in Motion: Lesbian and Transsexual Histories." In *The Transgender Studies Reader*, edited by Susan Stryker and Stephen Whittle, 420–433. New York: Routledge.

Brewer, Marilynn B. 1991. "The Social Self: On Being the Same and Different at the Same Time." *Personality and Social Psychology Bulletin* 17: 475–482.

Cavanaugh, Sheila L. 2010. *Queering Bathrooms: Gender, Sexuality, and the Hygienic Imagination*. Toronto: University of Toronto Press.

Chong, Dennis, and James N. Druckman. 2007. "Framing Theory." *Annual Review of Political Science* 10: 103–126.

Druckman, James N. 2004. "Political Preference Formation: Competition, Deliberation, and the (Ir)relevance of Framing Effects." *American Political Science Review* 98: 671–686.

Druckman, James N., Donald P. Green, James H. Kuklinski, and Arthur Lupia. 2011. *Cambridge Handbook of Experimental Political Science*. New York: Cambridge University Press.

Druckman, James N., and Justin W. Holmes. 2004. "Does Presidential Rhetoric Matter? Priming and Presidential Approval." *Presidential Studies Quarterly* 34 (4): 755–778.

Gerber, Alan S., and Donald P. Green. 2000. "The Effects of Canvassing, Telephone Calls, and Direct Mail on Voter Turnout: A Field Experiment." *American Political Science Review* 94 (3): 653–663.

Grant, Jaime M., Lisa A. Mottet, Justin Tanis, Jack Harrison, Jody L. Herman, and Mara Keisling. 2011. *Injustice at Every Turn: A Report of the National Transgender Discrimination Survey*. Washington, DC: National Center for Transgender Equality and National Gay and Lesbian Task Force. http://www.thetaskforce.org/downloads/reports/reports/ntds_full.pdf.

Haines, Elizabeth L., and Laura J. Kray. 2005. "Self-Power Associations: The Possession of Power Impacts Women's Self-Concepts." *European Journal of Social Psychology* 35 (5): 643–662.

Harrison, Brian F., and Melissa R. Michelson. 2012. "Not That There's Anything Wrong with That: The Effect of Personalized Appeals on Marriage Equality Campaigns." *Political Behavior* 34 (2): 325–344.

Harrison, Brian F., and Melissa R. Michelson. 2015. "God and Marriage: The Impact of Religious Identity Priming on Attitudes toward Same-Sex Marriage." *Social Science Quarterly* 96 (5): 1411–1423.

Harrison, Brian F., and Melissa R. Michelson. 2016a. "More than a Game: Football Fans and Marriage Equality." *PS: Political Science & Politics* 49 (4): 782–797.

Harrison, Brian F., and Melissa R. Michelson. 2016b. "He Said, She Said: Public Opinion toward Transgender Rights." Paper presented at the annual meeting of the American Political Science Association, Philadelphia, PA, September 1–4.

Harrison, Brian F., and Melissa R. Michelson. 2017. *Listen, We Need to Talk: Social Groups, Identity Priming, and LGBT Rights.* New York: Oxford University Press.

Iyengar, Shanto, and Donald R. Kinder. 1987. *News That Matters: Television and American Opinion.* Chicago, IL: University of Chicago Press.

Jeffreys, Sheila. 2014. "The Politics of the Toilet: A Feminist Response to the Campaign to 'Degender' a Women's Space." *Women's Studies International Forum* 45: 42–51.

Krosnick, Jon A., and Laura A. Brannon. 1993. "The Impact of the Gulf War on the Ingredients of Presidential Evaluations: Multidimensional Effects of Political Involvement." *American Political Science Review* 87: 963–975.

Lazarsfeld, Paul. F., Bernard Berelson, and Hazel Gaudet. 1948. *The People's Choice: How the Voter Makes Up His Mind in a Presidential Campaign.* 2nd ed. New York: Columbia University Press.

Levay, Kevin E., Jeremy Freese, and James N. Druckman. 2016. "The Demographic and Political Composition of Mechanical Turk Samples." *SAGE Open* 6 (1). doi:10.1177/2158244016636433.

McCall, Cade, and Nilanjana Dasgupta. 2007. "The Malleability of Men's Gender Self-Concept." *Self and Identity* 6 (2–3): 173–188.

McLeish, Kendra N., and Robert J. Oxoby. 2008. "Social Interactions and the Salience of Social Identity," IZA Discussion Papers 3554, Institute for the Study of Labor (IZA).

Rasinski, Kenneth A. 1989. "The Effect of Question Wording on Public Support for Government Spending." *Public Opinion Quarterly* 53: 388–394.

Rohall, David E., Melissa A. Milkie, and Jeffrey W. Lucas. 2013. *Social Psychology: Sociological Perspectives.* 3rd ed. New York: Pearson Higher Education.

Rudman, Laurie A., and Julie E. Phelan. 2010. "The Effect of Priming Gender Roles on Women's Implicit Gender Beliefs and Career Aspirations." *Social Psychology* 41 (3): 192–202.

Sniderman, Paul M., and Sean M. Theriault. 2004. "The Structure of Political Argument and the Logic of Issue Framing." In *Studies in Public Opinion*, edited by Willem E. Saris, and Paul M. Sniderman, 133–165. Princeton, NJ: Princeton University Press.

Sylvia Rivera Law Project. n.d. Accessed September 8 2016. http://srlp.org/resources/fact-sheet-transgender-gender-nonconforming-youth-school/.

Tajfel, Henri. 1981. *Human Groups and Social Categories.* Cambridge: Cambridge University Press.

Terry, Deborah J., and Michael A. Hogg. 1996. "Group Norms and the Attitude-Behavior Relationship: A Role for Group Identification." *Personality and Social Psychology Bulletin* 22: 776–793.

Race, gender, and media coverage of Michelle Obama

Ray Block Jr.

ABSTRACT
In this autobiographical essay, I discuss why I became a Michelle Obama scholar and what I've learned while investigating Mrs. Obama as a case study of the growing literature on Black female bodies.

For several years I have been participating in a joint research project with my colleague Christina Haynes on the media's treatment of First Lady Michelle Obama. This short essay presents my thoughts on why I am studying this topic and how it is enriching my development as a scholar. As a political scientist, I study identity politics, broadly defined. Before Barack Obama entered the national scene, I never considered studying the presidency. But in 2007, for the first time, a man of my race was seeking the highest office in the nation. As a political scientist, I was deeply interested in how race would shape analysis of his political career. I chronicled how Obama managed his identity during the 2008 presidential primaries and wrote about the role of social identity on the outcome of the general election (Block and Onwunli 2010; Block 2011).

In 2011, Christina Haynes approached me about doing joint research on the media's treatment of Michelle Obama. I jumped at the chance because I had realized that it was not possible to analyze Barack Obama's political career without understanding the role Michelle has played in his success. It was her identity as an African-American that convinced many Black voters to support her husband, whose racial identity was unusual and not well understood in this country. Black voters decided to trust Barack because they trusted Michelle. This was an unprecedented dynamic in presidential identity politics that fascinated me.

Christina studies education, particularly how Black women cope with daily microaggression in predominantly White institutions, and she was interested in why some media coverage of the First Lady was so harsh while other coverage presented her in a more positive light (Haynes 2011, n.d.). We agreed to conduct our work on Michelle Obama as a mutual side project, a welcome diversion from our main lines of scholarship that functions for us as the intellectual equivalent of dessert after a meal.

Very early in the first administration, it became clear that some media generators consistently focused on the First Lady's physicality (Gillespie, 2016; Guerrero 2011). Media elites in both the "mainstream" and Black press commented on Michelle Obama's height, curves, and muscle tone; the texture of her hair; and the sternness of her countenance. Regardless of intent, they reduced Michelle Obama to a collection of bodily traits. This kind of media coverage of a First Lady was unprecedented.

Another theme of media coverage draws upon insidious stereotypes of Black women (Collins 2004; Harris-Perry 2011). Bloggers have characterized her demeanor as she presented her public initiatives as angry and aggressive, tapping into the Sapphire stereotype (Springer 2007; Glanton 2012). Coverage that focuses on Michelle Obama's physicality often tap into Jezebel-inspired stereotypes; one example is an exchange between Erin Audrey Kaplan and Latoya Peterson about the First Lady's fuller, athletic figure (Kaplan 2008; Peterson 2008). When the First Lady announced that her first priority was her daughters, she was called a "feminist's nightmare," as if she was embracing the Mammy role instead of doing more "important" things (Harris-Perry 2013.)

All of this coverage is a way of questioning whether Michelle Obama belongs in the White House. She is one of the most prominent women in contemporary U.S. politics. Her status as First Lady has encouraged many voters, particularly those of color, to become more involved in civic life (Williams 2009). Her public initiatives have contributed to a reduction in child obesity and healthier school lunches (Vilsack 2012). Her White House garden has made healthy eating a national issue (Obama 2012). She is an effective campaigner for other Democrats and a talented public speaker (Joseph 2011). Yet the narrative the media presents often focuses on other issues than her political influence or the success of her initiatives. Because of her professional background, fashion choices, and political style, Michelle Obama departs from many traditions about who a First Lady is and how a First Lady behaves (Parks and Roberson 2008). All of these factors would be expected to shape media coverage of her tenure as First Lady. However, race touches much that is said and published about her (White 2011). Media generators seem to feel that because of her race they can write about Michelle Obama in ways that no First Lady has ever been covered. The scrutiny of Michelle Obama has gone far beyond what is typical.

Our research

Christina and I formulated what we call the Michelle Obama image transformation hypothesis: the argument that the First Lady's popularity changed once she began making an unprecedented number of television appearances. Supporters argue that this media blitz helped the First Lady soften her public image and increase her appeal for mainstream voters, while critics maintain that she ran the risk of overexposure and falling out of public favor. We set out to find which interpretation was right. Our methodology required an examination of aggregate polling results over time. We analyzed the content of over 100 summary documents of survey results from nearly a dozen commercial polls during the 2008 and 2012 presidential campaign cycles. We then merged that data with a chronology of Michelle Obama's media activities. We found that the First Lady's polling numbers were influenced by both the frequency and the type of television appearances she makes. Certain genres (i.e. musicals, children's shows, and reality TV) and viewing times (especially the early morning time slot, 6:00–9:00 am) were more influential than others in the sense that they increased or diminished Mrs Obama's popularity to varying degrees. We also found that scheduling multiple broadcast trips in the same week did not improve perceptions of the First Lady and that doing so might actually decrease her favorability ratings (Block and Haynes 2014).

In the course of this research, we developed a novel measure of Michelle Obama's media exposure. We mined entertainment news websites (rather than scholarly archives) for details about her television appearances. A keyword search for "Michelle Obama" on the Internet Movie Database (IMDb) revealed that the First Lady has a neatly organized filmography. We merged filmography data with the aggregate polling results to record not only the number of TV appearances Michelle Obama made during the week when a particular survey was in the field but also the types of appearances.

Christina and I have embarked on a second project that is a natural extension of our research on her image transformation. It examines how the First Lady used her media exposure to advance her political agenda. We studied a sample of the First Lady's political speeches to examine the rhetoric describing two of her signature policy initiatives: the "Joining Forces" program for military families and the "Let's Move" campaign against childhood obesity (Block and Haynes 2016). By building on the ideas Mary Kahl developed in her essay on the First Lady's strategic use of Mom-In-Chief rhetoric and making use of the resources in C-SPAN's Video Library, we gained insight into the First Lady's skill as an orator and agenda setter (Kahl 2009).

Our continuing research examines the impact of specific racialized stereotypes of Black women on perceptions of Michelle Obama (Block and Haynes, n.d.). We are using a framing experiment from a pilot study in which we alter the text of mock newspaper articles about the First Lady to show that voters tend to be more favorable toward Michelle Obama when the news story depicts her in a way that is consistent with Eurocentric notions of femininity. Alternative depictions – for example, those emphasizing her assertive demeanor (Sapphire), physicality (Jezebel), and parental choices (Mammy) – encourage opinions that are typically less positive, mainly because they conjure up negative stereotypes of Black women.

Concluding remarks

In her commencement speech to the spring 2015 graduates of Tuskegee University, Michelle Obama admitted that she was disappointed about the negative press she and her husband received (Obama 2015). The First Lady has spoken candidly about being characterized as a Sapphire by some and a Mammy by others (Gayle 2015). As we listened to the First Lady recount her experiences on the campaign trail and in the Oval Office, Christina and I had mixed feelings. As scholars of color, we salute Michelle Obama for challenging, if not transcending, negative stereotypes about Black women. But we feel it is unfortunate that racially inflected image politics continue to play such a large role on the perceptions voters have of Black political figures.

I began this research as a side project for my own pleasure. It feels good to do scholarly work on a black political leader, and both Christina and I feel that not enough academic research is being published about Michelle Obama. But as I dug into the work, I realized that the insights and new methods the project was generating enriched my other scholarship.

The methodology of combining summary results from public opinion polls and with documentation of a politician's media activities was so fruitful that I have used it in my research on Barack Obama (Block and Lewis, forthcoming). Analyzing the Obamas through the lenses of race and gender has peaked my interest in presidential studies – what would scholarship look like if all presidents were evaluated using race as the focus of analysis? Most important, this work has challenged what I thought I knew about race, gender relations, and electoral politics and the interconnections between those three vectors of analysis.

Disclosure statement

No potential conflict of interest was reported by the author.

References

Block, Ray, Jr. 2011. "Backing Barack Because He's Black: Racially Motivated Voting in the 2008 Election." *Social Science Quarterly* 92 (2): 423–446.

Block, Ray, and Christina Haynes. 2014. "Taking to the Airwaves: Using Content Analyses of Survey Toplines and Filmographies to Test the 'Michelle Obama Image Transformation' (MOIT) Hypothesis." *National Political Science Review* 16: 97–114.

Block, Ray, and Christina Haynes. 2016. *The Impact of Michelle Obama's "Mom-In-Chief Rhetoric" on Voters' Policy Attitudes*. Working Paper.

Block, Ray, and Christina Haynes. n.d. *The "Mammy", the "Sapphire", the "Jezebel", and Michelle Obama: Race-Gender Stereotypes and the Politics of Media Depiction*. Working Paper.

Block, Ray, and Angela K. Lewis. Forthcoming. "The 'Obama Effect' Revisited: A Macro-level and Longitudinal Exploration of the Influence of Barack Obama's Media Presence on Racialized Political Party Polarization." In *After Obama: African American Politics in the Post-Obama Era America*, edited by Todd Shaw, Robert Brown, and Joseph McCormick.

Block, RayJr., and Chinonye Onwunli. 2010. "Managing Monikers: The Role of Name Presentation in the 2008 Presidential Election." *Presidential Studies Quarterly* 40 (3): 464–481.

Collins, Patricia Hill. 2004. *Black Sexual Politics: African Americans, Gender, and the New Racism*. New York: Routledge.

Gayle, Damien. 2015. "Michelle Obama: I Was Knocked Back by Race Perceptions." *Guardian.com*, May 11. Accessed February 29, 2016. http://www.theguardian.com/us-news/2015/may/11/michelle-obama-i-was-knocked-back-by-race-perceptions.

Gillespie, Andra. 2016. "Race, Perceptions of Femininity and the Power of the First Lady: A Comparative Analysis." In *Distinct Identities: Minority Women in U.S. Politics*, edited by Nadia Brown and Sarah Allen Gershon, 234–251. New York: Routledge.

Glanton, Dahleen. 2012. "There's Reason to Be Angry about "Angry Black Woman" Stereotype. *Chicago Tribune*, January 17. http://articles.chicagotribune.com/2012-01-17/news/ct-talk-glanton-angry-0117-20120117_1_black-woman-black-women-michelle-obama.

Guerrero, Lisa. 2011. "(M)Other-In-Chief: Michelle Obama and the Ideal of Republican Womanhood." In *New Femininities: Postfeminism, Neoliberalism and Identity*, edited by Rosalind Gill and Christina Scharff, 68–82. New York: Palgrave Macmillan.

Harris-Perry, Melissa. 2011. *Sister Citizen: Shame, Stereotypes, and Black Women in America*. Cambridge, MA: Yale University Press.

Harris-Perry, Melissa. 2013. "Don't Call First Lady a 'Feminist Nightmare.'" MSNBC.com, November 23. Accessed February 22, 2014. http://www.msnbc.com/melissa-harris-perry/watch/dont-call-first-lady-a-feminist-nightmare-70871619713.

Haynes, Christina S. 2011. "'You Expect Me to Be That Way?' Academically Successful African-American Women's Counter-narratives to Stereotypical Images." *Enrollment Management Journal* 5 (Fall): 38–62.

Haynes, Christina S. n.d. *There's No Place Like Home? African American Women in the Residential Halls of a Predominantly White Midwestern University*. Working Paper.

Joseph, Ralina L. 2011. "Hope Is Finally Making a Comeback: First Lady Reframed." *Communication, Culture & Critique* 4 (1): 56–77.

Kahl, Mary L. 2009. "First Lady Michelle Obama: Advocate for Strong Families." *Communication and Critical/Cultural Studies* 6 (3): 316 320.

Kaplan, Erin Aubry. 2008. "First Lady Got Back." Salon.com, May 13. Accessed September 13, 2012. http://www.salon.com/2008/11/18/michelles_booty/.

Obama, Michelle. 2012. *American Grown: The Story of the White House Kitchen Garden and Gardens Across America*. New York: Crown Books.

Obama, Michelle. 2015. "Remarks by the First Lady at Tuskegee University Commencement Address." *White House: Office of the First Lady*, May 9. https://www.whitehouse.gov/the-press-office/2015/05/09/remarks-first-lady-tuskegee-university-commencement-address.

Parks, Gregory S., and Quinetta M. Roberson. 2008. *Michelle Obama: The 'Darker Side' of Presidential Spousal Involvement and Activism*. Cornell Law Faculty Working Papers. http://scholarship.law.cornell.edu/clsops_papers/39/.

Peterson, Latoya. 2008. "Salon: First Lady Got Back, Racialicious, the Intersection of Race, and Pop Culture." November 18. Accessed February 29, 2016. http://www.racialicious.com/2008/11/18/salon-first-lady-got-back/.

Springer, Kimberly. 2007. "Divas, Evil Black Bitches, and Bitter Black Women: African American Women in Postfeminist and Post-Civil-Rights Popular Culture." In *Interrogating Postfeminism: Gender and the Politics of Popular Culture*, edited by Yvonne Tasker and Diane Negra, 249–276. Durham, NC: Duke University Press.

Vilsack, Thomas J. 2012. "The Healthy, Hunger-Free Kids Act – Building Healthier Schools." *Childhood Obesity* 8 (1): 4–6.

White, Khadijah L. 2011. "Michelle Obama: Redefining the (White) House-Wife." *Thirdspace: A Journal of Feminist Theory & Culture* 10 (1): 1–19.

Williams, Verna L. 2009. "The First (Black) Lady." *Denver Law Review* 86: 833–850.

Bodywork in identity: passing as ethnography

Claire McKinney

ABSTRACT
Despite its centrality to organizing life sciences and identity politics, the body tends to disappear even when it is under scholarly consideration. The disappearing act of the body is supported by theoretical and methodological approaches that implicitly or explicitly see the body as an object that is acted upon and/or is the medium through which other concepts operate. A methodological approach that begins with bodywork allows us to understand the body not only as a site of action but also constitutive of the possibilities and limits of interacting with fields of power and ideology. Beginning with a consideration of the phenomenon of identity passing, the ethnography produced by bodies in action becomes apparent both to scholars and to those engaged in identity production and reaction.

When considering the place of the body in theorizing, two extremes become clear. First is the rendering of the body as invisible even as it is being studied. Sociologist Alan Radley (1995) argues that as social theory turned more and more to understanding how discursive practices and institutions focused on the body as an object of control, the agency of the body increasingly escaped the possibility of theorization. While the body is the object of control, its objective status remains crucially undertheorized because the dynamic nature of power and discourse draws the majority of scholarly attention. Second is the scientific desire to render the body as an object that is absolutely knowable and categorizable in hierarchies of physical worth (Riska 2010). Here, from a disembodied scientific gaze, the secrets of the bodies under scrutiny become transparent through techniques of categorization: "comparison, differentiation, hierarchization, homogenization, and exclusion" (Young 1990, 126). While the body has a central place in both these ways of thinking, the main focus is on rendering the body intelligible; that is, how to objectify the body such that it remains a stable object for study and manipulation.

But the body can also be a subject that makes experience possible and identity transformative. I propose a method of studying the body that begins with its active presence in the construction of and response to institutional orders that moves scholars beyond both the linguistic turn and scientific objectification. If we think of the body as being active in its own construction and reception in different fields of power, then a methodology I term *bodywork* can highlight unrecognized aspects of relational modes. In this brief piece, I apply my proposed method of bodywork to the phenomenon of "passing" to reveal how identity construction absent attention to the body's activity is incomplete and misleading. Passing denotes when a person assumes a group identity that, if certain information became public knowledge, would otherwise be denied them interpersonally and institutionally. For instance, the protagonist of Philip Roth's *Human Stain*, is Coleman Silk, an African American who has "passed" as white and Jewish for his entire adulthood. If the knowledge of his parent's ascribed race became public knowledge, his ability to be white and Jewish would cease. The passing body provides an opportunity for a methodology of the body to be reoriented away from understanding the body as an object. Passing under a bodywork methodology that understands the body as an active part of subjectivity troubles discursive overdetermination, scientific legibility, and the naturalization of identity. By focusing on the subjectivity of the body, we can begin to understand its active part in the creation of experience through a response to norms, institutions, and identity.

Methodology of bodywork

Gimlin (2007) has argued that body work in sociology has been used to describe four different types of work: the work people do on their own bodies, paid care labor focused on the bodies of others, the emotional labor of the service industry, and the production of the appearance of the body in the workplace. These four uses of the term body work, to varying degrees, participate in what I am terming the methodology of *bodywork*. I use this neologism to direct scholarly attention to what the body does in relation to institutional norms and procedures. For instance, while much of the sociology of work has focused on the effects of particular forms of labor on the body, such as the manifestation of repetitive stress in physical impairment, bodywork would begin with questions of how the body itself accustoms people to particular forms of work such as how one fidgets as a mechanism to expel physical energy while engaged in cognitive labor. The distinction here is nuanced but important in understanding bodily comportment as not just the effect of other actions but as causally related to making other processes operative.

Bodywork as a methodological approach begins from the following premises:

Premise 1: The body provides a horizon of possibility for experience and action.

Premise 2: The body acts to establish the terms of engagement with other bodies and institutions.

Premise 3: No aspect of the body is naturally given but is only intelligible within social and political contexts.

Young argues "it is the ordinary purposive orientation of the body as a whole toward things and its environment that initially defines the relation of a subject to its world" (2005, 30). This phenomenological insight is reflected in one of the more influential allegories of subject formation found in Louis Althusser's concept of interpellation. Althusser argues that ideology operates through apparatuses of power that render ideology material, producing an imagined and naturalized relation between the subject and her world. Althusser does not invoke bodywork in the way I have defined it. Rather, he imputes action to ideology in his allegory of the police officer hailing an individual on the street: "ideology 'acts' … in such a way that it 'recruits' subjects among the individuals … which can be imagined along the lines of the most commonplace everyday police (or other) hailing: 'Hey, you there!'" (1971, 174). But bodywork is implied in the characterization of the response of the person on the street: "the hailed individual will turn round. By this mere one-hundred-and-eighty-degree physical conversion, he becomes a *subject*" (1971, 174, emphasis in original). The bodily practice of turning around produces the individual as a subject of state power; the hailing of the police officer alone is insufficient for the production of a subject. In this sense, then, identity is not merely written on the body but requires particular bodily comportment to function.

From this phenomenological point, bodywork as methodology reveals the possibility of remapping social relations that contribute to the production of identity. The body is not infinitely malleable but its practices adapt to the conditions of multiple and contradictory institutional demands. Titchkosky (2003) has written about the disabled body as a body that is inscrutable to the normative order of typical behavior (how bodies should appear and act in social spaces and relations) and thus disabled bodies demand both accommodation and the reworking of normalcy. In relation to her husband's blindness, Titchkosky describes typical reactions of people driving when they see him with his guide dog: some people slow down to stare at his bodily presence only to jerk forward when they are done staring, endangering both him and his guide dog; others stop and wave him through the crosswalk, both acknowledging his blindness and acting based on the habits of the sighted. Blind comportment makes visible the normative work or assumptions of sightedness and disrupts that same normative order by rendering able-bodied bodily comportment strange in relation to non-normative bodily presence. Because the relation to the world happens through embodied practice, the body cannot just be the site of normative operation but actively produces its possibility or impossibility, allowing for a more nuanced and detailed picture of that normative order.

One difficulty in most attempts to disrupt the naturalization of the normal workings of institutions and social relations through attention to the body is that focus on certain modes of disruption seems to rely upon the naturalization of other aspects of the body. Alcoff's (2006) *Visible Identities* is instructive in this regard. Alcoff argues that the confusion and malleability around racial categorization and identity renders visible epidermal differences as determinative of classification but in ways that do not remain consistent over geography or time. But when she turns her attention to the question of gender difference, the danger of theoretical sex neutrality leads Alcoff to propose an objective basis of gender difference: "Women and men are differentiated by virtue of their different relationship to the possibility to biological reproduction, with biological reproduction referring to conceiving, giving birth, and breast-feeding, involving one's own body" (2006, 172). Alcoff argues that such an objective basis does not require normative conclusions, such as compulsory heterosexuality, but the desire to render the phenomenology of gendered identity transparent and contained wholly in women's potential relation to reproduction reveals that understanding of the body in action often falls back on an ideological assumption of the natural function of the body.

Transwomen and transmen cannot be said to be differentiated on the basis of different horizons of biological reproduction in terms of the imagined capacity to conceive, breastfeed, etc., and thus there is a normativity of these gender categories that would see trans* modes of being as violating the objective basis of gender. Here, then, history (feeling connected with one's mother's reproduction as a woman who shares that capacity) and memory (understanding the self as capable of carrying a child even if that never comes to pass) reify the meaning of gender in reproduction, rendering the possibility of trans* folk as belonging to a community of women or men an objective impossibility. Bodywork, by contrast, does not seek the naturalization of the function of the body taken to be outside of the phenomenological experience of the body at work. Being a pregnant woman is an embodiment that transforms the relation between the normative world and the self; being a transwoman disrupts normative gender ordering when such orders rely on the assumption that the objective status of women lies in their capacity to conceive.

Passing as ethnography

With these premises of a methodology of bodywork in mind, I now turn to examine how such an understanding could transform our evaluation of the phenomenon of identity "passing." Passing as a phenomenon requires the assumption that identity is natural, socially intelligible, and immutable. That is, a person has a true identity that they seek to hide from others through secret keeping or subterfuge. This definition requires identity to be something fixed and unchangeable; one is born, not made, a woman, as it were. But "passing" as a practice violates the notion that the body is an object with an objective meaning that cannot transform. A bodywork perceptive on passing challenges the stability of race, gender, and disability as well as sexuality, religion, age, and socioeconomic status.

Instead of seeing passing as requiring disavowal of the true self left behind, as a survival strategy to have access to identity privilege in an oppressive social world, or as a fundamentally unethical basis for relating to others, considering passing as a phenomenon of bodywork can reveal passing as a form of ethnography. Ethnography produces a corporeal knowledge of experience that is attuned to rendering intelligible the symbols and practices embedded in a particular time and place that makes experience possible in the first place. Passing as a practice is a folk ethnography, a field guide produced by participant-observation, because resisting the supposed naturalness of a true identity requires a working knowledge of the symbols, practices, and interactions of a time and place in relation to the body. Of course, ethnography as scholarly practice is aimed at better understanding as an end in itself; passing as ethnography is aimed at the possibility of bodily engaging the social world in ways that one's ascribed identity would seem to disallow.

Two examples may clarify the capacity of passing as folk ethnography. Titchkosky (2003) not only describes her husband's bodily comportment as a blind man in the world but also describes disability passing in two veins: her husband passing as sighted when he retained some visible acuity and her passing as blind when she and her husband traveled. An example of standpoint epistemology, Titchkosky argues that the ability of her husband to pass as sighted requires a knowledge of the norms of sighted society that is gleaned through the experience of one's own marginalization. Titchkosky's husband must be aware of the minutest expectations of others if he is to be able to act as sighted, such as recognition of a friend approaching from a distance (a feat he accomplished with the help of Titchkosky whispering the fact in his ear). By experiencing oneself as distant from normalcy, someone who can pass can judge what to do with the knowledge of the operation of the normal order based on their experience of a body that does not comport with the order's assumptions.

Titchkosky's own experience as passing as blind, however, reveals a different aspect of the work of embodied social norms. Titchkosky has moments where she acts as a sighted person does, such as sitting in a chair without feeling for the seat first, but the extreme visibility of the markers of blindness, such as sunglasses worn indoors and the presence of a service dog, overwhelm sighted people, making the discovery of her sightedness unlikely. As Titchkosky summarizes, "if openness to blindness was typical, I could not have been blind for ten days" (2003, 186). The dual passing, from a marginalized identity to a normatively typical one and vice versa, allows Titchkosky to produce a nuanced picture of sociability, institutional order, and barriers of embodied difference.

The second example comes from the recent furor over Rachel Dolezal, the NAACP chapter president who presented as black but then was "outed" as white by her parents. The controversy over the reality over Dolezal's race turned variably on her parent's ethnicity (race as heredity), her memory of a deep attachment to black culture from an early age (race as culture and history), and analogies and disanalogies to transgender embodiment through assertions of transracialism (analogies called on lived practice of identity and consciousness; disanalogies called on the difference between race and gender as marked by the function of power). But what is not considered is that prior to her "outing," Dolezal was understood to be black. The believability of her bodily comportment as the comportment of a black woman has been undertheorized, as commentators assert the truth of her identity to lie in more stable determinations of race found in biology or unchosen community. More careful attention to why and how Dolezal was taken to be black by her chosen community (as well as interpellating state authorities – Dolezal claimed a police officer during a traffic stop marked her race as black without asking (Samuels 2015)) could be more instructive about the actual operation of race in early twenty-first century Washington State. How Dolezal was able to navigate the contours of race in twenty-first century Washington such that she could be understood as black is evidence of a folk ethnography of the body. This was an ethnography that required work, to be sure, from tanning to mastering black hairstyles, but that work reveals the importance of the body as productive of identity, rather than merely the site upon which identity operates.

Examining passing through the methodology of bodywork demonstrates how we could produce new understandings of the relation between identity and institutions that take the body not as an object but as an active subject. Passing is an obvious application of such a methodology because the naturalized status of the body is troubled by the activity of the body. Bodywork can also transform how we think of the body in practice in a variety of institutional settings, including work, social movements, and anonymous interactions of the everyday. In each of these places, we assume the body, especially the marginalized body, is only worked upon instead of actively reworking the given terms of meaning and action. Bodywork would not take the normative order as the entry-point for investigation but rather would begin with the body itself and what it does in order to produce a dynamic understanding of the body in practice and in context.

The importance of the body has been recognized by the social sciences for decades and has especially grounded the importance of integrating feminist, disability, and race studies into the mainstream of academic work. Mere recognition of the body does not ensure that it does not become the inert stuff of objective analysis. Beginning with premises that recognize the body's place in active subjectivity, bodywork as methodology can deepen our appreciation of the creativity of the body while still recognizing the limits imposed on the body through the normative rules of behavior and the institutional practices that channel that behavior. As such we may come to know the body, sociality, and institutional practice as more nuanced, complex, and interdependent than previously posited.

Disclosure statement

No potential conflict of interest was reported by the author.

References

Alcoff, Linda. 2006. *Visible Identities: Race, Gender, and the Self.* Studies in Feminist Philosophy. New York: Oxford University Press.
Althusser, Louis. 1971. *Lenin and Philosophy, and Other Essays.* London: New Left Books.
Gimlin, Debra. 2007. "What Is Body Work? A Review of the Literature." *Sociology Compass* 1 (1): 353–370. doi:10.1111/j.1751-9020.2007.00015.x.
Radley, A. 1995. "The Elusory Body and Social Constructionist Theory." *Body & Society* 1 (2): 3–23. doi:10.1177/1357034X95001002001.
Riska, Elianne. 2010. "Gender and Medicalization and Biomedicalization Theories." In *Biomedicalization*, edited by Adele E Clarke, Laura Mamo, Jennifer Ruth Fosket, Jennifer R Fishman, and Janet K Shim. Durham: Duke University Press Books. http://www.myilibrary.com?id=306506.
Samuels, Allison. 2015. "Rachel Dolezal's True Lies." *Vogue*, July 19. http://www.vanityfair.com/news/2015/07/rachel-dolezal-new-interview-pictures-exclusive.
Titchkosky, Tanya. 2003. *Disability, Self, and Society.* Toronto: University of Toronto Press.
Young, Iris Marion. 1990. *Justice and the Politics of Difference.* Princeton, NJ: Princeton University Press.
Young, Iris Marion. 2005. *On Female Body Experience: "Throwing like a Girl" and Other Essays.* Studies in Feminist Philosophy. New York: Oxford University Press.

Queer sensibilities: notes on method

Jerry Thomas

ABSTRACT

This note characterizes queer methods developed in the humanities in ways that may be useful in social science and law. Since it is antithetical to queer theory's resistance to fixity to concretize queer methods into a metatheory, this note characterizes these methods as queer sensibilities. Queer sensibilities are useful for analyzing queer bodies in public spaces – physical spaces and democratic spaces – especially in research programs concerned with sexual citizenship. This note connects queer sensibilities to sculptures of Charles Ray. His work serves as both a metaphor for and substantive example of methods that replicate heteronormativity by erasing pubic queerness. Queer sensibilities leverage insights for how law and culture construct norms of sexual citizenship. At the heart of this note is a queer perspective on the extent to which men's naked and queer bodies enter the dialogic of sexual citizenship, when heteronormativity censors such bodies and silences sexual expression.

My research program examines queer bodies and sexual citizenship, that is, what citizens do with bodies that constitute queerness in connection with the extent to which citizens receive certain dignities, autonomies, liberties, and equalities based upon adherence to or transgression from sexual norms. Sexual citizenship norms are constructed through legal, cultural, and political technologies that are at once invisible and omnipresent in ways that construct and privilege heteronormativity. I am concerned with the erasure of queer bodies in public spaces – physical spaces and democratic spaces – where extant norms insist that sexualities remain private. Formally trained in political science and law, I draw upon queer theories developed in the humanities to construct queer theory in social science and law, disciplines scholars note a decided absence of queer theory (Halley and Parker 2011). This absence is related to methods. In this dialog associated with body politics, I discuss queer methods I find useful for constructing and analyzing social, political, and legal norms surrounding bodies in sexual citizenship. I characterize these methods as queer sensibilities.

As I describe methods I cull from many disciplines, I am cautious not to over-represent them as queer methods more broadly. Readers steeped in queer theory might recoil from attempts to reify a theory that refuses fixity. Notably, queer theorists suggest that situating queer theory into a metatheory would be "radically anticipatory" and "violently partial"

(Berlant and Warner 1995, 344). Too, few are polyglots who speak languages of art, poetry, literature, social science, law, politics, and queer theory, including me. I cannot feign omniscience in any one discipline, much less all of them. Still, I sense a responsibility to say something, at least, about queer methods; else, my silence may result in certain methodological deaths. If queer theorists know anything at all, we know from AIDS politics that "silence equals death." Voice is queer method's moxie, especially when the life of queer theory is like the embodied lives of queer citizens: both are set against pogroms that privilege heteronormative technologies – sciences, religions, socio-legal norms, and disdains for nonconformity. The trajectory of queer methods mirrors the trajectory of HIV and AIDS treatments: neither existed in certain moments; queers forced both into being. I acknowledge my aim to create what scarcely exists – a queer method useful in public law, politics, and social science inquiry. I also acknowledge that my methods and messages are not severable; I am concerned with disrupting method/message binaries, keenly aware that skeptic methodologists might view this disruption as undermining scientific standards similar to jurists who view message-based speech proscriptions as undermining constitutional principles of neutrality. Notwithstanding such skepticism, a strength of queer methods is disruption, if only to expose inherent politics and unquestioned assumptions in science, law, methods, and other programs that erase and exterminate queerness, even if unwittingly. In this essay, surely I mischaracterize queer theories and methods, neither being homogenous. Surely there are errors of omission.

Queer sensibilities

Queer "theory" is not theory consisting of deductions following formal propositions; instead, queer theories are like heuristics, commentaries, or sensibilities of the sort Susan Sontag describes in *Notes on Camp*. "A sensibility is almost, but not quite, ineffable. Any sensibility which can be crammed into the mold of a system, or handled with the rough tools of proof, is no longer a sensibility at all. It has hardened into an idea" (1982, 106). Sontag admits, "to talk about Camp … is to betray it" (105), yet she structures her essay as 58 notes that describe camp. She never defines that which defies definition, but her notes help us glean meanings of camp sensibility. Queer sensibility is like camp sensibility: it exists, even without pithy frames. Like Sontag's methods (descriptions, anecdotes, and lists), queer methods often consist of cataloging language, culture, narratives, and environmental externalities that construct sexualities and sexual citizenship in historical and contemporary moments and places. Here are a few notes that inform queer sensibilities.

Sexualities are culturally constructed. Queer theory is largely constructivist. Dominant political and legal discourses espouse sexual essentialism, viewing sexualities as inherent and immutable. Heterosexuals and homosexuals alike insist they are "born this way," despite bioethicist suggestions that biological determinism does not account for the considerable sexual variation among citizens (Nelson 2014). Queer theorists provide considerable etiological evidence that queer and non-queer sexualities are constructed through many technologies, such as memetic replication through literary narratives (Rohy 2015). The nature-culture debate is not shopworn; instead, the impasse is political, where heterosexuality is privileged through teleological arguments explaining heterosexuality's natural occurrences through unquestioned valuations of heterosexuality's product – human reproduction.

Queer is not synonymous with gay or lesbian. Citizens who engage in sexual conduct and form relations with same-sex others are queer inasmuch as queer defines itself against the normal; but queerness is not confined narrowly to gender and sex categories. Queer is capacious and pluralistic, often fluid and indeterminate, subjective and personal. Examples: voyeurism, autoeroticism, pansexualism, trichophilia, and library-sex-in-the-stacks are queer (perhaps).

Queer theory disrupts binarisms. Queer methods disrupt a host of binaries: gay/straight, man/woman, productive/waste, parody/pastiche, and public/private. Queer also disrupts methodological binaries: objective/subjective, qualitative/quantitative, and method/ message. Poet John Ashbery exposes artificial boundaries between *natural* (nonhuman-made environments and heterosexualities) and *unnatural* (built environments and queer sexualities) in the simple phrase "landscape architecture" (Schmidt 2014). It is incongruous to conceptualize shrubs planted by birds through their droppings as natural and shrubs planted by humans as unnatural. The fact that nature and sexualities are constructed does not mean they are unnatural. Queer and nature are not opposites; queer nature is not paradoxical.

Queer is a verb and an identity; but first it is a verb. To queer, in part, is to see, construct, and experience sex and sexuality in spaces, places, and ideas where dominant discourses insist they do not, cannot, and should not exist; quintessentially, some citizens see, construct, and experience same-sex relations, despite efforts to proscribe such relations. Sex and sexuality exist in many places. Michael Warner:

> Every person who comes to a queer self understanding knows in one way or another that her stigmatization is connected with gender, the family, notions of individual freedom, the state, public speech, consumption and desire, nature and culture, maturation, reproductive politics, racial and national fantasy, class identity, truth and trust, censorship, intimate life and social display, terror and violence, health care, and deep cultural norms about the bearing of the body (1993, xiii).

Queer sensibilities thrive in the inability to cease seeing queerness and anti-queer technologies operating nearly everywhere and in everything. Queer blurs sexual and nonsexual distinctions. Further, queer is "a political and existential stance, an ideological commitment, a decision to live outside some social norm or other" (Ford 2007, 345). While most queer theory is anti-identitarian, queerism as ideology can form queer identities much like commitments to heteronormative ideologies can form heterosexual identities. José Esteban Muñoz: "Queerness, like feminism, is an essentially performative endeavor, a mode of doing as opposed to being. This is not to say that being and performativity are easily unyoked" (2011, 149). Queer is a verb, a method. Queer transforms into identity when citizens commit, consciously or otherwise, to using queer methods.

Queer theory runs toward its criticism, not away from it. Preeminent queer theories confront technologies created to impede queer development: the barebacker's rectum is a grave (Bersani 2011), homosexuality spreads like a contagion (Rohy 2015), queers are waste (Schmidt 2014), queers have a death drive and no future (Edelman 2004), queers are not normal (Warner 1999), and we can bring kids up gay (Sedgwick 1991). Other queer theories sanitize themselves of such controversies and messes, I suspect, to make inroads with non-queer establishments who prefer to preserve the status quo of sexual erasure. There is a shred of truth in Michael O'Rourke's assertion about queer theory's "big secret:"

> Queer theory does not – despite what it tells itself – like the icky, sticky, yucky, viscous, gloopy, gunky, mascara-streaked, wet, bloody, sweaty, pissy, shItty, leaky, seeping, weeping, sploshing, spurting, spashing, milky. It needs to carefully mop up the messy, the dirty, the sexually disgusting. In order to remain squeaky clean it has to cast out that which it deems too perverse. (2014, 5)

Queer theories that acknowledge sexual messiness and do not shy away from otherwise debilitating criticisms and taboos markedly inform queer sensibilities and sexual epistemologies.

Queer itself is methodologically pluralistic. Queers and queer theorists use a number of techniques including parody, lists, excess, and repetition. Parody's humor makes palatable the taste of queerness, and parody's strength, like camp, exists when its replication obscures insincerity and sincerity, or in art terms, when parody slips into pastiche (Rogers 2006). Lists also obscure words' meanings as well as distinguish them. A related legal method, *noscitur a socci*, ascertains statutory meaning by referencing associated words, especially in lists. Queerness, like other sexualities, uses repetition to construct its own queerness. Judith Butler notes the importance of repetition: "hegemonic heterosexuality is itself a constant and repeated effort to imitate its own idealizations" (1994, 85). The archetypal and formidable Gertrude Stein used parody, lists, and repetition simultaneously and copiously to develop and describe the fetish of her wife's bodily functions and excrement. Using "cow" as a metaphor interchangeably for orgasm, feces, creativity, and body, Stein wrote:

> Have it as having having it as happening, happening to have it as happening, having to have it as happening. Happening and have it as happening and having it happen as happening and having to have it happen as happening, and my wife has a cow as now, my wife having a cow as now, my wife having a cow as now and having a cow as now and having a cow and having a cow now, my wife has a cow and now. My wife has a cow (Stein [1926] 1973).

Queer perspectivism stands on the shoulders of feminist perspectivism. It is no secret, via feminism, that the personal is political. Angela Harris (1990) juxtaposes subjective perspectives of individuals, namely black women, with the objective perspective of law: the Preamble of the U.S. Constitution speaks as if there is a single, unifying identity and voice of "We the People." Harris does not aim to replace one perspective with another; instead, she understands legal and literary discourses as complex struggles and perpetual dialogue among voices, a "multiple consciousness" recognizing no essentialized self, but "a welter of partial, sometimes contradictory, or even antithetical 'selves'" (584). Individual and collective consciousnesses are not fixed but are "process[es] in which propositions are constantly put forth, challenged, and subverted" (584). For Harris, essentialism silences black women's voices; in turn, black women's voices destabilize feminist essentialism that privileges white women's perspectives as universally woman. Similarly, queer perspectives – subjective perspectives – destabilize essentialist thinking about sexual bodies and reveal methods that privilege objectivity and heteronormativity. Queer subjects, even with poststructuralist deconstructions of the "subject" itself, compel alternate ontological bearings of the body different from universalizing bearings that define queerness by its absence or otherness in relation to heteronormativity and other dominant tropes of sexuality.

Queer is anti-assimilationist. While sexual citizenship concerns the extent to which citizens adhere to sexual norms, queer is frequently defined as transgression from sexual norms. That is, queer defines itself against the normal. Queerness and assimilation, then, are largely antithetical, even while queer resists binarisms. In *Obergefell v. Hodges (2015)*, the U.S. Supreme Court legitimated same-sex marriages nationwide. This decision recognizes gay and lesbian citizens' right to assimilate to heteronormativity's primary institution – marriage – despite queer thinkers' cautions that such assimilation would further entrench heteronormative power and culture.

Charles Ray sculptures of nude men: methods and messages of sexual citizenship

In summer 2015, when the *Obergefell* Court announced its decision, I spent the summer reading queer theory and visiting the Charles Ray exhibit at the Art Institute of Chicago. The exhibit included sculptures of, *inter alia*, six male nudes curated in a park-like setting on the entire second floor of the Modern Wing. These experiences shape my perspective and inform my work examining political and legal dynamics of seeing men's bodies – vulnerable, naked, and queer – in public spaces, democratic discourses, and sexual citizenship.

Nude men are virtually invisible in high art, queer men more so. The Guerrilla Girls have long noted lopsided visibilities in art, asking, "Do women have to be naked to get into the Met Museum?" Their 1989 poster shows a nude woman wearing a gorilla mask alongside the relatively unchanged statistic: "Less than 5% of the artists in the Modern Art sections are women, but 85% of the nudes are female." So it is not immaterial to see a naked 14-year-old white boy bending over next to a naked 28-year-old black runaway slave whose pubic hair and intact foreskin are at eye level (see Figure 1). What is negligible, however, is the controversy this particular sculpture aroused inside the Art Institute.

Huck and Jim, based upon Mark Twain's characters, is larger-than-life (150% scale); Ray designed the sculpture for public space, a fountain. The Whitney Museum commissioned and ultimately rejected the sculpture for the outdoor plaza at its new space in lower Manhattan, which is how it became part of the Art Institute's exhibit. *Huck and Jim*, like contemporary queerness, was too large to be crammed into the indoor space at the Art Institute, even if the metaphorical closet was a glass one: Ray's queer indoor park was flanked by walls of windows overlooking Millennium Park. Twain's novel is a recurring entry on lists of most banned books, so *Huckleberry Finn* is no stranger to censorship. Still, in 2015 the politics of Huck's queerness, including a racially charged queerness, once again denied publics unfettered access to Huck and his companion, Jim.

When the Art Institute (a private institution) curated Ray's naked and queer bodies in a park-like setting where visitors milled around the monochromatic sculptures, it constructed and modeled artificial nature – queer nature – where multiple consciousness existed; the space manifested seldom-realized queer possibilities in the full light of day when I, alongside queer and non-queer citizens, experienced without controversy queer bodies in sexual citizenship's infrastructure. Until then, this experience had been erased from my citizenship. I grew up in a poor, rural south, where there were neither

Figure 1. Charles Ray, Huck and Jim (2014), painted glass-reinforced plastic, Charles Ray: Sculpture, 1997–2014, May 15, 2015–October 4, 2015, Galleries 288, 291–299, The Art Institute of Chicago. Photography © The Art Institute of Chicago.

museums with nude or queer art nor the means to buy a ticket if such museums existed, so I experienced very little public art that was not a war hero on a horse. Ray's sculpture represents the queerness that was always present in Twain's classic American novel about two men, frequently naked on a raft, working together to escape their oppressors – systems of slavery and an abusive patriarch. Ray's retrospective queering (anachronistically identifying queerness in historical places and moments) revealed that Huck and Jim, in queer temporality language, were "always already queer." My understanding of sexuality would have been different if Main Street's principle art installation had been Ray's fountain. Citizens in contemporary New York City and Chicago might offer similar polemics.

Ray's exhibit is a metaphor for the politics of sexual citizenship, where men's naked bodies are censored from American culture and excluded from democratic discourses because dominant discourses capitalize on fears of queer increase. Heteronormative fictions reify in sexual citizenship by erasing from public view vulnerable men – naked and queer – because doing otherwise renders queerness legitimate and risks memetic queer reproduction and queer increase (Rohy 2015). Of the two dozen sculptures included in Ray's exhibit, only one, *Horse and Rider*, stood outside the Modern Wing in an outdoor plaza available to all passersby without paid museum admission. *Horse and Rider* depicts an aging Ray, fully clothed, sitting on an aging Hollywood horse, both beaten down from performing cultural tropes of masculinity: cowboys in denim riding horses to conquer adversaries and swoon women, never revealing their penetrable, vulnerable bodies. Ray's naked and queer bodies were visible only to those who had the means to pay admission and tacitly approved to see queerness. All others, especially children in the adjoining Millennium Park, were denied access to queer perspectives because Ray's sculptures, including those designed as outdoor public art, were not displayed permanently in public. Queer perspectives rarely receive dialogic representation in democratic discourses; here, Ray's queer perspectives were censored.

Unlike the young man I witnessed being denied entry into Ray's exhibit because he could not pay the $25 admission (or could not attend on Thursday evening when the Institute is open free of charge to Chicago residents), I had the means – a professor salary – to see queerness. I wish I had offered to pay his admission; hindsight, like retrospective queering, is full of possibilities. It is unfortunate the young man could not see for himself that the armature of *Huck and Jim* is the space between Huck's back and Jim's hand hovering over it. We never see Huck and Jim touch, but their queerness – interracial, inter-generational, homoerotic, and quintessentially American – is omnipresent in this absence, a space anything but empty.

I cannot affect what people saw and read contemporaneously in the past, but perhaps I can show through queer sensibilities and perspectives how law and culture operate to exterminate queerness in method and substance so that moving forward society might know the value of queer increase and bring into full view truths about bodies, queer and non-queer. Using these methods, I argue in my work that public sexual expression is not only protected in the First Amendment but also in Constitutional values whose purposes are to maximize democratic participation. When we understand sexualities as constructed and queerism as an ideological commitment to living outside social norms, we understand that silencing public sexual bodies – compartmentalizing and relegating them to private spaces – does violence to personhoods and creates heteronormative fictions unrepresentative of citizens' lived realities. Politics censored Ray's queer sensibilities and perspectives, leaving in place for most citizens ubiquitous cultural fictions that the bodies of Huck and Jim – a boy and a man – are not queer. Seeing Ray's sculpture, I know differently.

In addition to operating as a metaphor for the role of men's bodies in sexual citizenship discourse, Ray's exhibit is a substantive narrative of how heteronormative machineries control sexual constructions. Two private museums – Whitney and Art Institute of Chicago – chose not to display Ray's queer sculptures publicly. These decisions reveal that queer subjects have not yet transformed understandings of sexual bodies or sexual citizenship norms. Queer sensibilities help us understand why and how queer bodies are censored from publics: visible queerness increases queerness, unquestioned assumptions perpetuate essentialized views of heterosexuality, taboos surrounding children's sexualities prevent understandings that sexualities are constructed, and clothes sustain fictions that men's bodies are not vulnerable or penetrable. Law operates with similar heteronormative methods to shape and reinforce hegemonic bodily and sexual epistemologies. Queer sensibilities expose these methodological impurities.

Legions of perspectives are entangled necessarily with bodies. I am uninterested in disentangling these relationships since compartmentalizing and labeling, both central to identity politics and methods, are part of the problem in sexual citizenship. Forcing citizens to separate sex and sexuality from citizenship renders "queer citizen" paradoxical and inimical. I am interested, however, in articulating relationships between narratives and bodies, especially socio-legal norms that suppress expression and impede construction of certain queer sexualities. When sexualities are absent in publics, especially discursive ones that construct sexual citizenship, replication's key foundation is absent. That is, sometimes we do not understand X unless we first see X, including its erasure, and then see X again and again. Queer sensibilities help articulate the seemingly ineffable power of sexual bodies, as here when queer Huck and Jim were erased from public view, revealing heteronormativity's power to silence its other.

The trouble with constructing queer sensibilities and, concomitantly, queer sexual citizenship is when political, legal, and cultural forces curtail the expression of queer perspectives. Queerness thrives when exposed to other queerness, as when I fled pre-Internet, rural, heteronormative communities and found queer communities in larger cities. My queerness developed in new ways and thrived when I saw and emulated other queers. This ubiquitous expressive phenomenon is, of course, another narrative of closet politics. Visibility in all its forms – literary narrative, pop culture, visual art, and Internet pornography – assists in the construction of sexualities and sexual citizenship. Seeing publicly men's queer and naked bodies affects both. This observation lends credence to Carl Stychin's queer legal analysis, which, consistent with methods of queer repetition, merits repeating at length:

> Given the history by which access to the dialogue has been denied to some – to those who have not been allowed to publicly articulate an identity – the traditional right of free expression has been far from universal. Dialogic equality demands more than an unencumbered liberty to speak. Rather, the conditions for dialogue must be conducive to the manipulation, reworking, and redeployment of the signs and symbols by which our culture permeates our lives. The expressive right, then, has a positive connotation in that it demands that subjects have access to the cultural tools by which a meaningful contribution to the dialogue can be made. The articulation of identity connotes the ability to reconfigure, in a unique manner, the signs of dominant culture. In so doing, the ways in which we conceive of culture, the subject, and the community all may be radically altered such that the dialogic contributions of all subjects come to have meaning for all others. (1995, 28)

In summer 2015, I reeled at seeing Charles Ray's sculptures of naked men at the Art Institute, more so when I learned during the exhibit's closing lecture that *Huck and Jim* stirred little to no controversy among visitors. Ray and the Art Institute, it appeared, provided a cultural tool to contribute meaningfully to sexual citizenship dialogue. On reflection, I realized I was reeling simply because queerness had a place at the table, not acknowledging I was again settling for crumbs. Sexual citizenship norms kept Ray's sculptures out of public view, connoting that queers – often invited at the last minute to a dinner party, if they are invited at all – frequently eat only what heteronormativity serves. Queer sensibilities, as a method of and product of expressive freedom, continues to elude sexual citizenship, and I, like Berlant (2011), continue to be "starved" for queer theory, especially in legal and social science disciplines. To push the "eating" metaphor a bit more, I hope this note on queer sensibilities helps nourish dialogues about body politics, so queers might claim spaces as banquet hosts, not merely guests.

I conclude with a list of words associated with queer methods that honors queer theory's resistance to being fixed, a list that parodies method and might also slip into pastiche. Presented like a Paul Monette (1988) poem – an elegy for a lover lost to AIDS, written without punctuation or comma so readers might approximately know the despair of being trapped in grief, left alone in a body, itself dying of AIDS, not entirely unlike the isolated grief I experience making sense of and articulating queer methods – my methods are "queer-feminist-personal-perestoikan-deconstructionist-narrative-experiential-critical-legal-disruptive-anarchist-libertarian-pluralist-replicable-through-shared-experiences-transferrable-case-studies-angry-reflective-auto-ethnographic-dynamicslippages-perspectivist-qualitative-inimical-sexual-decentralized-diatribe-quantitative-counting-nude-male-bodies-voyeuristic-participant-observer-observer-participant-subjective-objective-stories-ecofeminist-political-erotic-honest-poetic-philosophical-constructivist-interpretive-dialectic-white-imaginary-jerry-centric-repetitive-elitist-anti-essentialist-tonality-non-anonymous-democratic-defensive-vulnerable-open-momentary-momentous-radically-anticipatory-violently-partial-sensibility-heuristic-transformational-intentional-multiple-consciousness-creative-disestablishmentarian-and-with-help-from-the-Art-Institute-of-Chicago-and-Charles-Ray-no-longer-dickless-internal-citations-omitted-as-if-perspectives-matter-only-when-other-scholars-have-already-published-as-much-ish."

Disclosure statement

No potential conflict of interest was reported by the author.

References

Berlant, Lauren. 2011. "Starved." In *After Sex? On Writing since Queer Theory*, edited by J. Halley and A. Parker, 79–90. Durham, NC: Duke University Press.

Berlant, Lauren, and Michael Warner. 1995. "What Does Queer Theory Teach Us about X?" *PMLA: Publications of the Modern Language Association of America* 110 (3): 343–349.

Bersani, Leo. 2011. "Shame on You." In *After Sex? On Writing since Queer Theory*, edited by J. H. A. A. Parker, 91–109. Durham, NC: Duke University Press.

Butler, Judith. 1994. *Bodies That Matter*. New York: Routledge.

Edelman, Lee. 2004. *No Future: Queer Theory and the Death Drive*. Durham, NC: Duke University Press.

Ford, Richard Thompson. 2007. "What's Queer about Race?" *South Atlantic Quarterly* 106 (3): 477–484. doi:10.1215/00382876-2007-006.

Halley, Janet, and Andrew Parker, eds. 2011. *After Sex? On Writing since Queer Theory*. Durham, NC: Duke University Press.

Harris, Angela P. 1990. "Race and Essentialism in Feminist Legal Theory." *Stanford Law Review* 42 (3): 581–616. doi:10.2307/1228886.

Monette, Paul. 1988. *Love Alone: Eighteen Elegies for Rog*. New York: St. Martin's Press.

Muñoz, José Esteban. 2011. "The Sense of Watching Tony Sleep." In *After Sex? On Writing since Queer Theory*, edited by J. Halley and A. Parker, 142–50. Durham, NC: Duke University Press.

Nelson, Jamie Lindemann. 2014. "Medicine and Making Sense of Queer Lives." *Hastings Center Report* 44 (s4): S12–S16. doi:10.1002/hast.364.

Obergefell v. Hodges, 135 S.Ct. 2584. 2015.

O'Rourke, Michael. 2014. "The Big Secret about Queer Theory." *Inter Alia: A Journal of Queer Studies* 9 (Bodily Fluids): 1–14.

Rogers, Henry, ed. 2006. *Art Becomes You: Parody, Pastiche and the Politics of Art*. Birmingham: Article Press (Birmingham City University).

Rohy, Valerie. 2015. *Lost Causes: Narrative, Etiology, and Queer Theory*. New York: Oxford University Press.

Schmidt, Christopher. 2014. *The Poetics of Waste: Queer Excess in Stein, Ashbery, Schuyler, and Goldsmith*. New York: Palgrave MacMillan.

Sedgwick, Eve Kosofsky. 1991. "How to Bring Your Kids Up Gay." *Social Text* 29: 18–27. doi:10.2307/466296.

Sontag, Susan. 1982. "Notes on Camp." In *A Susan Sontag Reader*. New York: Farrar, Straus, and Giroux.

Stein, Gertrude. (1926) 1973. *A Book Concluding with as a Wife Has a Cow a Love Story*. West Gloverton, VT: Something Else Press.

Stychen, Carl F. 1995. *Law's Desire: Sexuality and the Limits of Justice.* New York: Routledge.
Warner, Michael, ed. 1993. *Fear of a Queer Planet.* Minneapolis: University of Minnesota Press.
Warner, Michael. 1999. *The Trouble with Normal.* New York: Free Press.

Rape, apology, and the business of title IX compliance

Brooke Mascagni

ABSTRACT
This essay discusses the body politics of the contemporary student anti-rape movement, using the widely publicized 2016 case of Stanford Olympic hopeful and convicted sexual predator Brock Turner as an analytical departure point. My objective is to place the raced and gendered discourses of the Stanford case in the broader political debate about the rape crisis and Title IX compliance in higher education. My reading of the Stanford case and the cultural commentary generated by the rape survivor's letter suggests that students would be better served if university administrators (1) recognize that sexual assault has been normalized on their campuses, particularly in college athletics and fraternities, (2) acknowledge the dignity of student survivors of sexual violence by offering an institutional apology, and (3) initiate substantive cultural reforms that extend beyond Title IX legal compliance.

I thought there's no way this is going to trial; there were witnesses, there was dirt in my body, he ran but was caught. He's going to settle, *formally apologize*, and we will both move on. Instead, I was told he hired a powerful attorney, expert witnesses, private investigators who were going to try and find details about my personal life to use against me, find loopholes in my story *to invalidate me* and my sister, in order to show that this sexual assault was in fact a *misunderstanding*. That he was going to go to any length to convince the world he had simply been confused.

What has he done to demonstrate that he deserves a break? *He has only apologized for drinking and has yet to define what he did to me as sexual assault*, he has *revictimized* me continually, *relentlessly*. He has been found guilty of three serious felonies and it is time for him to accept the consequences of his actions. He will not be quietly excused.

He is a lifetime sex registrant. That doesn't expire. Just like what he did to me doesn't expire, doesn't just go away after a set number of years. It stays with me, *it's part of my identity*, it has forever changed the way I carry myself, the way I live the rest of my life. (Emily Doe, read aloud in Santa Clara County Superior Court addressing her assailant, Brock Turner, on June 2, 2016; italics added)[1]

Stanford University student and standout swimmer Brock Turner sexually assaulted an incapacitated Emily Doe[2] outside of a fraternity party one evening in January 2015. Two international graduate students cycling nearby witnessed Turner thrusting his body over an unconscious woman, who was half naked and lying behind a dumpster.

When the students approached, Turner immediately darted from the scene, leaving Emily behind, her body sprawled on the ground, her legs spread apart. Turner was tackled by the students and consequently arrested for raping Emily. When interviewed by a member of law enforcement, one of the graduate students "was crying so hard he couldn't speak because of what he'd seen." But as the passage that introduced this essay suggests, the criminal trial that followed (*People v. Turner*)[3] involved relentless shaming of Doe, relaying that the violent act was consensual and that "she liked it."

The three paragraphs aforementioned are excerpted from Emily Doe's statement to California's Santa Clara County Superior Court, which she read aloud to her assailant on June 2, 2016. The case garnered national and international attention when the letter was released to the public, flooding online social media news feeds. Within a few days, her statement had been viewed by over thirteen million people[4] and read on live television by CNN journalist Ashleigh Banfield.[5] Members of Congress have read parts of her statement on the floors of the U.S. House and Senate,[6] and Vice President Joe Biden has written a public apology[7] to Emily – a meaningful apology that stands in stark contrast to public statements delivered by Stanford University and her assailant. More recently, *Glamour* magazine named Emily Doe as one of their 2016 women of the year.[8]

In this essay, I discuss the body politics of the movement to prevent and end sexual violence on U.S. college campuses, using the statements of Emily Doe and her assailant as an analytical departure point. My objective is to place the raced and gendered discourses surrounding the Stanford case within the broader political debate about the rape crisis and Title IX compliance in higher education. Feminist theories of intersectionality explain how systems of power create political divisions (such as race, gender, citizenship, sexuality, and class) that shape individuals' lived experiences. In other words, the intersections of these differences empower some people while limiting the opportunities of others. I accordingly interrogate the intersectional identities of Emily Doe and Brock Turner to highlight how power is structured to perpetuate raced and gendered norms. More specifically, the analysis reveals how gender and racial hierarchies contribute to a discriminatory learning environment that has normalized sexual violence on college campuses.

I conclude by introducing the idea of political apology to the scholarship on body politics and gendered violence, borrowing from theories established by political philosophers (Griswold 2007). Theorizing about the role that an institutional apology could play in healing and reconciliation offers one route for shifting the way we think about campus sexual violence. My reading of the Stanford case and the cultural commentary generated by the rape survivor's letter suggests that students would be better served if college administrators (1) recognize that sexual assault has been normalized on their campuses, particularly in college athletics and fraternities, (2) acknowledge the dignity of student survivors of sexual violence by offering an institutional apology, and (3) initiate substantive cultural reform that extends beyond Title IX legal compliance. I now turn to the official statements written by Turner and Doe, integrating core ideas from the feminist scholarship on body politics to highlight the raced and gendered dimensions of the student anti-rape movement.

Raced and gendered bodies

Emily Doe read her statement aloud in the courtroom after having read her assailant's letter requesting leniency in his punishment. We have research dating back to the 1950s documenting college rape as a problem (Dirks 2015) but I suspect that the widespread dissemination of Doe's letter signifies a historic cultural moment. Her words, some of which were cited in the introduction to this essay, have been read or heard by millions of people across the globe. Emily describes in detail her horrific experience, allowing the reader to "experience the world through her body" (Merleau-Ponty 1962):

> My clothes were confiscated and I stood naked while the nurses held a ruler to various abrasions on my body and photographed them. The three of us worked to comb the pine needles out of my hair, six hands to fill one paper bag. To calm me down, they said it's just the flora and fauna, flora and fauna. I had multiple swabs inserted into my vagina and anus, needles for shots, pills, had a Nikon pointed right into my spread legs. I had long, pointed beaks inside me and had my vagina smeared with cold, blue paint to check for abrasions.

> After a few hours of this, they let me shower. I stood there examining my body beneath the stream of water and decided, *I don't want my body anymore. I was terrified of it, I didn't know what had been in it, if it had been contaminated, who had touched it.* I wanted to take off my body like a jacket and leave it at the hospital with everything else.

> In newspapers my name was "unconscious intoxicated woman," ten syllables, and nothing more than that. For a while, I believed that that was all I was. *I had to force myself to relearn my real name, my identity. To relearn that this is not all that I am.* That I am not just a drunk victim at a frat party found behind a dumpster, while you are the All American swimmer at a top university, innocent until proven guilty, with so much at stake. *I am a human being who has been irreversibly hurt,* my life was put on hold for over a year, waiting to figure out if I was worth something. (italics added)

Emily's language directs our attention to *her* body, *her* identity, and *her* value as a human being. Our sense of self – our personhood – is connected to the desire to be recognized. When rape survivors tell their stories, calling for sexual predators and institutions of higher learning to be held accountable, they are struggling "to be perceived as persons" (Butler 2004, 32).

Viscerally experiencing the world through a rape survivor's body complicates discourses that dominate the student movement to end sexual assault and harassment on campus. Emily was not a drunk girl who was "asking for it." She did not "enjoy" this horrifying violence executed on her flesh. On the contrary, she was forced to "assume the position of powerless victim, one who has no control over what is happening to her body" (Collins 2010, 90). The body is ours – in our possession – yet it also "is out of our control as it leaks, fails us, and gives us away" (Kosut and Moore 2010, 5). As she stood showering, mentally absorbing what had transpired, Emily no longer wanted her body. It was tainted. He had taken something from her, leaving a feeling of emptiness behind.

Feminist scholarship on embodiment has taught us that bodies are invested with cultural meanings. Theories of intersectionality argue that there is no marker of identity that can explain the complexities of human experience without considering it in relation to other socially constructed differences (Zinn and Dill 1996). While we are aware of Emily Doe's gender, her race has not been disclosed to the public. However, cultural critics and online comments consistently have noted the eloquence and grace of her prose, which might signify Emily's class.[9] Scholars of race and gender argue that whiteness is the "default racial category" through which gender, sexuality, class, and other categories of social difference are expressed (Carbado 2013, 823). In the Western social imagination, class privilege is associated with whiteness (Purdie-Vaughns and Eibach 2008). Although we cannot confirm Emily's racial identity, it is not unreasonable to assume that her "gender is intersectionally but invisibly constituted as white" by those who have read her statement (Carbado 2013, 824).

Situating Emily Doe's identity within an intersectional framework demonstrates how subjectivity is formed by interlocking spaces of race, class, sexuality, and gender. Our bodies are located at the intersection of multiple sites of inequality, rendering some bodies more vulnerable to violence than others. It is possible that Emily's assumed whiteness, cisgender, and class privilege – articulated by her sophisticated and lucid prose – have shaped how the public has experienced her trauma. As a result, an undue burden is placed on survivors of sexual violence: not only do they have to communicate the trauma they have experienced, but must do so eloquently in order to be heard.[10] This struggle to be perceived as a person is more difficult for individuals with "intersectional subordinate-group identities," such as women of color and LGBT/gender-queer students (Purdie-Vaughns and Eibach 2008, 383). National surveys demonstrate that women (disproportionately women of color) and LGBT/gender-queer students are more susceptible to sexual violence on U.S. college campuses, but these cases often are underreported and overlooked.

Alternatively, a person occupying intersecting axes of high-status – namely whiteness, maleness, and heterosexuality – maintains privilege that normalizes one's behavior. The demeanor of a white cisgender man, such as convicted sexual predator Brock Turner, is "normative not just because of *what* he is doing (i.e., his conduct) but because it is *he* who is doing it (i.e., his status)," (Carbado 2013, 818). Turner, the Stanford swimming champion, thrives in accordance with his white, male, cisgender, and class privilege. When the rape of Emily Doe was flooding the Internet, corporate news sites incessantly published articles highlighting Turner's exceptional swim times, lamenting that the assault charges could disqualify him from major competitions. The arresting law enforcement agency initially did not release his mug shot to media outlets, opting instead for a "respectable" class photo that pinpoints his elite status as a Stanford student from a "good family." Indeed, Turner's white skin, blond hair, blue eyes, and radiant smile in his school picture symbolize the All-American boy. Turner's social value was thereby predicated on his "muscular, sensory, and mental prowess," facilitating an image of the ideal body (Kosut and Moore 2010, 5; Russell 1998, 15).

This gendered line of thinking about embodiment is derived from socio-historical norms that associate female bodies with the primitive, while male bodies signify rationality and civility (Kosut and Moore 2010, 4). Men are suited for politics in the public realm, so the argument goes, whereas women are relegated to the private sphere for domestic and emotional labor. As a matter of fact, the distinction between the public and private self formed the basis of the field of political science until the 1970s when feminist scholars challenged this patriarchal aspect of the discipline (Carroll and Zerilli 1993).

Hegemonic gendered and raced discourses consequently assume that bodies like that of Turner command sensibility, while "other" bodies may be construed as too emotional to make reasonable decisions (Waylen et al. 2013). During the trial, Turner never admitted to sexual assaulting Doe. He continues to argue that the sexual act was consensual, despite eyewitness accounts confirming Emily's lack of consciousness. But the jury sided with Doe, finding Turner guilty of three felony counts (assault with intent to commit rape of an intoxicated woman, sexually penetrating an intoxicated person with a foreign object, and sexually penetrating an unconscious person with a foreign object).

Before his sentencing, Turner submitted a statement to the judge overseeing his case and beseeched leniency. The convicted sexual aggressor evidently perceives himself as a "voice of reason," and offers to become a spokesperson to teach young people about the dangers of "binge drinking and sexual promiscuity."[11]

> I want to show that *people's lives can be destroyed by drinking and making poor decisions while doing so*. One needs to recognize the influence that *peer pressure* and the attitude of having to fit in can have on someone. One decision has the potential to change your entire life. I know I can impact and change people's attitudes towards the culture surrounded by *binge drinking* and *sexual promiscuity* that protrudes through what people think is at the core of being a college student.

> I want no one, male or female, to have to experience the destructive consequences of making decisions while under the influence of alcohol. I want to be *a voice of reason* in a time where people's attitudes and preconceived notions about partying and drinking have already been established. I want to let young people know, as I did not, that things can go from fun to ruined in just one night. (Excerpts from Brock Turner's letter to the Court, in his plea for a lenient sentence from Judge Aaron Persky; italics added)[12]

Critics on social media and in online comments sections ridiculed Turner for blaming his rape of Emily Doe on alcohol, party culture, and peer pressure.[13] His misguided conflation of alcoholism and sexual behavior with rape demonstrates precisely how rape culture operates: sexual assault happens so frequently that the violent, nonconsensual act is interpreted as heavily drinking and "hooking up." When student survivors report the crime and seek accountability, narratives that epitomize rape culture clutter the discursive environment, typically resulting in a "he said/she said" debate that undermines the human dignity of the survivor. What if the two graduate students had not intervened, catching Turner in the aggressive act? I surmise that public commentaries would follow the usual pattern of blaming the victim and slut-shaming, questioning the integrity of Emily's alleged promiscuous behavior.

Turner's defenders maintain that a "minor" instance of a drunken sexual encounter should not ruin this man's promising swimming career. Indeed, Dan Turner, Brock's father, has been widely condemned for a statement submitted to the Court on behalf of his son. He asserted that a prison sentence was "a steep price to pay for 20 minutes of action out of his 20 plus years of life,"[14] reinforcing a narrative of "boys will be boys" that normalizes rape.

Based on his three felony convictions, California state law dictates Turner be sentenced to a minimum of two years in state prison, and the prosecutor in the case recommended the defendant serve six years. But Superior Court Judge Aaron Persky pronounced Turner an exception to the rule, claiming that prison would have a "severe impact on him. I think he will not be a danger to others."[15] Persky consequently used his judicial discretion to sentence Turner to only six months in county jail.[16]

Turner's light sentence was met with sweeping criticism. The editorial board of the *San Jose Mercury News* pronounced "Brock Turner's six-month jail term for sexual assault of an intoxicated, unconscious woman on the Stanford campus last year is a setback for the movement to take campus rape seriously."[17] Stanford Law Professor Michelle Dauber has led a recall campaign of Judge Persky; the petition to remove him from the bench has gathered over 1.3 millions signatures as of November 30, 2016.[18] *People v. Turner* additionally has prompted the passage of legislation in California that tightens the sentencing parameters of those convicted of sexual assault.[19]

The aforementioned intersectional analysis of Turner's white, cisgender male body helps explain Judge Persky's justification for his light sentencing of the former Stanford athlete. The judge is a Stanford alumnus, and like Turner, Persky is a white, cisgender man. Persky seemingly evaluated Turner's violent behavior in terms of his intersectional identities, which mirror his own (Carbado 2013, 818). To illustrate this differentiation, consider the case of Raul Ramirez, also a convicted sexual predator who was sentenced by Judge Persky in the same year as Turner. Both men were found guilty in their respective cases, yet Turner received a six-month sentence in county jail, whereas Ramirez will serve three years in a California state prison. Ramirez's social status starkly contrasts with the former Stanford swimmer; he was born in El Salvador and was raised in a poor immigrant family. Ramirez thereby is situated outside white normativity (Carbado 2013). Ramirez also confessed and apologized while Turner maintains his innocence. From Judge Persky's vantage point, Turner's white body is more relatable and presumably innocent, which in effect places greater value on whiteness than the guilty brown body of Ramirez. Defense attorney Alexander Cross, who briefly represented Ramirez, explained, "society is not exactly suffering a loss [for sending Ramirez to prison for three years]. At least, that's not how it's looked upon."[20] With Turner's conviction, however, Stanford lost a standout swimmer.

Institutional betrayal and apology

Emily Doe continues to wait for an acknowledgment from Turner that the violence he inflicted on her unconscious body was not consensual. In wake of the outcry generated by Turner's light sentence, Stanford University publicly stated that it "did everything within its power to assure that justice was served in this case." Jennifer Freyd, a professor of psychology known for her field-defining work on institutional betrayal (as well as a Stanford alumna) questioned the institution's disingenuous claim in an open letter to Stanford administrators and trustees:

> How sad to see Stanford squander the opportunity to actually do something within its power to contribute to justice: *issue a sincere apology*. Instead, its self-congratulatory and defensive stance is typical of *institutional betrayal*, a pattern of behavior that my students and I have been investigating for the past six years … when schools engage in acts of institutional betrayal, victims of sexual violence experience additional harm – harm that occurs above and beyond that caused by the sexual violence itself.[21] (italics added)

In terms of the contemporary college rape crisis, institutional betrayal refers to the "failure to prevent or respond supportively to wrongdoings by individuals (e.g., sexual assault) committed within the context of the institution," (Smith and Freyd 2013). Put differently, survivors of sexual violence relive the trauma produced by their assault when colleges fail to prevent or sufficiently respond to acts of sexual violence. Freyd's research on institutional betrayal corresponds with intersectional scholarship on gendered violence. Even if a survivor of rape is not physically injured, the emotional and psychological impact of the rape can be far more devastating, undermining one's sense of self and integrity (Collins 2010, 90). My advocacy work with faculty and student activists across the U.S. has led me to conclude that a sincere apology from Stanford potentially could serve as a way of psychological and emotional healing through institutional accountability. When an institution of higher learning acknowledges that sexual violence has been normalized, particularly at fraternities and in collegiate athletics, it signals that they have *not* done everything that they could to ensure a learning environment free of gender and sex discrimination, but that they are initiating substantive programs to challenge the rape culture that pervades their campus – to try to *prevent* it from happening again.

Some players in what I call the *Title IX Compliance Industry* approach the college rape crisis differently. Multiple factors have fostered the growth of this booming, profit-driven business. In the same year that Yale University was undergoing scrutiny for its mishandling of sexual assault cases, the U.S. Department of Education (DOE) issued its 2011 "Dear Colleague Letter," communicating to colleges and universities that the federal agency was taking steps to ensure an educational environment free of sex discrimination, which is mandated by Title IX of the 1972 Education Amendments. Shortly thereafter, student activists from multiple universities formed online coalitions and began bombarding the DOE with Title IX Complaints.

Media coverage of student protests, campus screenings of *The Hunting Ground* (the critically acclaimed documentary on the current rape crisis in higher education) and The White House's 2014 initiative to end sexual assault on college campuses[22] have mounted pressure on colleges to take steps to comply with Title IX.[23] Universities subsequently have spent millions, facilitating the for-profit industry of legal experts and consultants specializing in Title IX lawsuits.[24]

When business interests regulate the bodies of student rape survivors, their lived experiences are reduced to statistics. Bodies that are "registered bureaucratically and demographically via binary categories" are managed as liabilities, resulting in dehumanizing discourses directed towards bodies that have been scarred by sexual violence (Kosut and Moore 2010). Student complainants from colleges and universities across the country have communicated that high-profile Title IX legal "experts" are hired by educational institutions to "clean up messes by paying lip service to federal compliance." Some argue that expensive firms specializing in Title IX risk-management actually are used as weapons to silence victims and their allies,[25] allowing universities like Stanford to declare that they are "doing everything within their power" to ensure justice for survivors.[26]

Professor Freyd's open letter generated a pointed response from Brett Sokolow, a key player in the Title IX Compliance Industry. The Founder and President of The National Center for Higher Education Risk Management (NCHERM) and Executive Director of the Association of Title IX Administrators (ATIXA)[27] posted a response to ATIXA's online forum in June 2016, part of which is excerpted here:

> I'm ticked off by this, both logically and emotionally … In this open letter, she is just feeding the "one more thing'ers" as I call them … If Stanford had apologized, the one more thing'ers would be demanding admission and free tuition for the victim. Just one more thing until you satisfy my external litmus test for whether you did enough. Of course, *the one more thing'ers are never satisfied*. I don't see that Stanford's failure to apologize to the victim is an example

of institutional betrayal ... It might be humane for Stanford to express sadness or remorse about the crime, and it might be healing for Stanford to do so, *but this takes it too far* and fails to recognize all that Stanford has already done.

Situating Sokolow's whiteness, maleness, and class privilege within an intersectional framework sheds light on the problematic ways that university administrators and business interests have regulated the bodies of student survivors of sexual violence. Like Brock Turner and Judge Persky, Sokolow occupies intersecting axes of high social status. His condescending language directed towards Freyd reproduces a gendered and raced narrative that privileges the white male's "sensibility" over the distinguished professor's expertise. Protesting that an apology "takes it too far" implies that Freyd may be too emotional and irrational to adequately evaluate the Stanford case (Waylen et al. 2013). Sokolow does not express interest in the human dignity of Emily Doe; the self-proclaimed Title IX expert instead applauds the procedural steps taken by Stanford to become legally compliant with Title IX directives issued by the DOE.

Peter Lake, Stetson University Law Professor, warns of allowing lawyers like Sokolow to lead the movement to combat sexual violence on college campuses: "I'm a lawyer, but it scares me to death that we are lawyering up higher ed ... We're legalizing this field very quickly with little attention being paid to how it will affect victims."[28] In a similar vein, Freyd reacted to Sokolow's e-mail, suggesting that privatizing Title IX compliance will not heal a learning environment scarred by rape culture. Elsewhere in his e-mail, Sokolow claimed that an apology from Stanford could facilitate a lawsuit against the university. Freyd subsequently responded:

> Perhaps such an apology would open some door for something to be used in some lawsuit. Perhaps so. However, I also think universities do their students and their own future a disservice when they attend too much to risk management and too little to doing the right thing. In my opinion, *there are more important values for universities to promote than always prioritizing the reduction of lawsuit risk.* (I say that and at the same time I know that apologies also reduce the probability a lawsuit will be filed in the first place – so in fact, such a forward bold step may not even increase legal liability on average even if it does in one particular case) ... I don't think we will see either academic excellence or culture change without some risk taking. *I worry the corporate university has made us more and more risk adverse to the point we are promoting mediocrity and cowardice.*

Theorizing about the role that an institutional apology could play in healing and reconciliation offers one avenue for shifting the way we think about campus sexual violence. In her response to Sokolow, Freyd suggested that Stanford must find a way to "move from institutional betrayal to institutional courage." And on September 2, 2016, Stanford *finally* issued an apology. Lauren Schoenthaler, recently appointed Senior Associate Vice Provost for Institutional Equity and Access, states in the *Stanford News*: "Emily Doe should not have been sexually assaulted anywhere, and she should not have been sexually assaulted at Stanford. On behalf of the Stanford community, I offer my heartfelt apology that this happened to her."[29] Despite this gesture, however, Stanford's apology lacks substance; it does not offer the possibility that the university's campus culture was in any way related to Turner's sexual aggression.

How a rape case was handled at Oregon State University (OSU) provides one example of an institution accepting blame for its inability to foster a learning environment free from discrimination and taking positive steps to challenge rape culture. Brenda Tracy had been gang raped by OSU athletes over a decade ago, and in 2015, she reached out to OSU, inquiring about the consequences of her case. OSU President Ed Ray was appalled by how his university had handled the accusations: the student athletes were found responsible for the violent rape, but received a light punishment and were allowed to continue playing football. Acknowledging the egregious institutional betrayal committed by OSU, Ray recalls asking, "What does it make sense to do as a human being?"[30] OSU subsequently confronted its mistakes head on, issuing a public apology to Tracy and the university community.

Political theorists have developed a body of scholarship that highlights the utility of understanding apology as a political concept (Digeser 2001; Griswold 2007). To publicly apologize is to initiate a process of reconciliation, thereby rectifying the past injustice. In other words, a public apology could restore the relationship between the two parties (i.e., the college and the sexual assault survivor) in a positive, respectful way.

OSU did not simply apologize to Tracy; Ray initiated the process of reconciliation by hiring Brenda as a consultant to improve the university's handling of cases involving sexual assault. Tracy has delivered presentations to OSU students on campus rape and healthy masculinity, which have helped her overcome feelings of resentment towards the institution for its past unwillingness to hold student athletes accountable. OSU finally had recognized her value as a human being. The institution's determination to disrupt college rape culture signifies that the bodies of sexual assault survivors count as viable subjects (Butler 2004, 28). Ray explains:

> One reason why a lot of institutions get it wrong with very real, very personal human tragedies like this is they forget it's not about the institution. It's *not about damage control*. It's about trying to understand what the situation is, regardless of whose watch it was on. (President Ed Ray, on why he offered an apology, italics added)

Focusing on the lives of vulnerable bodies and restoring a sense of self starkly contrasts with the Title IX Compliance Industry's emphasis on legal compliance. Rather than engaging in damage control, silencing Tracy and other survivors of sexual violence, OSU has recognized the utility of institutional apology and reconciliation. In addition to bringing Tracy back into the OSU community, Ray initiated a public dialogue with university administrators and athletic directors in the Pac-12 Conference and succeeded in changing the conference's policy on student athletes who had been found responsible for sexual assault. As a result of Ray and Tracy's collaboration, the Pac-12 universities no longer allow student athletes who have been suspended or expelled for an act of sexual violence to continue their athletic careers by transferring to another school.[31]

The power of a public apology has not been lost on student survivors active in the movement to prevent and end campus rape. Shortly after Emily Doe's letter had gone viral online, students initiated a petition demanding Stanford issue an apology to Emily Doe; the petition has received almost 170,000 signatures as of the time of this publication.[32] And in August 2016, national survivor activists Wagatwe Wanjuki and Kamilah Willingham co-founded "Survivors Eradicating Rape Culture" and introduced the #JustSaySorry campaign.[33] The movement is described as

> a grassroots campaign led by survivors of campus gender-based violence and allies demanding apologies from the schools that failed them. It aims to highlight the inadequacy of

schools' silence and to demand apologies for their widely recognized and almost universal failures to prevent and meaningfully respond to sexual violence.[34]

Key findings from the 2015 Inside Higher Ed Survey of College and University Presidents reveal the significance of Wanjuki and Willingham's campaign: Of 647 American college presidents surveyed, "32% agree campus sexual assault is a problem. But only 6% agree it's a problem on *their* campus."[35] The #JustSaySorry campaign notes that only one university leader has admitted to its egregious mishandling of sexual violence cases and has issued a sincere public apology, University of Alaska-Fairbanks Interim Chancellor Mike Powers.[36] Similar to President Ed Ray of OSU (who apologized for the mishandling of Brenda Tracy's case that was conducted under former leadership a decade prior), Chancellor Powers mustered the institutional courage to accept full responsibility for the university's grossly inadequate response to reports of what he called "heinous violence." He states that for several years,

> we failed to follow our own student discipline policies for the most serious violations of the student code of conduct … We investigated reports of rape, and often took informal action like removing the accused from dorms or campus. But, until recently, students were not being suspended or expelled for sexual assault, or for any major violation of our code of conduct … I am deeply sorry for how our lack of action affected our students and their friends and families … As the brother of someone who was similarly violated 40 years ago, I am incensed that our communities still have not adequately dealt with this opportunistic and cowardly behavior. It's time for this to end.[37]

Significant to the chancellor's apology is his implied condemnation of rape culture, the term I have used to describe the way our communities "tolerate a broad range of behaviors that create an environment where sexual offenders are not held accountable for their actions, and victims are blamed instead."[38] This "boys will be boys" mentality objectifies women and LGBT/gender-queer bodies as a source of male entitlement, whereas survivors are often dismissed through victim-blaming and slut-shaming. I have argued that Emily Doe's impact statement and Brock Turner's letter requesting leniency profoundly capture the ways that rape culture has been normalized on U.S. college campuses. Instead of teaching men not to rape, victim-blamers shamefully place the onus of responsibility on survivors, arguing that they could avoid becoming targets by abstaining from drinking alcohol or wearing modest clothing.[39] Racial undertones often shape this discourse, condemning women of color who are deemed exotic and hyper-sexualized – thereby excusing the behavior of sexual predators who "just cannot help themselves" (Anderson 2010, 651–652; LaFree 1989). Students embodied with "intersecting subordinate identities" correspondingly are even more vulnerable to experience gendered violence, undermining their self-worth (Purdie-Vaughns and Eibach 2008; Strolovitch 2007).

Rape culture and the U.S. Presidential election

The timing of this essay's publication begs the question: how will rape culture on college campuses fare over the next four years? I would be remiss not to address the current historical moment in American politics: the President of the United States is an accused sexual predator and misogynist. President Donald Trump epitomizes rape culture,[40] specifically when he intimates that he cannot help himself when he meets beautiful women:

> I just start kissing them. It's like a magnet. Just kiss. I don't even wait. And when you're a star, they let you do it. You can do anything … *Grab "em by the pussy. You can do anything."*[41] (italics added)

The now infamous leaked *Access Hollywood* tape is only one of several documented instances of Trump's grotesque misogyny on display. We have recordings of the President of the United States calling women "'pigs,' 'slobs,' 'fat,' and 'ugly."[42] A powerful campaign video created by the team of Trump's primary opponent, Hillary Rodham Clinton, plays a voiceover of some of his crudest remarks while young girls look at their reflections in mirrors:

> I'd look her right in the fat ugly face of hers. She's a slob; she ate like a pig. A person who is flat-chested is very hard to be a "10." Does she have a good body? No. Does she have a fat [redacted]? Absolutely. [in response to Howard Stern's question, Do you treat women with respect?] Ugh, I can't say that either.

The 30-second video, which has been viewed over 5.5 million times on YouTube, ends with the question, "Is this the president that we want for our daughters?"[43] For many Americans, the answer is a resounding "No!" as the country grapples with an administration that does not appear to take sexual assault and harassment seriously.

Confronting rape culture and ending violence against vulnerable bodies poses major challenges: first, prove that it exists, and second, convince others that it is wrong (Elman 2013, 239). Not surprisingly, the election of an accused sexual predator to the country's highest office makes the anti-rape work of student and faculty activists exceedingly more difficult.[44] The White House and the Department of Education's Office for Civil Rights have been the movement's greatest allies, and advocates fear that a Trump administration will reverse President Obama's historic initiatives to fight sexual violence in higher education.[45] In the Trump-era, the urgency for college administrators to summon the institutional courage cannot be overstated. The very nature of Title IX compliance could become a non-issue if a Trump administration reverses the Department of Education's Title IX guidelines. This essay thereby concludes with a call to action. Students and faculty, demand that your institutions (1) recognize that sexual assault has been normalized on your campuses, particularly in college athletics and fraternities, (2) acknowledge the dignity of student survivors of sexual violence by offering an institutional apology, and (3) initiate substantive cultural reforms that extend beyond Title IX legal compliance. We cannot allow rape culture to continue in higher education, regardless of who sits in the Oval Office.

Notes

1. Emily Doe's 12-page victim-impact statement was first published online at BuzzFeed News. See: Katie Baker, "Here is the Powerful Letter the Stanford Victim Read to Her Attacker," *BuzzFeed News*, June 3, 2016, https://www.buzzfeed.com/katiejmbaker/heres-the-powerful-letter-the-stanford-victim-read-to-her-ra?utm_term=.skvVrQ7MKR#.gsw3DWv2bN.
2. The rape survivor's given name has not been disclosed to the public.

3. The court documents are available online: "Court Documents: Stanford Rape Case," *Los Angeles Times*, http://documents.latimes.com/stanford-brock-turner/.

4. Melissa Batchelor Warnke, "Rape Survivors Shouldn't Have to Be Eloquent to Get Justice," *Los Angeles Times*, June 10, 2016, http://www.latimes.com/opinion/opinion-la/la-ol-week-in-review-20160609-snap-story.html.

5. Frank Pallotta, "Why Asheligh Banfield Read Stanford Rape Victim's Letter on CNN," *CNN*, June 6, 2016, http://money.cnn.com/2016/06/06/media/ashleigh-banfield-cnn-stanford-letter/.

6. Jasmine Aguilera, "House Members Unite to Read Stanford Rape Victim's Letter," *New York Times*, June 16, 2016, http://www.nytimes.com/2016/06/17/us/politics/congress-stanford-letter.html.

7. Tom Namako, "Joe Biden Writes an Open Letter to Stanford Survivor," *BuzzFeed News*, June 9, 2016, https://www.buzzfeed.com/tomnamako/joe-biden-writes-an-open-letter-to-stanford-survivor?bftwnews&utm_term=.tcNBpVar4#.deve4XQo5; Jonah Engel Bromwich, "Biden Calls Victim in Stanford Rape Case a 'Warrior,'" *New York Times*, June 9, 2016, http://www.nytimes.com/2016/06/10/us/biden-calls-victim-in-stanford-rape-case-a-warrior.html?_r=0.

8. Maggie Mallon, "Stanford Sexual Assault Case Survivor Emily Doe Speaks Out at Glamour's Women of the Year Awards," *Glamour*, November 15, 2016, http://www.glamour.com/story/stanford-sexual-assault-case-survivor-emily-doe-speaks-out-at-glamours-women-of-the-year-awards.

9. Rebecca Makkai, "The Power and Limitations of Victim-Impact Statements," *New Yorker*, June 8, 2016, http://www.newyorker.com/culture/culture-desk/the-power-and-limitations-of-victim-impact-statements.

10. See Note 4.

11. Matt Payton, "Stanford Rape Case: Brock Turner Blames Assault on 'Alcohol' and 'Party Culture,'" *Independent*, June 9, 2016, http://www.independent.co.uk/news/world/americas/stanford-rape-case-brock-turner-blames-sexual-assault-on-alcohol-and-party-culture-swimmer-victim-a7072691.html.

12. Sam Levin and Julia Carrie Wong, "Brock Turner's Statement Blames Sexual Assault on Stanford's 'Party Culture,'" *Guardian*, June 7, 2016, https://www.theguardian.com/us-news/2016/jun/07/brock-turner-statement-stanford-rape-case-campus-culture.

13. Ibid.

14. Christina Cauterucci, "Brock Turner's Father Sums Up Rape Culture in One Brief Statement," *Slate*, June 5, 2016, http://www.slate.com/blogs/xx_factor/2016/06/05/brock_turner_s_dad_s_defense_proves_why_his_victim_had_to_write_her_letter.html.

15. Liam Stack, "Light Sentence for Brock Turner in Stanford Rape Case Draws Outrage," *New York Times*, June 6, 2016, http://www.nytimes.com/2016/06/07/us/outrage-in-stanford-rape-case-over-dueling-statements-of-victim-and-attackers-father.html?_r=0&version=meter+at+0&module=meter-Links&pgtype=article&contentId=&mediaId=&referrer=http%3A%2F%2Fwww.nytimes.com%2F2016%2F06%2F07%2Fus%2Foutrage-in-stanford-rape-case-over-dueling-statements-of-victim-and-attackers-father.html&priority=true&action=click&contentCollection=meter-links-click.

16. In early September 2016, Turner was released from custody after having served three months.

17. Editors, "Stanford Sexual Assault Sentence Was Too Light," *San Jose Mercury News*, June 2, 2016, http://www.mercurynews.com/2016/06/02/mercury-news-editorial-stanford-sexual-assault-sentence-was-too-light/.

18. Petition to Remove Judge Aaron Persky from the Bench for Decision in Brock Turner Rape Case, at *change.org*, https://www.change.org/p/california-state-house-impeach-judge-aaronpersky.

19. Sarah Larimer, "In Aftermath of Brock Turner Case, California's Governor Signs Sex Crime Bill," *Washington Post*, September 30, 2016, https://www.washingtonpost.com/news/grade-point/wp/2016/09/30/in-aftermath-of-brock-turner-case-californias-governor-signs-sex-crime-bill/?utm_term=.16e299fc7815.

20. Sam Levin, "Stanford Trial Judge Overseeing Much Harsher Sentence for Similar Assault Case," *Guardian*, June 27, 2016, https://www.theguardian.com/us-news/2016/jun/27/stanford-sexual-assault-trial-judge-persky.

21. Jennifer J. Freyd, "Open Letter To the Administration and Trustees of Stanford University," *Huffington Post*, June 21, 2016, http://www.huffingtonpost.com/jennifer-j-freyd/open-letter-to-the-admini_b_10577338.html.

22. The White House Taskforce to Protect Students from Sexual Assault, *Not Alone*, April 29, 2014, https://www.notalone.gov/assets/report.pdf.

23. Amanda Hess, "How the Internet Revolutionized Campus Anti-Rape Activism," *Slate*, March 20, 2013, http://www.slate.com/blogs/xx_factor/2013/03/20/occidental_college_sexual_assault_case_how_the_internet_revolutionized_campus.html.

24. Anemona Harocollis, "Colleges Spending Millions To Deal with Sexual Misconduct Complaints," *New York Times*, March 29, 2016, http://www.nytimes.com/2016/03/30/us/colleges-beef-up-bureaucracies-to-deal-with-sexual-misconduct.html.

25. Katie Baker, "Rape Victims Don't Trust the Fixers Colleges Hire to Help Them," *BuzzFeed News*, April 25, 2014, https://www.buzzfeed.com/katiejmbaker/rape-victims-dont-trust-the-fixers-colleges-hire-to-help-the?utm_term=.glMkjLr972#.ckMy6×1X2Y.

26. Freyd (2016).

27. See Sokolow's full bio and list of credentials here: https://www.ncherm.org/consultants/brett-sokolow/.

28. Tyler Kingkade, "Students Want Stanford to Apologize for Brock Turner's Sexual Assault," *Huffington Post*, June 8, 2016, http://www.huffingtonpost.com/entry/stanford-brock-turner-apology_us_57589064e4b0ced23ca6f901.

29. Q&A: Sexual Violence Prevention and Response at Stanford, *Stanford News*, September 2, 2016, http://news.stanford.edu/2016/09/02/sexual-violence-prevention-response/.

30. Tyler Kingkade, "What It Looks Like When a University Truly Fixes How It Handles Sexual Assault. *Huffington Post*, April 7, 2016, http://www.huffingtonpost.com/entry/oregon-state-university-sexual-assault_us_56f426c3e4b02c402f66c3b9.

31. Ibid.

32. Stanford Association of Students for Sexual Assault Prevention (ASAP), Letter to Stanford University in support of survivor of Brock Turner case. Online petition, June, 2016, https://www.change.org/p/letter-to-stanford-university-in-support-of-survivor-of-brockturner-case?utm_source=embedded_petition_view.

33. Survivors Eradicating Rape Culture, http://eradicaterape.org/justsaysorry/.

34. Ibid.

35. The full report is available for download at: https://www.insidehighered.com/booklet/2015-survey-college-and-university-presidents.

36. Tyler Kingkade, "This University Leader Showed How Colleges Should Own Up to Failures on Sexual Assault Cases," *Huffington Post*, October 22, 2015, http://www.huffingtonpost.com/entry/college-president-apology-sexual-assault_us_5628fc90e4b0443bb562ddc0.

37. Ibid.

38. Clare Foran, "Donald Trump's Cynical Exploitation of Rape Culture," *The Atlantic*, October 13, 2016, http://www.theatlantic.com/politics/archive/2016/10/donald-trump-women-accusations-sexual-assault/504089/.

39. See, for example: Emily Yoffe, "College Women: Stop Getting Drunk," *Slate*, October 15, 2013, http://www.slate.com/articles/double_x/doublex/2013/10/sexual_assault_and_drinking_teach_women_the_connection.html.

40. Dana Liebelson, "The Man You Say Assaulted You Will Be President. Here's What That's Like," *Huffington Post*, November 16, 2016, http://www.huffingtonpost.com/entry/donald-trump-assault-allegations_us_582b8abae4b0e39c1fa6df11.

41. "Transcript: Donald Trump's Taped Comments about Women," *New York Times*, October 8, 2016, http://www.nytimes.com/2016/10/08/us/donald-trump-tape-transcript.html

42. For a thorough examination of Trump's vulgar comments and behavior, see: Claire Cohen, "Donald Trump Sexism Tracker: Every Offensive Comment in One Place," *Telegraph*,

November 9, 2016, http://www.telegraph.co.uk/women/politics/donald-trump-sexism-tracker-every-offensive-comment-in-one-place/; Eve Ensler, "The Undeniable Rape Culture of Donald Trump," *Huffington Post*, October 4, 2016, http://www.huffingtonpost.com/entry/the-undeniable-rape-culture-of-donald-trump_us_57ee5879e4b0c2407cdd4c92; Jia Tolentino, "Donald Trump's Unconscious, Unending Sexism," *New Yorker*, October 10, 2016, http://www.newyorker.com/culture/jia-tolentino/donald-trumps-unconscious unending-sexism.

43. The campaign video can be viewed on YouTube: https://www.youtube.com/watch?v=vHGPbl-werw (last accessed November 30, 2016). Also see: Melissa Batchelor Warnke, "Turning the Mirror Back on Donald Trump," *Los Angeles Times*, September 26, 2016, http://www.latimes.com/opinion/opinion-la/la-ol-mirror-donald-trump-hillary-clinton-20160926-snap-story.html; Inae Oh, "Clinton's Newest Ad Shows Girls Looking in the Mirror While Trump Mocks Women's Appearances," *Mother Jones*, September 23, 2016, http://www.motherjones.com/politics/2016/09/hillary-clinton-ad-donald-trump-mock-women.

44. Sam Levin, "'It's Going To Silence People': Setback Feared in Fighting Campus Sexual Assault," *Guardian*, November 11, 2016, https://www.theguardian.com/us-news/2016/nov/11/campus-sexual-assault-title-ix-civil-rights-universities-rape.

45. Tovia Smith, "Obama Championed the Fight Against Sexual Assaults. Will Trump?" *NPR*, heard on *Morning Edition*, November 24, 2016, http://www.npr.org/2016/11/24/503236223/activists-worry-trump-s-education-secretary-won-t-champion-sexual-assault-issues; Nick Anderson, Emma Brown, and Moriah Balingit, "Trump Could Reverse Obama's Actions on College Sex Assault, Transgender Rights," *Washington Post*, November 23, 2016, https://www.washingtonpost.com/local/education/trump-could-reverse-obamas-actions-on-college-sex-assault-transgender-rights/2016/11/21/44e0e9b4-ab4e-11e6-8b45-f8e493f06fcd_story.html; James Hoyt, "Donald Trump's Election Alters the Playing Field for Sexual Assault Awareness on Campuses," *USA Today*, November 21, 2016, http://college.usatoday.com/2016/11/21/trump-election-sexual-assault-on-campus/.

Disclosure statement

No potential conflict of interest was reported by the author.

Funding

This work was supported by a postdoctoral research fellowship awarded by the American Association of University Women.

References

Anderson, Michelle J. 2010. "Diminishing the Legal Impact of Negative Social Attitudes Toward Acquaintance Rape Victims." *New Criminal Law Review* 13 (4): 644–664.

Butler, Judith. 2004. *Undoing Gender*. New York: Routledge.

Carbado, Devon W. 2013. "Colorblind Intersectionality." *Signs: Journal of Women in Culture and Society* 38 (4): 811–845.

Carroll, Susan J., and Linda M. G. Zerilli. 1993. "Feminist Challenges to Political Science." In *Political Science: The State of the Discipline II*, edited by Ada W. Finifter, 55–76. Washington, DC: American Political Science Association.

Collins, Patricia Hill. 2010. "Assume the Position: The Changing Contours of Sexual Violence." In *The Body Reader: Essential Social and Cultural Readings*, edited by Lisa Jean Moore and Mary Kosut, 80–107. New York: New York University Press.

Digeser, P. E. 2001. *Political Forgiveness*. Ithaca, NY: Cornell University Press.

Dirks, Danielle. 2015. Confronting Campus Rape. Paper presented at the annual meeting of the American Sociological Association, Chicago, IL.

Elman, R. Amy. 2013. "Gender Violence." In *The Oxford Handbook of Gender and Politics*, edited by Georgina Waylen, Karen Celis, Johanna Kantola, and S. Laurel Weldon, 236–258. New York: Oxford University Press.

Griswold, Charles L. 2007. *Forgiveness: A Philosophical Exploration.* New York: Cambridge University Press.

Kosut, Mary, and Lisa Jean Moore. 2010. "Introduction: Not Just the Reflexive Reflex: Flesh and Bone in the Social Sciences." In *The Body Reader: Essential Social and Cultural Readings*, edited by Lisa Jean Moore and Mary Kosut, 1–26. New York: New York University Press.

LaFree, Gary. 1989. *Rape & Criminal Justice: The Social Construction of Sexual Assault.* Belmont, CA: Wadsworth Publishing.

Merleau-Ponty, Maurice. (1962) 2005. *Phenomenology of Perception.* London: Routledge.

Purdie-Vaughns, Valerie, and Richard P. Eibach. 2008. "Intersectional Invisibility: The Distinctive Advantages and Disadvantages of Multiple Subordinate-Group Identities." *Sex Roles* 59 (5): 377–391.

Russell, Marta. 1998. *Beyond Ramps: Disability at the End of the Social Contract.* Monroe, ME: Common Courage Press.

Smith, Carly Parnitzke, and Jennifer Freyd. 2013. "Dangerous Safe Havens: Institutional Betrayal Exacerbates Sexual Trauma." *Journal of Traumatic Stress* 26: 119–124.

Strolovitch, Dara. 2007. *Affirmative Advocacy: Race, Class, and Gender in Interest Group Politics.* Chicago, IL: University of Chicago Press.

Waylen, Georgina, Karen Celis, Johanna Kantola, and S. Laurel Weldon. 2013. "Body Politics." In *The Oxford Handbook of Gender and Politics*, edited by Georgina Waylen, Karen Celis, Johanna Kantola, and S. Laurel Weldon, 161–164. New York: Oxford University Press.

Zinn, Maxine Baca, and Bonnie Thornton Dill. 1996. "Theorizing Difference from Multiracial Feminism." *Feminist Studies* 22 (2): 321–331.

Index

137; educational attainment 138; face-to-face interviews 137; gendered leadership stereotypes 132–3 (*see also* gendered leadership stereotypes); gender quotas 145; hierarchical logistic regression models 142–3, **143**; household wealth 138; human development 145n4; institutional causes 132; labor force participation 144; labor market participation 141; leadership stereotypes 139, *139*; leftism 138; multivariate analysis 138; multivariate hierarchical models 141–2, **142**; national economy 137; non-authoritarians

141; partisanship levels 144; policy consequences 132; presidential candidates **151**; pro-female stereotype 133, 142–3, 145; pro-male stereotype 133; social desirability bias 139–40, 144; support for democracy 138; support for the political system 138; voting models 138

Wong, Cara 89

Young, Iris Marion 32, 167

Zerilli, L. 1

Made in the USA
Middletown, DE
08 February 2023

24401571R00121